The Huayan University Network

THE SHENG YEN SERIES IN CHINESE BUDDHIST STUDIES

THE SHENG YEN SERIES IN CHINESE BUDDHIST STUDIES
Edited by Daniel B. Stevenson and Jimmy Yu

Funded jointly by the Sheng Yen Education Foundation and the Chung Hua Institute of Buddhist Studies in Taiwan, the Sheng Yen Series in Chinese Buddhist Studies is dedicated to the interdisciplinary study of Chinese language resources that bear on the history of Buddhism in premodern and modern China. Through the publication of pioneering scholarship on Chinese Buddhist thought, practice, social life, and institutional life in China—including interactions with indigenous traditions of religion in China as well as Buddhist developments in South, East, and Inner/Central Asia—the series aspires to bring new and groundbreaking perspectives to one of the most historically enduring and influential traditions of Buddhism, past and present.

For a complete list of titles, see page 275.

THE HUAYAN UNIVERSITY NETWORK

The Teaching and Practice of
Avataṃsaka Buddhism
in Twentieth-Century China

ERIK J. HAMMERSTROM

COLUMBIA UNIVERSITY PRESS   *NEW YORK*

Columbia University Press
Publishers Since 1893
New York   Chichester, West Sussex
cup.columbia.edu
Copyright © 2020 Columbia University Press
All rights reserved

Library of Congress Cataloging-in-Publication Data
Names: Hammerstrom, Erik J., author.
Title: The Huayan University network : the teaching and practice of Avataṃsaka Buddhism in twentieth-century China / Erik J. Hammerstrom.
Description: New York : Columbia University Press, 2020. | Series: The Sheng Yen series in Chinese Buddhist studies | Includes bibliographical references and index.
Identifiers: LCCN 2020011464 (print) | LCCN 2020011465 (ebook) | ISBN 9780231194303 (hardback) | ISBN 9780231550758 (ebook)
Subjects: LCSH: Hua yan Buddhism—China—History—20th century.
Classification: LCC BQ8212.9.C6 H35 2020 (print) | LCC BQ8212.9.C6 (ebook) | DDC 294.3/9209510904—dc23
LC record available at https://lccn.loc.gov/2020011464
LC ebook record available at https://lccn.loc.gov/2020011465

Columbia University Press books are printed on permanent and durable acid-free paper.
Printed in the United States of America

Cover art: © Wikimedia Creative Commons
Cover design: Milenda Nan Ok Lee

For Aimee
and for all of my ancestors

Contents

Preface ix

Introduction 1

PART ONE

ONE Huayan as a School of Chinese Buddhism 17

TWO The Huayan Universities 47

THREE Second- and Third-Generation Programs 72

FOUR The Huayan University Network After 1949 104

PART TWO

FIVE Huayan Doctrine in Republican China 125

SIX A Common Curriculum 155

Conclusion 180

CONTENTS

List of Chinese Characters   185

Notes   201

Bibliography   239

Index   261

Preface

THIS STUDY GREW out of my desire to better understand Huayan, an enduring component of the pan–East Asian Buddhist tradition. I have been fascinated and inspired by the imagery and metaphors of Huayan Buddhism since I was an undergraduate at Sarah Lawrence College. Its vision of the overwhelming complexity and intimate harmony of the universe took hold of me and never let go. As befits the philosophy of its founders, Huayan is not one thing but can be many things depending on the perspective from which it is viewed. This book focuses on a single aspect of the history of Huayan, telling the story of one group of Buddhists who devoted their lives to studying and teaching its complex philosophy during a period of great change in China's recent past.

As this book deals in part with the philosophy of causes and conditions, it is only right for me to acknowledge the causes involved in its production. This book has been years in the making, so there are many people I wish to thank for helping me write it. T. Griffith Foulk, my teacher at Sarah Lawrence, was the first person to model for me what it means to pursue the rigorous study of Buddhism. He also recommended I read Robert Buswell's book *The Zen Monastic Experience*, which sparked my interest in the Huayan (Hwaŏm) underpinnings of Korean Sŏn thought, and introduced me to the monk Ŭisang's 義湘 (625–702) fascinating summary of that philosophy, *Diagram of the Huayan One Vehicle Dharmadhātu* (*Hwaŏm ilsŭng pŏpkye do* 華嚴一乘法界圖). Buswell's book sent me to Korea, where I studied Buddhism for several years. Although I did not go on to specialize in Korean Buddhism, I continue to return to Ŭisang's writings, and when I began to study classical Chinese in earnest at Portland State University, for my first big project I chose to produce an annotated translation of that text. I was guided in this course by Professors Jonathan Pease and Stephen Wadley, whom I thank for giving me a solid foundation in that language. Several years later I wrote a paper on Huayan hagiography for a graduate course on saints taught by Robert Campany at Indiana University, and some of that research appears in this book. I am thankful for him and the other mentors I had at Indiana, John McRae, Jan Nattier, Aaron Stalnaker, and especially Stephen Bokenkamp. With their support, I researched and wrote my first book, which was not about Huayan at all.

I was able to return to my earlier interest in Huayan through the support of many people and institutions. My school, Pacific Lutheran University (PLU), is deeply committed to the best principles of Lutheran Higher Education: critical inquiry, freedom of conscience, and a value-filled education that emphasizes equality and service. At PLU, I have been able to pursue my studies in an atmosphere of support and affirmation. I thank the school for a sabbatical and a Regency Advancement Award, which provided the temporal and financial support necessary to complete the first draft of this book. I also thank my departmental colleagues, especially Kevin O'Brien, for their comments and advice as I considered how or even if I should undertake this project. I am grateful to our school's librarians, Ann Dodge, Kathy Honsberger, and Katie Wallis, whose skill with the InterLibrary Loan system transformed our modest holdings into a world-class library. They were wonderfully patient in tracking down rare materials I needed in English, Chinese, Japanese, and even Korean. In the same vein, I thank for their assistance Kristina Troost, who aided me during several visits to the Duke University Library, and Hyokyoung Yi at the University of Washington's East Asia Library.

Outside of PLU, I have been supported by a wide group of scholars, including Gregory Adam Scott, my longtime collaborator. I have also received various forms of encouragement, assistance, and advice from a number of people during the long period of this project's completion. In particular, I thank Raoul Birnbaum, Richard Jaffe, Ishii Kosei, Hwansoo Kim, Victoria Montrose, Jin Y. Park, Jeff Schroeder, Lina Verchery, and the Venerable Xiandu. Others have offered substantial support and advice, without which this book would not have been possible. I thank the series editors Dan Stevenson and Jimmy Yu for their unwavering support for this project from its early stages as well as all but one of the anonymous reviewers, whose timely comments improved this work tremendously. Jason Clower and Stefania Travagnin provided extensive advice on various aspects of the project. Finally, the most significant help I received has been the inspiration and insight I received from Lei Kuan Rongdao Lai, a consummate scholar and human being. Her ideas and work showed me that this was a book that could be written, and her comments and advice played no small role in its current form. To all of these scholars: thank you, I have listened to you as best as I have been able. Any errors that remain are, of course, solely my own.

Life is not just about scholarship, so I also thank my regular role-playing gaming group for all the laughter and the chance to relax on a regular basis. I thank my *sangha* at the Tacoma Buddhist Temple, a community of kind, dependable, and diverse Buddhists who are keeping the tradition alive. They have provided me a Buddhist home and a place of purpose. A special thanks goes to Rev. Kojo Kakihara and Tetsuo "Ted" Tamaki, who welcomed me and brought me into the community. Great thanks must also go to my parents, who gave me my love of Buddhism: my mom, who showed me the life of the heart and taught me to ask big questions and take delight in the variety of the universe; my father, who showed me the life of the mind and taught me to ask precise questions and

PREFACE

trust the learning and expertise of disciplined minds. And finally, thanks to my wife, Aimee, for all of her immeasurable support. She helped me with timely and precise advice, a keen eye for my blind spots, and a listening ear for my frustrations when the project was mired in yet another delay.

* * *

A note on terminology: For the title of this book I have chosen to translate the Mandarin Chinese term "Huayan 華嚴" with the Sanskrit word "Avataṃsaka." I have done this so that scholars of other forms of Buddhism will be able to recognize at a glance what this book is about. I am well aware that some scholars believe this to be an incorrect usage. The majority of textual scholars agree that the three versions of the Huayan Sutra (Huayanjing 華嚴經), from which the Huayan School takes its name, were created through the concatenation of multiple smaller, independent sutras. This means there is no complete Sanskrit version to check for a proper title. The two primary choices for what this large sutra would be called in Sanskrit are "Avataṃsaka" and "Gaṇḍavyūha." I chose to use the former for pragmatic reasons: "Avataṃsaka" has become the consensus term used by most Buddhists and scholars since the twentieth century, and it is a term supported by textual evidence.[1] The latter term, though favored by the third and fourth patriarchs of the Huayan School, probably more accurately refers to the "Entering the Dharmadhātu" ("Ru fajie pin" 入法界) section of the text, which comes at the end of the sixty- and eighty-volume versions of the sutra (the forty-volume version of the Huayan Sutra is simply an expanded version of the "Entering the Dharmadhātu" section).[2] I have chosen to use "Avataṃsaka" in the title of my book because it is more recognizable by nonspecialists; however, because the current study deals exclusively with the Chinese version of the text and the Chinese Buddhist School associated with it, outside of this book's title I use the Mandarin term "Huayan."

Cascadia
Winter 2019

Introduction

ON THE FIRST day of 1912, in the city of Nanjing, newly elected president Sun Yat-sen proudly declared the establishment of the Republic of China (1912–1949), ending more than two millennia of imperial rule and ushering in a period that would witness changes across virtually every sphere of Chinese life. That same year, nearly two hundred miles downriver in the cosmopolitan hub of Shanghai, the monks Yuexia 月霞 (1858–1917) and Yingci 應慈 (1873–1965) launched the first monastic school of the era, aimed at improving the education level of the Buddhist monastic community. It was located in a garden on the grounds of the estate of Liza Roos and Silas Hardoon, and its student body of around sixty young monks followed a full daily schedule involving the study of sutras and commentaries, meditation, and strict adherence to the monastic rule. Named after the Huayan Sutra (Huayanjing 華嚴經), the most voluminous scripture in the Chinese Buddhist canon, the school was called Huayan University (Huayan Daxue 華嚴大學). It was the first monastic school of China's new era.

Scholars of modern Chinese Buddhism have long recognized that educational reform was a central issue for Buddhists during the Republican period, but their analysis has a tendency to reproduce uncritically the categories used by the people of that time. Buddhist education in early twentieth-century China is still often discussed in terms of tradition versus modernity or simply old versus new models of education. The first is meant to include the mandatory training course monastics had to undergo at a Vinaya monastery directly before their ordination as well as forms of education centered on earlier educational models, such as that of the Guanzong Research Society (Guanzong Yanjiu She 觀宗研究社), founded in 1918 by the modern Tiantai 天台 master Dixian 諦閑 (1858–1932). The second category, "modern" or "new" education, is usually used to describe the Wuchang Buddhist Institute (Wuchang Foxueyuan 武昌佛學院) and programs related to it. Criteria for being considered "modern" often include the teaching of secular subjects (foreign languages, natural science, history, etc.) within the curriculum; use of the apparatus of modern education such as blackboards, tests, and diplomas; and the presence of both lay and monastic students in the same classrooms. By these criteria, Huayan University would be a clear example of "traditional" monastic educational program. However, the picture is far more complex. Fully a decade before the founding of the Wuchang Buddhist Institute, Huayan University was the first school of the Republic to take up the legacy of the Jetavana Hermitage (Zhihuan Jingshe 祇洹精舍), which ran from 1908 to 1910 and is widely regarded as the wellspring of modern Buddhist education in China.

There is some utility in sorting Chinese Buddhist education in the twentieth century into "modern" and "traditional" or in placing various institutions on a spectrum that takes these two paradigms as its poles, but in this study I follow an approach suggested by Stefania Travagnin, who has argued that we can fruitfully study modern Buddhist education by engaging in the microhistorical study of specific educational networks. Travagnin is particularly concerned that historians move beyond the "Taixu paradigm," which tells the story of modern Chinese Buddhism strictly in relation to the activities, associates, and ideas of the famed monk Taixu 太虛 (1870–1947).[1] This book moves beyond the Taixu paradigm by telling the history of one specific network within modern Chinese

Buddhism, the network of Huayan-centered educational programs that originated from the first Huayan University.

Students at the Huayan University acquired a firm foundation in the study of the Huayan Sutra, but they also built a network of colleagues whom they called upon as they carried on university's educational legacy throughout the Republican period. They identified their teacher, Yuexia, as the source of their own authority as they taught a third generation of monastic students during the tumultuous years of the 1920s and 1930s. The teaching that Yuexia initiated continued with each generation, and many of the Chinese monastics today who have made a name for themselves through their diligent study of the Huayan Sutra also place themselves within a lineage originating from Yuexia. This is not a monastic lineage in the traditional sense but one formed through bonds of education and erudition, which were the basis for a Huayan University network that had a significant but overlooked impact on Buddhist education in China in the 1920s and 1930s and that continues to the present day.

The Study of Huayan Buddhism During the Republic

Huayan University got its name from Yuexia's traditional lecture series on the Huayan Sutra that served as the school's central curriculum. It is widely held within Chinese Buddhism that the Huayan Sutra is a record of the first teachings given by the Buddha after his enlightenment. The Huayan Sutra is also the longest single sutra in East Asian Buddhism. This sutra is said to reflect more accurately than any other scripture the full reality that the Buddha perceived at the moment of his awakening, and for this reason it is often referred to as the "king of sutras" (*jingzhong zhi wang* 經中之王, *jingwang* 經王, etc.). It addresses the full range of Mahāyāna Buddhist teachings as it describes, in vast and complex detail, the world of the Buddha's enlightenment. Parts of this text became important in Buddhist devotional practice in East Asia, and its mythology of a central cosmic Buddha was incorporated into the premodern political ideologies of China, Korea, and Japan.² Exegesis on the Huayan Sutra in China during the Sui and Tang dynasties (581–618 and 618–907 CE) also led to the formation of a distinct school of Buddhist thought and practice, which is usually known by the same name as the sutra. The ideas and writings of this Huayan School (Huayanzong 華嚴宗) spread to all of the other nations of East Asia, where they have been studied and taught up to the present.

The period from the late nineteenth century to the mid-twentieth century saw massive changes in the social, political, economic, religious, and intellectual lives of the people of China. As Buddhists navigated these changes, they absorbed, adapted, and deployed new resources and concepts. New printing technologies facilitated the spread of novel ideas about Buddhism. Trends in the social-scientific study of religion, then being developed in the West and in Japan, came to China,³ and lost texts of the Chinese Buddhist tradition were returned to circulation through the work of new publishing houses. Debates about what Buddhism ought to be took place among members of urban lay study groups, students in new monastic educational programs, and the authors of histories and introductory textbooks on Buddhism. The identity of Chinese Buddhism, including the identities of its component parts, such as Huayan, was the subject of much discussion.

Chinese Buddhists believed that the Huayan School was an essential and meaningful component of their tradition that deserved to be conserved and studied. For most Buddhists, their engagement with Huayan occurred primarily through devotional practice and the reading of the summary presentations of Huayan given in the new general texts on Buddhism. Lay and monastic Buddhists alike continued to engage in the traditional merit-making practices of reciting, printing, and copying by hand (in ink, gold, or their own blood) the entire Huayan Sutra or a few select chapters. New printing technologies made it easier to own copies of the sutra and its commentaries, though older-format printings remained prized for their aesthetic value. Printing and expanded literacy gave rise to an increasing number of introductory textbooks on Buddhism. These books, pitched to the literate nonspecialist, popularized a condensed-version of Huayan doctrine and history.

When discussing Huayan Buddhism during the Republican period, scholars have tended to focus on three main themes. The first is the interest displayed by a number of reform-minded politicians in Huayan in fin-de-siècle China.[4] The second is the personal interest that the great lay Buddhist publisher and educator Yang Wenhui 楊文會 (1837–1911) had in Huayan, which led him to focus on the writings of that tradition as he worked to recover and reprint lost Buddhist texts in the late nineteenth century. The third theme is the tendency to treat Yuexia and Huayan University as both the epitome and the source of a revival of Huayan Buddhism in the Republic of China.

Just as I avoid using the terms *traditional* and *modern*, I generally avoid the question of "revival," which has been a key focus in the scholarship on Republican Buddhism since at least as early as Holmes Welch's foundational work *The Buddhist Revival in China* (1968). Although he wrote this book to critically question the very notion of a revival in China, it is still a common theme in scholarship on that period. An overemphasis on revival has led to a tendency among some scholars to critique Huayan and other Buddhist activities of the period according to these activities' level of innovation or lack thereof. This tendency is related to a catch-22 into which Sinophone scholars of late-imperial Chinese Buddhism often place their subjects: on the one hand, those who adhered closely to classical texts in their study and teaching are treated as simply going through the motions as they promoted a dead and lifeless tradition; on the other hand, those who created new ideas and interpretations are deemed to have gotten it all wrong by departing too greatly from the tradition.[5] In studying the Republican period, it is important to avoid making such judgments, which animate the work of some who look beyond Yuexia and the Huayan

University to assess the academic study and the scholastic exegesis of classical Huayan thought over the span of the entire twentieth century.⁶

Holmes Welch (1924–1981) discussed Huayan (which he refers to as "Avataṃsaka") Buddhism several times in *The Buddhist Revival in China*. Although it was not a primary topic of inquiry for him, he did see Huayan as playing an important role in the Buddhism of the period. He identified the revived interest in the Huayan School and the Consciousness-Only School (Weishi Zong 唯識宗) as one of the reasons behind the surge in Buddhist printing activities that took place at the time. He also claimed that interest in those two schools, alongside Tiantai, was so great that by the late 1930s the three had begun to supplant study of more basic sutras at some major monastic centers, such as Tianning 天寧 Temple.⁷ Aside from this, most of Welch's comments on Huayan center on Yuexia, Yingci, and the Huayan University. The late scholar-monk Shi Dongchu 釋東初 (1908–1977) deals with many of the same ideas as Welch. He provides information on a greater number of people and institutions involved with Huayan during the period in his history of modern Chinese Buddhism, but his information is still brief.⁸ Chen Bing 陳兵 and Deng Zimei 燈子美 discuss Huayan University and some of the activities of its graduates in their general history of twentieth-century Chinese Buddhism. Their book is one of the few sources I have seen that includes the monk Shouye 壽冶 (1908–2001) among its list of Huayan worthies.⁹ Although Shouye is not widely recognized for his scholarship and did not study under Yuexia or Yingci, he was highly committed to the recitation of the Huayan Sutra, and his brand of practice and devotion should be considered as much a form of "Huayan Buddhism" as the scholastic studies of those other monks.

Yao Binbin's 姚彬彬 recent work has added much to our understanding of modern Huayan. For the most part, he deals with the same issues as earlier scholars but does so with a greater range of data and in a much more theoretically sensitive manner. Yao also includes an analysis of the ways in which Huayan thought was used to address contemporary issues. For example, he finds that some in China linked Huayan to modern political discourses of equality.[10] This was not unique to China because Huayan thought also was used to support the idea of equality in other parts of East Asia.[11] Yao also discusses the philosophical uses to which Huayan was put to by thinkers associated with Neo-Confucianism. King Pong Chiu has studied them in much greater depth in his examination of the Huayan thought of Thomé H. Fang (Fang Dongmei 方東美, 1899–1977) and Tang Junyi 唐君毅 (1909–1978).[12]

Why Huayan University?

Every general study of Republican Chinese Buddhism mentions the importance of the Huayan University, but the exact nature of that importance is rarely explained. The university is sometimes described as a mostly unsuccessful attempt to create a modern Buddhist seminary. At other times, it is cited either as evidence for the existence of a distinct Huayan School in Republican China or merely as an example of a limited resurgence of Huayan studies in modern China. Regardless of how it is framed, any discussion of the university is usually brief. This study seeks to provide a fuller picture of both the Huayan University and the larger Huayan School by locating them in relation to several major concerns of Republican Buddhism. Here I focus on individual monks, the programs they ran, and the curriculum of their programs to show that Yuexia and Huayan University became the origin and putative center of authority for a loose network of monastics who taught Huayan doctrine and meditation from the 1920s to the present day. We see, for example, that two of the school's graduates, Cizhou 慈舟 (1877–1958) and Zhiguang 智光 (1889–1963), were treated as celebrated masters of Huayan in the Republican Buddhist press. And, like them, other members of the school's first class went on in the 1920s and 1930s to found nearly a dozen monastic study programs whose curricula centered on the study of classical Huayan thought.

INTRODUCTION

These programs in turn produced a third generation of Huayan specialists who carried this tradition of Huayan education to Taiwan, Vietnam, Hong Kong, and the United States and then back to mainland China as Buddhism revived in the wake of the repression of religion carried out during the Cultural Revolution (1966–1976). Even beyond the actual graduates of the school, Huayan University was so influential in the 1920s that programs with no direct link to the original program adopted its name and curriculum. Even today in China, the Huayan University is generally regarded as the root institution for modern Huayan studies.

Study of the Huayan University network sheds light on Republican-era Chinese Buddhism as a whole. The philosophy of the Huayan School focuses on the truth of the Buddhist doctrine of interdependence, which means that if you look closely enough at any one phenomenon, you can see all of reality reflected within it. This doctrine is most famously illustrated with the metaphor of Indra's net, a giant net that is said to hang over the entire universe. At each node in this net, there is a perfectly smooth, round, and reflective jewel. If you choose one jewel and look deeply enough into it, you can see all of the other jewels in the net reflected within its face. Causality works the same way in that all of the things and events of the universe have to happen just as they happen in order for any one thing to be the way it is. This idea is also mooted in history in the use of case studies. This book is one such case study, with its specific case, its limited node of meaning, being the people and activity that surrounded and produced Huayan education in the first half of the twentieth century.

Huayan education is linked to a number of important topics related to Chinese Buddhism in the modern period, including the antisectarian trend, the recovery of lost scriptures, and ongoing regionalism within Chinese Buddhism. The very idea that Huayan was a school in need of reviving was closely connected to the rhetoric of "revival" prevalent in the period. The supposed atrophy of the Huayan School and Huayan studies was taken as evidence of the sad state of Chinese Buddhism as a whole. The revival of schools such as Huayan was tied to the strongly antisectarian language that was popular during the period.[13] There is something fishy about this antisectarian trend, however: many people spoke against sectarianism, but very few spoke in favor of it, and a careful study of the people most invested in teaching Huayan turns up no examples of a person promoting the idea that Huayan is superior to other forms of Buddhism. The monks teaching Huayan, the people most likely to engage in the partisan support decried in the Buddhist press, repeatedly went out of their way to deny such claims, even stating that Huayan and Tiantai, a supposed historical rival of Huayan, are in perfect harmony. So where was the sectarianism that Chinese Buddhists were fighting so hard against? It was probably no closer than the Buddhism of Japan, which has a history of sectarianism and which exerted a strong influence on Chinese Buddhists during the republic.

Japanese Buddhism was the source of the rhetoric of a sectarian threat, but it was also a valuable source of lost texts. Scholars of modern Chinese Buddhism often make a great deal of the publishing activities of the scriptural presses active during the period. They point to the new technologies used by these presses and how they made rare and lost works more available. The Buddhist press of the early twentieth century did make available again a number of Huayan texts that had been lost in China, but these texts had a limited impact. Newly recovered texts were rarely if ever discussed, and the public teaching of Huayan consisted mostly of lecture series on the Huayan Sutra given by monastics using the commentaries written upon it by the fourth patriarch of the Huayan School, Qingliang Chengguan 清涼澄觀 (737–838). Even these lectures were fairly rare: Yingci, the most famous master of the Huayan Sutra during the period, completed only a couple of lecture series on either of the two full versions of the Huayan Sutra during the three decades between 1920 and 1949. Even the Huayan-centered educational programs of the Republican period did not engage in the study of newly recovered classical texts, choosing to center their curriculum instead on the Huayan Sutra and its traditional commentaries, which they usually supplemented with two summaries of Huayan teachings written by the early Qing dynasty (1636–1912) monk Xufa 續法 (1641–1728). Despite being criticized by such important Buddhist figures as Yang Wenhui and Taixu, Xufa's work was highly influential in Huayan studies throughout the Republican period.

Sources and Structure of This Study

The spread of mechanized printing, the proliferation of networks for the distribution of printed material, and rising literacy expanded the audience for Buddhist texts. But many of the texts available to the novice for the study of Buddhism were Buddhist scriptures, which were difficult to understand. To remedy this, a growing number of introductory texts to Buddhism appeared in the 1910s with titles including the words *chuxue* 初學 (beginning study), *rumen* 入門 (introductory), and *gangyao* 綱要 (general outline).[14] These works were written for an abstracted general readership, which Jan Kiely refers to as a "mass collectivity" of shared readers, and they were designed to spread generalized ideas about Buddhism among the greatest number of people.[15] They are a good place to look for information on what the Huayan School was popularly understood to be. These texts were most often quite broad in nature, but some of the shorter introductory works examined here focus specifically on Huayan, including summaries of Huayan written by some of its more prominent monastic exponents, such as Changxing 常惺 (1896–1939) and Nanting 南亭 (1900–1982).[16]

Beyond works written to serve as introductory texts, Chinese students of Buddhism in the 1920s and 1930s could also consult new works on the general history of Buddhism. These histories were often organized by school and thus provide much material for the study of emic definitions of Huayan. Such works are sometimes classified as *shi* 史 (histories) or *tongshi* 通史 (general histories).

Although they were meant to be comprehensive in breadth, they were not necessarily meant to provide depth, as indicated by the fact that their titles often featured the term *lüe* 略 (abbreviated) or *gang* 綱 (outline). General histories of Buddhism did exist before the modern period, but the modern period saw the emergence of new conventions and new genres of Chinese Buddhist history.[17] The writings of Yang Wenhui, which were influenced by Japanese scholarship, were important in establishing the sectarian model within modern Chinese Buddhist historiography. Several specific early Japanese histories were also particularly influential in establishing this trend in China.[18]

For this study, I have also used a number of textbooks and general histories on Buddhism published during the period to describe the common understanding of Huayan in the culture at the time. There is much overlap between the two genres, the introductory text and the general history, and a hard distinction is not needed here. Within and even across genres, there are many commonalities in these works' treatment of Huayan, sometimes to the point of direct copying.[19] Even when not copying other works, all of the sources examined here hold a fairly consistent line on the nature of the Huayan School. More significantly, as is common practice, I have made extensive use of Buddhist periodicals from the 1920s and 1930s. The essays, lecture transcripts, notices of current events, and institutional curricula they contain are invaluable for reconstructing the history of Chinese Buddhism in the early twentieth century

This study is divided into two parts. Part I deals with the institutions and individuals of the Huayan University and the network of programs it inspired, and part II discusses the doctrinal and practical content of the education that they provided. Each part starts with a general chapter in which Huayan Buddhism is situated within Republican Buddhist history, first institutionally (chapter 1) and then doctrinally (chapter 5). Both of these framing chapters aim to elucidate the emic conception of Huayan: how

Buddhists themselves understood and articulated the meaning of Huayan Buddhism during the Republican period.

Chapter 1 summarizes the origin and history of the Huayan School of Chinese Buddhism. As scholars have noted, one must be careful when using the notion of "schools" (*zong* 宗) such as Huayan when writing the history of Chinese Buddhism, so this chapter begins with a critical reflection on this issue of Buddhist schools in China. It argues that the idea of *zong* had great conceptual power in early twentieth-century Chinese Buddhism, and for this reason we should take it seriously in our study of the period even though there is no evidence of Huayan-centered sectarianism. Chapter 2 lays out the core event of this book: the founding of Huayan University. It locates the school's founding within a general drive toward monastic education in the period. It recounts the tumultuous years of the school, which had to move twice in less than four years, and briefly summarizes how a foundation was built to carry on the original school under a new name. Chapter 2 closes by assessing the nature of the network formed by the graduates of the original Huayan University. Even as they claimed authority by citing their tutelage under Yuexia, they formed a network of mutual connection characterized by strong peer relationships rather than a hierarchical one under a single master.

Chapters 3 and 4 trace the formation of a network of programs and teachers who carried on the legacy of the Huayan University. Chapter 3 begins with an assessment of the career of Yingci. When Yuexia died in 1917, the mantle of leadership could have been passed to Yingci, but Yingci made other choices. Although he did go on to have a celebrated career lecturing on sutras, he refused to serve as a center of authority for the network of graduates of the original Huayan University. This refusal led to the formation of a network that was diffuse, not centralized. This chapter recounts the histories of nearly a dozen Huayan-centered institutes between 1920 and 1940. Most of them were founded by graduates of the original Huayan University, but several, including the Huayan University of Yangzhou, were merely inspired by it.

INTRODUCTION

Although all of these institutes were relatively short-lived, they taught a next generation of monks to be teachers in their own right. Out of these institutes came a number of figures active in Chinese Huayan between 1950 and 2000, whose activities are discussed in chapter 4. These students of the second-generation academies carried the Huayan tradition beyond mainland China, where they preserved it and helped reintroduce it after liberalization began in the 1980s.

In part II, the book shifts from an emphasis on individuals and institutions to teaching and doctrine. It seeks to answer the following questions: What did a "Huayan" education consist of in Republican China, and how did the Huayan University network contribute to it? Chapter 5 describes the doctrines most commonly ascribed to the Huayan School by the general Buddhist population during the Republican period. They included its doctrinal classification scheme (*panjiao* 叛教, which was a point of some debate during the Republican period) as well as some but not all of the doctrinal concepts discussed by Xianshou Fazang 賢首法藏 (643–712) and Chengguan. Huayan was not merely a point of doctrine for Republican Buddhists, however, so the chapter begins with a brief summary of some of the devotional activities and other modes of Buddhist practice that took place in the 1920s and 1930s around the Huayan Sutra. These activities were evenly split between monastics and the laity, and they typify the strong continuation of traditional Chinese Buddhist praxis through the early-modern period. Chapter 6 compares the printed curricula of the various Huayan-centered educational programs and finds several common patterns. Despite the new availability of many overlooked and lost Huayan texts, most academic curricula focused their Huayan studies on three things: the Huayan Sutra, which was invariably studied using the commentaries of Chengguan; Fazang's *Treatise on the Five Teachings* (*Wujiao zhang* 五教章),[20] which was studied using the writings of the Qing dynasty Huayan master Xufa as a guide; and the practice of Huayan meditation. The chapter closes with a reconsideration of the nature of Huayan meditation and argues against the Tiantai notion that Huayan lacks such a practice.

In the wake of the closure of the original Huayan University, its graduates carried its legacy forward to form a loose network of individuals and institutions. This Huayan network was always diffuse, but though it lacked a formal spiritual lineage, an authoritative leader, and a geographic and institutional center, it did produce a lasting pattern of education and affiliation. The impact of Huayan University on Chinese Buddhism continues to this day.

PART ONE

ONE

Huayan as a School of Chinese Buddhism

IN ORDER TO understand the Huayan University and its network of descendent institutes, it is necessary to have a general sense of what the term *huayan* or the name "Huayan" means in the context of Chinese Buddhism. This chapter focuses on the notion of the "Huayan School," a name that appears widely in premodern and modern Sinitic Buddhist texts. Rather than create a stipulative definition of the term, this chapter aims to describe its emic meaning, especially the meaning ascribed to it by the historians of Buddhism and promoters of Huayan who were active during the first half of the twentieth century. This chapter analyzes academic Buddhist histories and textbooks as well as brief summaries and outlines to determine as precisely as possible what Chinese Buddhists meant when they referred to Huayan Buddhism.

Huayan Sutra and Huayan School

The Sinitic term *huayan* 華嚴 refers to the act of adorning something or someone with flowers as a way to show respect.[1] It can also refer to the adornments themselves, which are generally understood to be garlands of flowers, including those used to honor people and deities in South Asia, Polynesia, and many other parts of the world.² This practice spread with Buddhism out of India into other parts of Asia. In Sinitic East Asia, it took on a variety of meanings, becoming a polyvalent sign that can be used in many different but related ways. In its grandest sense, *huayan* is a metaphor for the totality of reality that surrounds and is none other than the body of Vairocana (Pilushe'na 毘盧舍那), the great cosmic Buddha. "Huayan" is the name for three sutras that describe that reality as well as an umbrella name for the commentaries written on those texts. As a bibliographic category in the Sinitic Buddhist canon, it also includes treatises written by Chinese authors that do not even discuss that sutra as well as manuals for repentance rites centered on the Huayan Sutra. It is the name of a philosophical school and the title for at least one dharma lineage in China that originates from that school's founders. It is also used as the name of many sacred Buddhists sites in China, including temples and geographic features. In other words, "Huayan" is a thing that one can visit, chant, study, practice, and realize.

Because of the wide range of meanings the name "Huayan" holds within the Sinitic Buddhist tradition, it is important to take care in its use. In this study, when "Huayan" is used by itself, it signifies the broadest, least-determined range of its meanings, as is done in Chinese-language materials. I use the phrases "classical Huayan," "Huayan thought," and "Huayan tradition" to refer more narrowly to a philosophical and practical tradition founded in China in the second half of the first millennium. This tradition is also referred to as the "Huayan School." The name "Huayan" is used adjectivally in Sinophone materials, and I sometimes use it in this fashion as well in ways that I have attempted to make clear from the context. Of course, I also make frequent mention of the Huayan Sutra, which is the central trunk from which all of these other branches have grown. When I use "Huayan Sutra" in an unqualified manner, I am referring to all three versions of that text.

Modern textual scholars agree that the Huayan Sutra was created in China starting in the fifth century CE through the amalgamation of a number of smaller, independently circulating Mahāyana sutras.[3] The sheer size of the Huayan Sutra as well as its origins in a handful of disparate texts make it difficult to summarize, but several key themes run through it. In the most basic and abstract terms possible, this text describes the nature of supreme enlightenment and lays out the practices necessary for attaining it. The text identifies Vairocana Buddha as the king of all buddhas, a cosmic Buddha whose body is coextensive with the universe and who is the very manifestation of truth. The Huayan Sutra describes his realm of perfect enlightenment, the Flower Store World (Huazang Shijie 華藏世界), and outlines in great detail the stages of practices through which a bodhisattva passes before it ultimately perceives and manifests this realm of enlightenment. The Huayan Sutra puts forward two ideas that would be particularly important for the theorists of the Huayan School. First, it proclaims the nonduality of the absolute and the phenomenal by stating that Vairocana's perfect and magnificent Dharma Realm, or Dharmadhātu (Ch. *fajie* 法界), is identical with the troubled ordinary world of sentient beings. Second, it puts forth a limited version of the idea of the identity of the one and the many (*yi xiang ru duo* 一相入多) when it states that each one of the bodhisattva practices contains all of the other practices.[4] Later Huayan thinkers expanded on this idea by using it to refer to the relationship between each single phenomenon and all of reality.

Soon after the Huayan Sutra's appearance in China, an exegetical tradition developed around it. Some of the most important figures in this tradition were later identified as the founders of a Huayan School, which is generally treated as espousing a unified philosophical position. Although there is certainly some logic to the way the core ideas of the Huayan School were derived from the Huayan Sutra, Huayan School thought and the ideas put forth in the Huayan Sutra are not the same. For this reason, most contemporary historians of Huayan are careful to draw a distinction between the study and exegesis of the Huayan Sutra, on the one hand, and the teachers and teachings of the Huayan School, on the other.[5] Although I fully accept this distinction and feel it to be valuable when studying the historical development of Huayan in China, in this book I do not emphasize this difference. Here I am concerned primarily with the definition, study, and practice of Huayan Buddhism in early twentieth-century China, and this distinction was not one that most Chinese Buddhists of this period cared to make. This scholarly distinction does not help us in understanding how Chinese Buddhists *themselves* thought of Huayan.

Name and Founders of the School

One can begin an examination of the received identity of the Huayan School where its exegetes most often begin: with the names they use to describe it. The Huayan School and the variety of names used to refer to it provide a useful framework for explaining how Chinese Buddhists thought about its basic identity. If a *zong* is a group organized around a central text, idea, or founder, what kind of *zong* is the Huayan School? The Chan School (Chanzong 禪宗) is named after its central method, meditation (*chan* 禪); the Pure Land School (Jingtuzong 淨土宗) is named for the aim of its practice, rebirth in the Pure Land (*jingtu* 淨土); and the Tiantai School is named after the school's primary founder, Tiantai Zhiyi 天台智顗 (538–597), who was often referred to using the name of Mt. Tiantai, where he resided. These, however, are only the most common names for the schools, and each is known by multiple names.

There are at least five different names used for the Huayan School, but only two were commonly used in the premodern and modern periods: Huayan School (Huayanzong) and Xianshou School (Xianshouzong 賢首宗). A few modern texts report that there were some who referred to Huayan as the Qingliang School (Qingliangzong 清涼宗), a reference to Qingliang Chengguan. Yang Wenhui said that although some people did this, they were mistaken, and the school should be known as the Xianshou School because Fazang was far more important than Chengguan.⁶ Despite Yang's comments, I have not seen any evidence that the name "Qingliang School" was much in use in the early twentieth century, and his statement may have simply been rhetorical. The same is true of "Dharmadhātu School" (Fajiezong 法界宗) and "Perfect School" (Yuanzong 圓宗), which are mentioned as alternate names for the school but were rarely used.

The name "Huayan School," which is used widely by both premodern Buddhists and the modern Buddhists studied here, adds to the legitimacy of the Huayan School by representing it as simply a school focused on the teachings of the Buddha as expressed in his own profound words within the Huayan Sutra. This emphasizes the idea that the Huayan School and the Huayan Sutra are coextensive. The name "Huayanzong" dates to the Tang dynasty and the writings of the school's putative fourth and fifth patriarchs, Chengguan and Guifeng Zongmi 圭峰宗密 (780–841), who used it to signal that they took the teachings of the Huayan Sutra as the central tenet (*zong*) of their thought. The other common name for the school came into regular use during the Northern Song (960-1127) when some started to refer to it as the "Teaching of the Patriarch Xianshou" (*Xianshou zujiao* 賢首祖教) or simply the Xianshou School.⁷ "Xianshou" was another name for Fazang, the third of the Huayan School's five putative founding masters. By referring to this school using Xianshou's name, one emphasizes his central role in establishing its main ideas. In this case, *zong* can be used in the sense of "familial or religious lineage," "the group descended from the ancestor (or *zong*) Fazang," but it is also used in the sense of "central philosophical tenet," as "the school that takes the thought of Fazang as its central tenet (*zong*)." Using this name thus elevates Fazang above the school's other founding figures.

Most authors writing during the Republican Period used only one name to refer to the school, choosing either "Huayan School" or "Xianshou School," and there is a noticeable pattern among those who chose to use one or the other name: Japanese authors and those who extensively copied their work, such as Jiang Weiqiao 蔣維喬 (1873–1958) and Huang Chanhua 黃懺華 (ca. 1890–1977), all follow the medieval Japanese Kegon monk Gyōnen 凝然 (1240–1321) in referring to it as the "Huayan School." Interestingly, Yang Wenhui, though strongly influenced by Gyōnen's work *Essentials of the Eight Sects* (*Hasshū kōyō* 八宗綱要, 1268) in other respects, uses "Xianshou School" primarily (following, perhaps, the influential Buddhist history *Chronicle of the Buddhist Patriarchs* [*Fozu tongji* 佛祖統紀], 1269).[8] Most of the Chinese authors who came after Yang in the early twentieth century, such as Taixu and Changxing, followed his lead and also chose to use the name "Xianshou School."

In the school's most common formulation, the five Huayan patriarchs are: Dushun 杜順 (a.k.a. Fashun 法順, n.d.), Zhiyan 智儼 (602–668), Chengguan, Fazang, and Zongmi. With only a few exceptions, each of the premodern and modern writings I examined identifies the Huayan School as having been established in China by these five masters.[9] I do not summarize their lives here as a number of useful studies are available on the life and thought of each of these figures (with the exception of Dushun, for whom very little dependable biographical data are available).[10] What is important here is the list as a whole and its role as an element of the core identity of the Huayan School. A few have argued that Zongmi created the first list of Huayan patriarchs by identifying the continuity between Dushun, Zhiyan, and Fazang; however, most scholars acknowledge that it was Jinshui Jingyuan 晉水淨源 (1011–1088) who created the list of the five founders and who was responsible for establishing a lineage of Huayan masters. Faced with the growing popularity of Tiantai and Chan, each of which created their own lineages in the Song dynasty (960–1279), Jingyuan argued for a comparable lineage within Huayan. His lineage began with two popular Indian Buddhist philosophers, Nāgārjuna and went through the five figures listed earlier. Not all of Jingyuan's contemporaries agreed with his list. His contemporary the Huayan exegete Guanfu 觀復 (n.d.) included Vasubhdandu as one of the Indian patriarchs, for example.[11] Later texts included other founding figures as well. The *Chronicle of the Buddhist Patriarchs* adds the lay scholar Li Tongxuan 李通玄 (645–740).[12] Regardless of such variation, Jingyuan's basic Huayan model of five patriarchs became the standard for later treatments of the Huayan School.

The lineage of five Huayan patriarchs as outlined by Jingyuan is important, but it should not be taken as a statement of historical fact. Scholars have serious doubts about the role that the supposed first patriarch Dushun played in creating the Huayan School.[13] And it is widely recognized that Fazang died twenty-five years before Chengguan was born, meaning that the two could never have met face to face. That said, authority within the Huayan lineage does not depend on an unbroken succession of teachers and students, as one finds within the Chan Schools, so such gaps are not a major problem for the school's proponents. The Huayan School's general lack of insistence on an unbroken lineage was probably one of the factors that allowed Yuexia, who was not a student of any recognized master of the Huayan tradition, to become regarded as the preeminent figure in that school in the Republican period. Regardless of the idea's historicity, all of the modern works examined here invoked the Huayan patriarchs in their description of the school. With few exceptions, they mention the five founders of classical Huayan. Some works also mention other important figures. Gyōnen and much later Nanting follow Jingyuan in adding Nāgārjuna and Aśvaghoṣa. Several others, notably Shimaji Mokurai 島地默雷 (1838–1911) and Oda Tokunō 織田德能 (1860–1911), follow the *Chronicle of the Buddhist Patriarchs* and include Jingyuan and his teacher Changshui Zixuan 長水子璿 (965–1034) in *A Brief History of Buddhism of the Three Nations* (*Sangoku Bukkyō ryakushi* 三國佛教略史), which was published in Japan in 1890 and was quite influential in China.[14] In the Republican period, such additions were the exception rather than the norm, and in their efforts to define the Huayan School the vast majority of modern authors simply referred to the five patriarchs.

PART ONE

Popular Practices of the Huayan Sutra

The Buddhists who are the focus of this book took it as axiomatic that the doctrine of the Huayan School, as explained by its five founders, is more or less identical to the teachings contained in the Huayan Sutra. Much of their work did center on the preaching and study of sections or the entirety of the Huayan Sutra, but as the scholar and nun Guo Cheen (Guoqin) 果琴 points out, since the Song dynasty Chinese Buddhists have rarely studied or taught the Huayan Sutra without the aid of the commentaries written by the Huayan School's founders, especially those written by Chengguan.[15] These commentaries interpret the Huayan Sutra using categories and concepts central to Huayan School thought, and their usage has reinforced the identity of the school and the sutra. As the years went by, the Huayan School founders' ideas deeply affected popular exegesis of the Huayan Sutra. As a result, although it is important for historians of early Huayan Buddhism to draw a distinction between the Huayan School and the exegetical tradition of the Huayan Sutra, it is not a distinction that matters as much after the end of the first millennium CE because the Chinese Buddhist tradition in general and proponents of the Huayan School in particular have tended to elide the difference between the two. They treat Huayan thought as it developed in China in the sixth through ninth centuries CE as more or less the same thing as the ideas of the text for which it is named. For this reason, though the current study focuses on institutions, doctrine, and text, it is important to also recognize that in discussing the status of "Huayan Buddhism" within early modern China, it is not accurate to separate the various activities centered on the sutra from those more narrowly focused on the school's doctrine and practice.

Given the lack of a clear distinction between the Huayan Sutra and the Huayan School within Chinese Buddhism, any account of either that does not include devotional practices would be incomplete. This assertion is supported from within the tradition itself, where the inclusion of devotional practice was integral to Huayan

Buddhism from the start. Huayan patriarchs Fazang and Chengguan incorporated in their commentaries on the Huayan Sutra tales of miracles associated with chanting and copying it.[16] Some of the most well known of these miracles are included in the *Record of the Transmission of the Huayan Sutra* (*Huayanjing zhuanji* 華嚴經傳記), which was started by Fazang and completed by his disciples after his death.[17] This text is a history of the Huayan Sutra in China, and it relates the stories of famous individuals who translated, commented upon, recited, and chanted it. Many of the stories in the collection feature miraculous events and are meant to support the idea of the power of the sutra. The *Record* attempts to prove that by venerating and chanting the Huayan Sutra, one can obtain the support and protection of buddhas and bodhisattvas. As with other sutras, collections of Huayan miracle tales were produced well into the late-imperial period.[18]

The identity of Huayan as commonly articulated in early twentieth-century China was closely tied to the founders and doctrines of the Huayan School, but in the religious lives of ordinary Chinese Buddhists the Huayan Sutra had a much broader impact than that school. In everyday Buddhism, the Huayan Sutra was more important as an object of and vehicle for devotional activity than as the inspiration for a school of doctrine. Lay and monastic Buddhists chanted, bowed to, or copied by hand the entire sutra. Because of the Huayan Sutra's length, such undertakings were a serious commitment of time, and reporters in the Republican period described with respect and praise those who chose to perform them. Beyond major acts of devotion centered on the entire text, portions of the Huayan Sutra were also used in more regular, small-scale devotions. In particular, one of its chapters, the "Chapter on the Practice and Vows of Samantabhadra" ("Puxian xingyuan pin 普賢行願品"), has circulated widely as an independent text in China.

Recitation of the entirety of the Huayan Sutra was done both individually and communally. The Republican Buddhist press records a number of examples of groups of lay people and monastics, often in combination, who formed temporary Huayan Assemblies (Huayanhui 華嚴會) to chant and occasionally to study the Huayan Sutra. Because the Huayan Sutra is the longest single Chinese Buddhist sutra, such events were newsworthy. Once organized, these assemblies took anywhere from several weeks to several months to chant the entire sutra, with the longest I have seen mentioned being a 120-day recitation carried out by the Shanghai Lotus Society (Shanghai Lianshe 上海蓮社) in the first months of 1930.[19] Recitation took such a long time both because of the length of the sutra and because these assemblies rarely consisted of all-day meetings in that they, at least the ones recorded in the press, were mostly lay-centered affairs, so recitation took place for only a few hours a day or even only for a few hours each week. For example, when the Nanjing Buddhist Pure Karma Society (Nanjing Fojiao Jingyeshe 南京佛教淨業社) decided to recite the entire sutra in 1936, they agreed to meet each day at 2:00 p.m. to chant four sections of the sutra, setting Sundays aside for longer chanting sessions.[20] At that rate, they would have finished the entire sutra in two to three weeks, depending on which of the three versions they were chanting. Daily gatherings of this kind seem to have been uncommon among lay assemblies, however. Individuals also undertook to recite the entire Huayan Sutra, though these cases were rarely recorded in the press. Solo recitation sometimes involved bowing to a sutra as one chanted it, which was usually accomplished by chanting one character of the text, making a full prostration, chanting the next character, and so on. Although this practice could be done with any sutra, it is particularly associated with the Huayan Sutra.[21] Chanting of the entire sutra was often paired with the practice of copying the sutra by hand.

Altogether, half-a-dozen cases of individuals copying the Huayan Sutra by hand are recorded in the Republican Buddhist press. Given the amount of time and effort involved in such a practice, it was most often undertaken by monastics who had entered a period of sealed confinement for the purpose of religious cultivation, called *biguan* 閉關. The duration of the confinement is determined in advance, with the most customary length being three years.[22] A number of prominent monks of the Republican era entered periods of *biguan*, including Taixu and Yingci, though neither did so to chant and bow to the Huayan Sutra. There are a few records of monks who did make this the goal of their *biguan*, however. Changguan 常觀 (n.d.) of Xiaozaogou Township 小棗溝 in Shanxi, who had ordained relatively late in life, began his monastic career on October 26, 1934, with a three-year retreat devoted to this practice.[23] Another monk, Xiding 習定 (n.d.), entered a period of *biguan* to chant and bow to the Huayan Sutra in 1937, a year after he had returned from a pilgrimage to Mt. Wutai 五台.[24] Wutai is a sacred location to both Chinese and Tibetan Buddhisms generally as well as to Huayan in particular. It is believed to be the earthly home of the Bodhisattva Mañjuśrī, and because the Chinese tradition sees Dushun, the first patriarch of Huayan, as a manifestation of Mañjuśrī, Mt. Wutai has been an important site for Huayan since at least the time of Jingyuan in the Song dynasty.[25]

Most people could not afford the time to enter a period of sealed confinement, but one could still copy the Huayan Sutra by hand in a more intermittent fashion. Copying a sutra by hand was the only way to reproduce it before the advent of xylographic printing in the ninth century, but even after the invention of printing the practice of hand copying of sutras endured as a popular merit-making activity in Sinitic Buddhism among both the laity and the monastics. One need not copy an entire sutra, however. The Huayan Sutra was a popular source for writing out shorter sections and phrases by hand. For example, Hongyi 弘一 (1880–1942) is famed for the beauty and balance of his calligraphy. During his life, he brushed, among many other works, a number of paired couplets (*duilian* 對聯) that have been carved into the columns of temples in the Fujian region. Most of these couplets are passages drawn from the Huayan Sutra. Although Hongyi is best known as a master of Vinaya studies, he was also a devout student of that text and wrote essays about it.[26]

PART ONE

Copying small parts of the Huayan Sutra was fairly common and, apart from famous examples such as Hongyi, often went unremarked. Stories about copying the entire sutra, however, were noteworthy and thus better recorded in the Republican Buddhist press. Tales of earlier examples of sutra copying were circulated during the Republican period. In 1923, for example, the long-running journal *Sound of the Sea Tide* (*Haichao yin* 海潮音, hereafter *HCY*) carried a preface written years earlier by the layman Zhou Guoren 周果仁 (a.k.a. Mo'an 默庵, 1839–1902) for the work of a monk who copied out the entire Huayan Sutra by hand. In 1885, Zhou was in Changsha, where he heard about a local abbot named Shaodian 少顛 (n.d.), who was chanting and bowing to the Huayan Sutra as he copied it out.[27] Such stories are not limited to monastics; laypeople also took up the practice of copying the entire Huayan Sutra by hand. Between 1932 and 1935, Su Zhouchen 蘇宙忱 (n.d.) wrote out the entire eighty-volume version of the sutra in the highly legible *kaiti* 楷體 calligraphic script in order to make merit in support of a lay Buddhist society he helped found in northern Suzhou in the spring of 1932.[28] A more talked-about instance of the hand copying of the Huayan Sutra was that of another Suzhou layman, Cao Songqiao 曹崧喬 (n.d.), a refuge disciple of the famous Pure Land master Yinguang 印光 (1862–1940), who began his work on New Year's Day in 1934.[29] It apparently took him two or three years to make his copy, which was fifty-three volumes in length.[30]

Although most of these men probably copied out the Huayan Sutra with conventional inks, the most celebrated method was to use one's own blood, either by itself or mixed with ink. This particular practice has historically been closely associated with the Huayan Sutra owing in large part to the fact that the forty-volume version of the text includes a passage that describes how Vairocana Buddha used his own skin as paper and his blood as ink to copy Buddhist scriptures. The latter was never a widespread practice, but there are a few examples of both lay and monastic Buddhists doing it. One of the most notable is the celebrated late Ming dynasty (1368–1644) master Hanshan Deqing 憨山德清) (1546–1623),

who finished copying the entire text in blood in 1577.[31] The only person I know of to write the entire Huayan Sutra in blood during the Republican period was the monk Shouye, whose long monastic career was closely tied to the practice and teaching of Huayan. Shouye, working intermittently, copied out the entire sutra between 1936 and 1940.[32] Shouye's life and activities, including his efforts at copying out the entire Huayan Sutra in his own blood, went unremarked in the Buddhist Republican press. He was also not associated with any of the most well-known Huayan teachers or programs of the period discussed in this book, but he was an important figure in disseminating Chinese Huayan studies first in Vietnam and then in the United States and for reviving them on the mainland after 1980.

Shouye was not alone in combining devotion to the Huayan Sutra and study of the Huayan School. The monk Kefa 可法 (n.d.) also attempted to copy the sutra while in *biguan*, though he finished only twenty volumes of the text before he had to hand the work over to his disciple Zongliang 宗量 (n.d.).[33] Prior to this, Kefa had been abbot at Tianning Temple in Yangzhou, where he taught the Huayan Sutra and Huayan doctrine in the early 1920s.[34] Although less celebrated than Cizhou, Yingci, and Yuexia, he is still considered to have been an important teacher of Huayan at the time. Other Buddhists of the late Qing and Republican period drew explicit connections between their devotions and the philosophy of the Huayan School. Zhou Guoren (Mo'an), in his report on Shaodian, noted that the monk had chosen the character *shao* 少, meaning "small" or "few," for his name because the Huayan Sutra teaches, through the doctrines of the Six Characteristics (*liuxiang* 六相) and the Ten Profound Gates (*shixuanmen* 十玄門), that no thing, no matter how defiled or how small, is separate from the body of Vairocana Buddha. In the same way, Shaodian felt that he was not separate from Vairocana even though he was very small in comparison. The Six Characteristics and the Ten Profound Gates, which are explained further in chapter 5, are central teachings of the Huayan School. Shaodian's very identity was rooted in the teachings of Huayan thought, at least in Zhou Guoren's biography.³⁵

Most of the announcements of Huayan Assemblies in the Republican press also framed the practice of recitation of the Huayan Sutra with explicit reference to the doctrines of the Huayan School. For example, reporting on the Huayan Assembly in Shanghai in 1930, the famous lay Buddhist publisher Fan Gunong 范古農 (1881–1951),³⁶ apparently a participant in the assembly, wrote that the Huayan Sutra contains a full account of the Buddha's complete explanation of the nature of the Dharmadhātu (*fajiexing* 法界性), or the nature of reality. Claiming that it adopts the position that "all things are identical with one thing, and one thing is identical with all things [*yiqie ji yi, yi ji yiqie* 一切即一, 一即一切]," Fan emphasized the comprehensive nature of the Huayan Sutra, which he maintained describes completely every practice and every form of realization found within Buddhism.³⁷ Fan's point here is that if one chants the entire Huayan Sutra, one is chanting the entirety of the Buddhadharma because there is no teaching that is not included within that sutra. Despite such comments about the universality of the Huayan Sutra, Fan and other Buddhists of the Republican period did believe in the existence of a distinct Huayan School, one that was badly in need of revival.

Huayan Sectarianism and Modern Japanese Scholarship

It is now widely acknowledged among scholars that Chinese Buddhism, especially during the Tang, should not be understood as a collection of institutionally distinct sects (*zong*) and that one must exercise care when writing Chinese Buddhist history lest one apply an inaccurate sectarian frame to one's subjects. Some may even argue that a study such as this one is at best passé because the field of Chinese Buddhist studies has grown beyond outdated categories such as "Huayan School." I do not agree. Although the concept of

Buddhist schools may not reflect the historical realities of the Tang, it has been important for Chinese Buddhists themselves and has been embedded within their own understandings of the nature of Buddhism since the Northern Song dynasty. Furthermore, as described later, the *zong*-centric model of Chinese Buddhist historiography took on added significance in China from the start of the twentieth century. The idea that Chinese Buddhist history is exactly a history of the development of distinct sects is indeed a fable, but throughout the twentieth century it was a fable that had a real impact on how Chinese Buddhists thought about their tradition. It also had an impact on the fate of Huayan studies. For this reason, we must not ignore the emic importance of the concept of *zong*.

Here I render the Chinese term *zong* as "school." The character *zong* 宗 has a long pedigree in Chinese and can express a range of meanings. It was originally created to depict an ancestral shrine in which votive or memorial tablets were held and wherein ceremonial offerings to the ancestors were made. *Zong* as "ancestral shrine" was also used as a metonym for the ancestors present within the shrine. From this sense of *zong*-as-ancestor, the meaning of the character developed along roughly two different but related lines. In the first, the idea of a biological progenitor was abstracted to refer to the origin, root, or central basis for something. In philosophy and religion, the character *zong* came to refer to the central thesis or doctrine of a text or school, the "root" concept or argument from which it sprang. *Zong*-as-ancestor also became a synecdoche for the larger clan descended from that ancestor. In this way, *zong* came to mean "family" or "family lineage." Within the context of Buddhism, *zong* is used in multiple ways, reflecting all of these meanings.

Stanley Weinstein describes in an article on the schools of Chinese Buddhism for the *Encyclopedia of Religion* (which is perhaps best known for being cited by T. Griffith Foulk in an article on Chan historiography in 1992) at least three distinct meanings of *zong* in the Buddhist context: a "specific doctrine or thesis"; the

PART ONE

"underlying theme, message or teaching of a text"; and a "religious or philosophical school."³⁸ Using the etymology of *zong* I have outlined, I would argue that the first and second meanings defined by Weinstein are not functionally distinct: in the first two, *zong* refers to the central or "root" idea of a text or argument; in the third, it refers to a religious "family" of some kind. The ambiguity of the term *zong* creates challenges for scholars who wish to analyze its use as a historiographic category or who wish to deploy it, as I do here. Although one can see how a group of like-minded individuals could gather around a core doctrine (*zong*) and thus form a school (*zong*) around that doctrine, one must be careful about reading too much of a historical reality into the claims of the independence of such schools, especially in the context of China.

Since at least the 1980s, scholars of Buddhism in the West have been conscious that Japanese Buddhist scholarship has affected the ways in which we understand the history of Chinese Buddhism. Owing to a variety of factors, Japanese Buddhism has developed into a highly sectarian religion in which the various sects (*shū* 宗 or *shūhai* 宗派) of Buddhism are institutionally separated, with each sect possessing different styles of ritual dress, objects of veneration, sacred texts, temple networks, lineages, and even distinct communities of ordained clergy. For example, to be ordained a Kegon (i.e., Huayan) monk in Japan meant that one was very clearly *not* a Tendai or Zen monk. In China, however, this kind of sectarianism was the exception rather than the norm.³⁹ The various schools of Buddhist thought and practice were rarely separated at the institutional level, and there was a general continuity of ritual, ritual dress, and objects of veneration across the Chinese Buddhist world. When one ordained as a monastic in China, one ordained not as a Huayan Buddhist or Chan Buddhist but as a Buddhist, and one could and often did participate through practice or study in many of the "schools" of Buddhism present in China without barrier, even while residing in a single monastery.

The chief problem scholars see in using *zong* as a historiographic category in the context of Chinese Buddhism is that it can lead one to erroneously imagine Chinese Buddhist history as nothing more than the sum total of the separate histories of institutionally distinct sects. It is perhaps not surprising that many of the scholars who have been most vocal about this issue are specialists in the study of the Chan School, which has the most highly developed internal narratives about both its lineal coherence and its separateness from the rest of Buddhism.[40] In Japan, these narratives exerted a great deal of influence on the academic study of Zen history, where claims of lineage were often accepted without critique until the latter part of the twentieth century. Despite the prevalence of the general *zong*-centric model, even a century ago there were scholars in both Japan and China who were suspicious about applying it to Chinese Buddhist history. As Erik Schicketanz notes, both the Japanese scholar Ui Hakuju 宇井伯壽 (1882–1963) and the Chinese historian Tang Yongtong 湯用彤 (1893–1964) voiced their misgivings about the applicability of this model to China.[41] For the most part, however, the sect-centered view of Buddhism broadly affected how nineteenth- and twentieth-century Japanese scholars told the history of Chinese Buddhism, which in turn affected Chinese Buddhists' views of their own tradition.

The evidence does seem to indicate that there were no institutionally distinct *zong* in China during the Tang dynasty and that many of China's supposed *zong* never existed as distinct entities in history (among them, one could point to the Chengshizong 成實宗 and the Dilunzong 地論宗). This is important, but we need to be cautious about how far we go in turning the idea that "there were no sects in China" into a *rule* of history. Although the concept of distinct sects or schools does not really apply to Chinese Buddhism during the Tang, they did come to exist in some fashion during the Song. At that time, the government began to associate certain temples with particular schools of Buddhism.[42] As a result, Chan and Tiantai formulated lineage histories in order to legitimize their standing as distinct schools worthy of controlling temples. Although the practice that occurred within those temples did not vary from school to school as widely as they did in Japan,[43] the schools did begin to articulate distinct self-identities. Huayan also constructed lineages in pursuit of institutional recognition.

The government was only one factor promoting the formation of Buddhist schools during the Song. Wang Song 王頌 argues that we must also consider membership, institutional structures, religious teachings, and social power.[44] By analyzing the writings and activities of monastics associated with Huayan in China's Jiangnan 江南 region, Wang finds that there was indeed a self-conscious and institutionally distinct Huayan School. Much of the activity of this school took place among a network of actors and sites centered on the monk Jingyuan and his headquarters, Huiyin 慧因 Temple, which was officially designated a Huayan temple by the Song government. Jingyuan lived during a time of acute conflict between the proponents of Huayan and those of Tiantai. In his efforts to garner legitimacy for Huayan as a school of Chinese Buddhism, Jingyuan created a lineage of founding figures, just as Chan and Tiantai writers had done for their schools. He also collected the writings of these founders, and, most importantly, he received imperial permission for those writings to be included in the officially sanctioned Buddhist canon, which was the most significant form of legitimization within Chinese Buddhism.[45]

The exact impetus behind the creation of Buddhist canons in China is not yet completely understood, but we do know that by the end of the sixth century CE, Chinese scholars had begun to compile catalogs of all of the Buddhist texts translated into Chinese, often along with the names of their authors and translators, and whether they were considered reliable. These catalogs organized the scriptures, commentaries, and other texts of Buddhism into different categories. One such catalog, found in Dunhuang, organized the canon according to the Huayan doctrinal classification scheme of the Five Teachings (*wujiao* 五教, discussed in detail in chapter 5). This schema for organizing the canon of Buddhist writings did not become popular, however. Instead, the most influential catalog for later canons was the *Catalog of Buddhist Works Compiled During the Kaiyuan Period* (*Kaiyuan shijiao lu* 開元釋教錄),

written in 730 by Zhisheng 智昇 (n.d.). Its method for organizing the canon became standard among all Buddhist canons in East Asia until the twentieth century. Zhisheng's catalog begins with five classes of Mahāyāna texts, and he included the Huayan Sutra and the shorter texts related to it as the fourth class.[46] From this point on, Huayan was treated as a distinct category within the Buddhist canon, but it was only because of Jingyuan's efforts that the writings of classical Huayan thinkers were included within the canons.

The Huayan School never developed a large institutional presence in China, and even the general institutional basis for the differentiation of Buddhist schools waned after the Song, returning to something of its pre-Song state. Nevertheless, the Song remains an important era for the story being told in this book. Jingyuan was successful for a time at establishing a Huayan School in China, but his most lasting contributions proved not to be institutional but ideological in that he was responsible for defining the basic identity of the Huayan School, which continues to the present.

The *zong*-centric model for understanding Chinese Buddhist history has its limitations. Most of the *zong* that are commonly discussed never existed in China in any meaningful way (institutionally or otherwise), and those that did developed later than their own pious histories claim. And after the Song, what few clear dividing lines there were between schools blurred to the point where the concept of *zong* loses much of its value as a category of historical analysis. Nevertheless, it is important for the study of modern Chinese Buddhism because by the 1910s Chinese Buddhists believed in the historical reality of such schools within their tradition. This belief had everything to do with Japanese scholarship.

Japanese academic Buddhist scholarship developed significantly amid the modernization that began during the Meiji period (1868–1912). Under the influence of Western scholarship and in response to pressures applied to Buddhism by a government that did not entirely approve of it, Japanese Buddhist scholars began to write new histories of Buddhism. These histories were often aimed at demonstrating that Japanese Buddhism represented the final, most advanced phase in the evolution of Buddhism. Some of these histories served as textbooks at the new institutions of higher education that Japan's major Buddhist sects founded at the end of the nineteenth century in order to educate their clergy and to demonstrate their value to the state. Most of these histories adopted one or both of two common organizational structures, chronological and/or institutional. Chronological narratives of the development of Buddhism charted its evolution first in India, then in China, then in Japan (the so-called Three Kingdoms, Jp. *sangoku* 三國). Institutional narratives described the development of Buddhism as a process of the emergence of specific schools (*shū* or *shūhai*) over time. Both of these historiographic conventions were adopted from the writings of the medieval Kegon monk Gyōnen. His work *Record of the Transmission of the Buddhadharma Through the Three Nations* (*Sangoku buppō denzū engi* 三國佛法傳通緣起, 1311) provided the template for the first structure, but of far more importance here is his earlier work *Essentials of the Eight Sects*, which provided the basic structure for the second type of Buddhist history[47] and which exerted a tremendous influence on East Asian Buddhist historiography in the twentieth century.[48] Many of the schools of Buddhism that Gyōnen identified were also recognized in China. For example, the *Chronicle of the Buddhist Patriarchs* includes sections on various schools of Buddhism. This text was produced in stages by several Tiantai partisans, so Tiantai features prominently, but there are also sections on the Chan, Huayan, Yogācāra (Cienzong 慈恩宗), and Vinaya Schools (Lüzong 律宗). One does not see in Chinese Buddhist histories an eight- or ten-school model, like the one outlined by Gyōnen, until the very end of the nineteenth century, although they did list some of the same schools.[49]

In May 1891, the great Chinese lay Buddhist scholar and publisher Yang Wenhui received a copy of Gyōnen's *Essentials of the Eight Sects* from his friend the Japanese Buddhist priest Nanjō Bunyū 南條文雄 (1849–1927).[50] Yang was committed to retrieving and printing as many of Chinese Buddhism's lost texts as possible, and Nanjō sent him copies of many texts during his lifetime. Although Yang had a particular devotion to Pure Land and Huayan Buddhism,[51] he wanted to strengthen and modernize all Chinese Buddhism through education and publication. He used the *Essentials of the Eight Sects* as the template for his own "Brief Explanation of the Ten Schools" ("Shizong lüeshuo 十宗略說").[52] It was also an essential organizing framework that Yang added to *A Primer on Buddhism* (*Fojiao chuxue keben* 佛教初學課本).[53] Both of these works promote the idea of the ten schools of Chinese Buddhism.[54] Yang used the latter work as a textbook at his short-lived but highly influential Buddhist school the Jetavana Hermitage.[55] There, it would have influenced a number of important monks of the early twentieth century.

Through his school and his various writings, Yang was particularly influential in spreading in China the *zong*-centered model of Buddhism laid out in Gyōnen's work and propagated in Japanese Buddhist scholarship, but the model spread through other channels as well. Both Yang's *A Primer on Buddhism* and Gyōnen's *Essentials of the Eight Sects* were reprinted in China several times during the 1930s, and the former was serialized in toto in the Buddhist press in 1941.[56] Other important thinkers of the day also promoted the model of Buddhism espoused in these works. Liang Qichao 梁啟超 (1873–1929) wrote about it from 1911 on, and the famous monk Taixu, who had been a student at Yang's school, regularly used both the eight- and ten-school models in his writings.[57] Finally, from the 1920s on, Chinese versions of Buddhist histories written by modern Japanese scholars further helped to promote this model within the Chinese Buddhist world.

These, therefore, are some of the facts concerning the concept of *zong* and *shū* (in Chinese and Japanese Buddhist historiography, respectively). The astute reader will have noticed that in the preceding pages I have used both the words *sect* and *school* to translate the Chinese character behind these terms. I have used *sect* for *shū* in Japanese Buddhism because *sect* is in common usage by scholars and because it fairly reflects the situation there. When translating the Chinese term *zong* here and in the remainder of this book, I use *school*. In this usage, I follow T. Griffith Foulk's advice that we use the latter term when referring to "movements or groups within Chinese Buddhism that are made of real persons united in a self-conscious manner by a common set of beliefs, practices, and/or social structures." He uses *school* in contradistinction to the term *lineage*, which refers to a "spiritual clan conceived as a group of individuals related by virtue of their inheritance of some sort of Dharma from a common ancestor."[58]

No Huayan Sectarianism in Republican China

Under the influence of Japanese scholarship, Huayan may have been construed as a distinct school of Sinitic Buddhism, but this construal did not lead to the appearance of a new Huayan sectarianism. As I argue in the next chapter, even the Huayan University network should not be thought of as a sectarian movement. Both those within and without the network instead continued to see Huayan as but one part of a larger, unified Chinese Buddhism.

In his discussion of the status of Buddhist schools in modern China, Holmes Welch notes, "While the popularity of sects rose and fell during the Republican period, there was also a new trend against thinking in terms of sect at all. Monks and monasteries announced that they belonged to no sect or to every sect."[59] The very idea that Chinese Buddhism could be thought of as composed of discrete "sects" was due primarily to the influence of Japanese Buddhist scholarship, and the appearance of the "anti-sectarian trend" (to use Welch's words) was actually a result of the popularity of Japanese sectarian historiography in China and not of any real sectarianism among Chinese Buddhists. Although Chinese Buddhism has rarely if ever been truly sectarian, the popularity of the school-centered model of Chinese Buddhist history convinced people in China that it had been and that this sectarianism needed to be stopped. In adopting an aggressively antisectarian stance, modern writers were thus actually arguing against a Chinese Buddhism that had never been. There were certainly new arguments to be had in modern Chinese Buddhist circles about the legitimacy of this or that text or doctrine, but these arguments rarely manifested as forms of sectarianism. This was especially true for Huayan.

Yang Wenhui was particularly disposed toward the study of Huayan doctrine, but one cannot call him a Huayan partisan. The output of his publishing house, the Jinling Scriptural Press (Jinling Kejingchu 金陵刻經處), included texts from every branch of Sinitic Buddhism. Although he favored Fazang's interpretation of the *Awakening of Faith in the Mahāyāna* (*Dasheng qixinlun* 大乘起信論),[60] in his introductory textbook *A Primer on Buddhism* he wrote of his great displeasure with people around him who he felt took Fazang's Five Teachings classification scheme too much to heart and minimized the teachings of other Buddhist schools.[61] I have not been able to determine exactly whom he was referring to in these comments. It is possible that he was making an oblique reference to Xufa, whose writings had been so influential in late-imperial Huayan studies (and would go on to become central to Republican-era Huayan curricula). In the preface to his press's published collection of recently recovered Huayan texts, *Xianshou Dharma Collection* (*Xianshou faji* 賢首法集), Yang chided Xufa for misinterpreting Fazang's Five Teachings because of his desire to refute the Tiantai School.[62] We cannot be certain that Xufa was Yang's main target, however, and Yang may have had someone else in mind when he wrote those words in *Primer*. I have found no evidence of Huayan sectarians who were active in fin-du-siècle China, so I am inclined to believe that his comments were more rhetorical than a reflection of historical fact. A similarly aggressive ecumenism can be seen in the writings of his student, the era's most famous and prolific monk, Taixu.

In 1924, Taixu published an article titled "A Brief Discussion of the Meaning of the Xianshou [School]" ("Lüeshuo Xianshou yi 略說賢首義"). It began as a fairly straightforward summary of Huayan thought, but about two-thirds of the way through Taixu offered a series of comments on the status of Huayan in China in the 1920s. He claimed that some people were at that time engaged in arguments about Huayan, Tiantai, and Yogācāra in various Buddhist journals, including his own journal *HCY*. Among the issues he identified as central in these arguments were: the One Vehicle (*yisheng* 一乘) versus the Great Vehicle (*dasheng* 大乘), the supremacy of Yogācāra texts versus the Sutra of Perfect Enlightenment (Yuanjue Jing 圓覺經), and whether the teachings of Tiantai or Yogācāra are superior.[63]

Those familiar with the history of Republican-era Chinese Buddhism will no doubt see that Taixu was referring to a heated debate that took place among Chinese and Japanese Buddhist intellectuals in the early 1920s on the status of the *Awakening of Faith in the Mahāyāna*. The tradition attributes this work to the Indian Buddhist monk Aśvaghoṣa, but there have long been doubts about its authorship, and by the early 1920s some Japanese scholars used modern text-critical methods to argue that this text was actually composed in China. This debate was important because the *Awakening of Faith* is a central text in the Sinitic Buddhist tradition, and its teachings about Buddha nature were foundational to Chan and even more so to Huayan.[64] Whereas in Japan the provenance of the text was the main focus of debate, Chinese Buddhists were more interested in "the philosophical and doctrinal teachings of the *Awakening of Faith* and their compatibility with what they understood as the authentic Buddhist teaching."[65] In the 1920s, Ouyang Jingwu 歐陽境無 and members of Faxiang University (Faxiang Daxue 法相大學) in Nanjing (then still called the Chinese Inner Studies Institute [Zhina Neixueyuan 支那內學院]), were critical of this text and its interpretation of Buddhism. Ouyang felt that the teaching of Buddha nature it contained helped give rise to Huayan and Tiantai, which fueled the general ignorance about Buddhism among Chinese people that was one of the contributing factors to the decline of Buddhism in China.[66] Ouyang and his supporters saw the study of Yogācāra as the solution to the generally sorry intellectual state of Chinese Buddhism caused by the popularity of Huayan, Chan, and Tiantai.[67]

Despite Ouyang's critique of Huayan and Taixu's characterization of these debates as centering at least in part on Huayan, the participants in the debates actually wrote almost nothing about Huayan. Looking through the more than one-dozen articles that record this debate, there is virtually no mention of Huayan. In his summary of Japanese scholarship on the issue in 1922, the famed reformer and intellectual Liang Qichao 梁啓超 stated in passing that the *Awakening of Faith* was important in the historical foundation of Huayan doctrine, but he did not elaborate on this point.[68] Even the monk Changxing, an important figure in the Huayan University network, simply stated that the *Awakening of Faith* supports both the Tiantai doctrine of "nature inclusion" (*xingju* 性具) and the Huayan doctrine of "nature origination" (*xingqi* 性起), two doctrines that have traditionally been seen as contradictory and central to the conflict between Huayan and Tiantai.[69] None of the other writers made any reference whatsoever to Huayan or its doctrine, and, despite Taixu's claims, it was not a specific topic of the debate; much of the argument instead revolved around whether the teachings of Dharma Nature (*faxing* 法性) was a legitimate Buddhist teaching. In other words, at least among the participants of these famous and important doctrinal debates, Huayan was not important as a topic by itself.

When Taixu published his essay on Huayan in 1924, it thus occurred in the midst of debates about the validity of core Sinitic Buddhist doctrines. Did he perhaps do this as an attempt to set the record straight about Huayan teachings within the context of these debates? Even if that were one of his goals, his primary argument was that one should not treat Huayan thought as better than other forms of Buddhist doctrine. At the conclusion of his article, he stated that one should not teach just Huayan but respect all of Mahāyāna Buddhism, as he himself did.[70]

For his part, Taixu was strongly antisectarian, which showed through in his defense of the *Awakening of Faith* and of Sinitic forms of Buddhism more generally.[71] It also colored his interpretation of Huayan's doctrinal classification schemes. Five years earlier Zhang Taiyan 章太炎(1868–1936) had submitted an article to one of Taixu's periodicals in which he attacked Zongmi's *Huayan Inquiry Into the Origin of Humanity* (*Huayan yuanren lun* 華嚴原人論).[72] As discussed in chapter 5, the *Inquiry Into the Origin of Humanity* is generally considered to be a Huayan text; in it, the fifth Huayan patriarch Zongmi laid out his own doctrinal classification scheme. Taixu was unwilling to let Zhang's criticisms appear in print without editorial comment, and he appended his own rebuttal to Zhang's article. Although the *Inquiry* actually says very little about classical Huayan doctrine, Taixu argued in his comments that Zongmi had indeed meant to hold Huayan up as the highest teaching of Buddhism, but Zhang was mistaken in taking Zongmi too seriously in this regard. Taxiu contended that the teachings of Buddhism are unified, and he criticized Zhang for mistakenly treating Zongmi's *provisional* ideas about the types of Buddhist teachings as an actual attempt to divide Buddhism into better and worse teachings.[73] Taixu did not disagree with the general concept that Zongmi's doctrinal classification scheme identified Huayan as holding the highest Buddhist teachings, but he was opposed to any attempt to use it to divide Chinese Buddhists along sectarian lines.

Taixu lectured and wrote about Huayan several times in the 1920s and 1930s. Though he proved competent in his exploration of Huayan doctrine, he remained consistently antisectarian in his treatment of it. His ecumenism ran so deep that he even sought to rehabilitate the Tang monk Huiyuan 慧苑 (673–743) within the Huayan tradition. Jingyuan had excised Huiyuan from the lineage due to Huiyuan's removal of the Sudden Teaching (*dunjiao* 頓教) from his master Fazang's Five Teachings scheme. Taixu felt, however, that some of Huiyuan's criticisms of his teacher Fazang were appropriate and that his model was better than Fazang's. Nevertheless, he felt that people who followed Fazang's teachings needed to realize that even Fazang knew that all teachings are just provisional words and that he never intended for people to reject the other teachings.[74]

Taixu continued his efforts to reconcile Huayan and Tiantai doctrine. He lectured on this topic again in 1932 at the World Buddhist Library (Shijie Foxueyuan Tushuguan 世界佛學苑圖書館), a kind of graduate-level Buddhist seminary that succeeded the Wuchang Buddhist Institute.[75] In these lectures, which were recorded by his disciple Fafang 法舫 (1904–1951), Taixu attempted to reconcile apparent differences between the doctrines of Huayan and Tiantai as articulated by Fazang and Zhiyi, respectively. To do this, he made both doctrinal and historical arguments. For example, Taixu noted that each system speaks of a different Perfect Teaching of the One Vehicle (*yisheng yuanjiao* 一乘圓教), but really they are talking about two aspects of the same thing. Whereas the version of the Perfect Teaching that is taught in the Lotus Sutra is perfect as a teaching designed to liberate sentient beings, the Perfect Teaching of the Huayan Sutra is perfect because it perfectly teaches the content of the Buddha's enlightenment. Buddhism needs both teachings. Regarding any differences between Fazang and Zhiyi's thought, Taixu noted that because Zhiyi lived much earlier than Fazang, he did not have access to certain texts that were important for Fazang, such as the *Daśabhūmika-bhāṣya* (*Shidi jinglun* 十地經論, Commentary on the Sutra of the Ten Stages).[76] As much as he praised Fazang and Zhiyi, he still faulted both men for their sectarianism. He closed his lecture by stating that each man was too focused on promoting his own favored sutra and establishing his own school of thought. Because of this, neither was able to unite the teachings of Mahāyāna and Hīnayāna, Dharma Characteristics (*faxiang* 法相) and Dharma Nature, or exoteric and esoteric Buddhist teachings. In this article, he again decried those who were promoting Huayan over other forms of Buddhism.[77]

Both Yang Wenhui and Taixu warned against trying to promote Huayan over and above other forms of Buddhism in a sectarian manner. Taixu's comments in particular, which came at a time when the various Huayan University–derived programs were at their most active, could be read as evidence that the members of the network displayed such sectarian tendencies, but based on the analysis offered here this was likely not the case. All of the programs in the network featured non-Huayan texts as important elements of their curricula. Many also required students to participate in Chan meditation or recitation of the Buddha's name. An examination of the biographies and writings of key figures in the network, such as Changxing, Cizhou, Yingci, Yuexia, and Zhiguang, shows that their study and promotion of Huayan was rooted in a typically ecumenical approach to Chinese Buddhism.

Yuexia left virtually no written works for us to consult, but it is well known that he received dharma transmission in a Chan lineage, and during his career he lectured on a variety of texts, including the Diamond Sutra (Jin'gang Jing 金剛經), the Perfect Enlightenment Sutra (Yuanjue Jing 圓覺經), the Vimalakīrti Sutra (Weimojie Jing 維摩詰經), and the Śūraṅgama Sutra (Lengyan Jing 楞嚴經).[78] Yingci, like Yuexia, was an ardent supporter of Chan practice, and he lectured extensively on a variety of Buddhist scriptures, including the Diamond, Perfect Enlightenment, Lotus, and Śūraṅgama Sutras, as well as on the *Awakening of Faith*. His published works include commentaries on the Vimalakīrti and Heart Sutras (Xin Jing 心經).[79] Yuexia and Yingci's student Cizhou also displayed little Huayan sectarianism. He lectured extensively and apparently exclusively on the Huayan Sutra and its commentaries throughout the 1920s and 1930s, but he is also well known for his study and promotion of Vinaya. Cizhou was not particularly well known until at least the late 1920s, however. He is not mentioned at all in the Buddhist periodical press until after 1926, and even then he is not regularly connected to Huayan. Cizhou's classmate Changxing was at least as ecumenical as Yuexia and Yingci in his study and promotion of Buddhism. After graduating from the Huayan University, he studied Chan at Tianning Temple in Changzhou and Tiantai under its great modern master Dixian at Guanzong 觀宗 Temple.[80] And in 1924, he was finishing his time overseeing the eclectic curriculum of the Anhui Monastic School (Anhui Seng Xuexiao 安徽僧學校), which supplied the curriculum and most of the students for the Minnan Buddhist Institute (Minnan Foxueyuan 閩南佛學院), which he started in 1925. The Minnan Buddhist Institute would go on to become the longest-running and most influential Buddhist seminary of the Republican period, and its curriculum was decidedly ecumenical.

Yuexia, Yingci, and Changxing may have favored Huayan, but they did not favor it in a sectarian manner to the exclusion of other forms of Buddhism. Perhaps there were others who did engage exclusively in Huayan. A good candidate might be Keduan 可端 (n.d.), the founder of the Huayan University of Yangzhou. Keduan, however, would make a very poor example of Huayan exclusivism. We have enough material to get a clear sense of his views on Huayan and even to get some sense of what he taught his students about Huayan. These materials show us that Keduan was no more sectarian that Yingci or Changxing. There was a clear focus on the study of Huayan in the curriculum of Keduan's university, befitting its name, but he was no partisan. This fact can be seen in the university's magazine *Buddha's Light* (*Foguang* 佛光). Keduan was the chief editor of the magazine as well as one of its main contributors. Although he wrote almost exclusively about Huayan-related matters for the magazine, he included articles on other topics written by notable Buddhists of the day. Each issue featured at least one piece on Tiantai doctrine written by Keduan's former teacher Dixian, and there were also articles on a wide range of topics, including the *Awakening of Faith*, the Lotus Sutra, and Yogācāra thought, written by famous Buddhists such as Jiang Weiqiao, Mei Guangxi 梅光羲 (1880–1947), Tang Dayuan 唐大圓 (ca. 1890–1941), and Zhang Taiyan.

Keduan's approach to *Buddha's Light* reflects the ecumenical attitude he brought to his program. As was the custom for Buddhist seminaries at the time, the inaugural issue of the magazine in 1923 contained an article describing the history of the university's founding, its primary aims, and its planned curriculum. There, Keduan gave a brief history of the Huayan School. Just as Taixu did in his lectures in 1932, Keduan acknowledged that Tiantai and Huayan rely on different texts for and thus have different ideas about the Perfect Teaching, but, he emphasized for the reader, this does not mean that their teachings do not lead to the same goal. The Four Teachings (*sijiao* 四教) of Tiantai and the Five Teachings of Huayan, he said, all elucidate the truth. Like Taixu, he argued that Buddhism is one, and he lamented the fact that there were people arguing about whether the teachings of Dharma Nature or of Dharma Characteristics were better.[81]

* * *

It was widely agreed upon in Republican China that Huayan was a distinct school of thought and that it was fundamental to Chinese Buddhism, but there is little evidence of a sectarian Huayan movement during the period. Even those figures most closely associated with the teaching of Huayan in the Republican period were not sectarian in their understanding of the relationship between Huayan and other forms of Sinitic Buddhist thought and practice. The Huayan University network was not a sectarian enterprise aimed at re-creating an institutionally or doctrinally distinct Huayan School of Chinese Buddhism.

TWO

The Huayan Universities

THE HUAYAN SUTRA was highly revered throughout Chinese Buddhist history, but the Huayan School only ever had a weak existence as a distinct institution. Even the efforts Jingyuan made in the Song dynasty to establish the school in specific temples were only nominally successful. Although there were some notable masters of the school over the years, Huayan teachings were mostly subsumed within the larger body of Chinese Buddhist doctrine. The arrival of the modern era in East Asia, however, reinforced the idea that Huayan was one of several separate schools of Chinese Buddhism, each of which contributed its own distinct lineages, doctrines, and practices to the larger tradition. Even though Huayan should not be treated as a distinct school in the sense described in chapter 1, a network of teachers and programs dedicated to its study did develop in the Republican period. This network originated in the first Huayan University, which was founded in 1912, the same year as the Republic of China, through the collective action of several monks and laypeople based in Shanghai. After a rocky first few years, it continued under other names through the 1930s, and attempts were made to reestablish it in the 1940s. This chapter examines the origination and early expansion of a Huayan network by focusing on several Huayan Universities that operated in Jiangsu and Hubei Provinces in the 1910s and

1920s. When people refer to *the* Huayan University, they mean the original institute that Yuexia and Yingci ran in the 1910s. I follow this usage here.

Education and the Modern Chinese Buddhist "Revival"

From the start of the twentieth century, there was a push to expand education among Buddhist monastics. This movement went hand in hand with the general desire for education reform that had begun to motivate the country's governing elite. Starting around the turn of the century, the threat posed by the power of colonial nations such as Japan and European countries inspired many in the government to accept the idea of reforming Chinese education along modern lines. For Buddhists, a combination of governmental pressure, interreligious friction with highly trained Christian missionaries, and an internal drive to raise the intellectual level of the *sangha* (community of Buddhist monks, nuns, and laity) led to the founding of an increasing number of programs for the education of monks and in a few cases nuns. In this endeavor, Chinese Buddhists were heavily influenced by their Japanese peers, who in the face of similar pressures back home had begun to establish Buddhist seminaries and universities from the late 1870s on. These Japanese Buddhists' goal was to create a knowledgeable and politicized priesthood that, trained in history, science, and a variety of religious perspectives, would be able to effectively promote Buddhism in Japan's rapidly modernizing society.[1] The schools founded during this period remained the primary loci for the study of Buddhism until the 1910s, when the focus shifted to Buddhist studies programs established at Japan's public universities and in the private universities set up by the various Buddhist sects.[2]

In China, there had of course been traditional structures within Buddhism for the training of monks and nuns prior to 1900. These structures centered on the major public monasteries, or *conglin* 叢林, but only a minority of monastics participated in them.

Although the Chinese Buddhist *sangha* was probably not as illiterate and uneducated as either Chinese Confucians or foreign Christian missionaries made them out to be,[3] the overall level of literacy and knowledge of Buddhist doctrine was probably not very high among the vast majority of monastics. To remedy this, Buddhists created a variety of new models for monastic education that departed to a greater or lesser degree from the *conglin*-centered model. The first major attempt to create a new type of monastic education were the monastic schools (*seng xuextang* 僧學堂) of the 1900s. Formed through collaboration between clergy and local gentry, these schools established a precedent for later Buddhist education programs. Most were located in the relatively wealthy region of Jiangnan, and they self-consciously looked to Japan for models of modern Buddhist education.

Most scholars have tended to overlook the role played by these monastic schools. This is due in part to the paucity of historical source material available for their study, but it has also been informed by the attitude of many of the monks who founded the next generation of Buddhist schools, including the outspoken and influential Taixu. The monastic schools were more influential than they are generally given credit for being and are deserving of more careful scrutiny. A number of monks who had large impacts on later Buddhist education went through these schools. For example, for the purposes of the current study, we might look to the monk Zhiguang, who served an important role in transmitting the modern Huayan tradition to Taiwan. He had his first taste of Buddhist education at a monastic school run by Wenxi 文希 (n.d.) at Tianning Temple from 1906 to 1908.[4] When Wenxi was arrested by the imperial government for collusion with the Japanese, Zhiguang traveled to Nanjing, where he joined Taixu as a student at the Jetavana Hermitage. When the hermitage closed abruptly in 1910, both Zhiguang and Taixu enrolled at the Jiangsu Monastic Normal School (Jiangsu Seng Shifan Xuetang 江蘇僧師範學堂), which ran from 1909 to 1911.[5] That school included on its faculty none other than Yuexia, who learned much as a teacher there. Yuexia and

PART ONE

Zhiguang were not unique in the impact that the monastic schools had on their careers because the schools gave them and many other important figures of modern Huayan experience teaching and studying in new types of Buddhist educational programs.

Scholars may dismiss the overall importance of the monastic schools, but the larger issue of modern Buddhist education has been a topic of scholarly interest since the 1920s. For the most part, scholars have tended to focus on three schools, which they have treated as the most innovative and thus the most representative of "modern" Chinese Buddhist education.[6] The first is the Jetavana Hermitage that Zhiguang and Taixu attended. The hermitage was the brainchild of Yang Wenhui, who established it in 1908 in Nanjing on the site of Jinling Scriptural Press. Although the hermitage ran for less than two years and had only a small student body of monks and laymen, many of its graduates went on to lead careers of great influence within modern Chinese Buddhism. Yang was committed to reforming Buddhist education, and the hermitage was a laboratory where he could try out his ideas, which included educating his students in foreign languages and modern secular subjects. Most scholars view this school as the start of modern Buddhist education in China:[7] its curriculum served as a model for many later Buddhist programs, and it was the direct predecessor of the two most famous Buddhist institutes in Republican China.

In 1922, Yang Wenhui's student Ouyang Jingwu started a new institute on the former site of the Jetavana Hermitage with the help of a number of prominent lay Buddhists. He initially called his program the Chinese Inner Studies Institute but changed it to Faxiang University in 1925, perhaps in reference to the Huayan University or to differentiate it from the more religiously inclined schools of his rival Taixu, which were also called "institutes" (*xueyuan* 學院).[8] (I refer to Ouyang's institute as Faxiang University hereafter in deference to its more long-standing name.) The Faxiang University curriculum centered on the philosophical study of Buddhist doctrine, with an emphasis on Yogācāra. Although the institute did attract some monastic students, its curriculum lacked both the more traditional aspects of Buddhist education, such as spiritual cultivation and the study of Buddhist precepts, as well as some of the more modern subjects, such as history and science, that had been taught at the Jetavana Hermitage. Language study was included in the curriculum, but Buddhist canonical languages such as Sanskrit were emphasized over modern languages. This institute continued for many years and was undoubtedly one of the most important centers for the development of a tradition of rigorous academic study of Buddhism in modern China.

As Ouyang was laying the groundwork for Faxiang University in Nanjing, one of his classmates from the Jetavana Hermitage was working with lay Buddhists to realize his own vision for a modern Buddhist seminary in a city three hundred miles to the west. Although the monk Taixu was not solely responsible for its founding, the Wuchang Buddhist Institute was heavily influenced by his opinions, and he served as the institute's principal from its founding in 1922 to 1924, when a disagreement with the school's lay board led him to resign. The institute was something of a hybrid institution that combined elements of traditional Buddhist education and modern educational practices. Its curriculum followed some of the innovations introduced by Yang Wenhui and included study of a wide range of secular subjects (Western philosophy, psychology, foreign languages) along with a basic grounding in Chinese and early mainstream Buddhist thought.[9] Unlike Faxiang University, the Wuchang Buddhist Institute struggled in its early years, and it closed entirely in 1926 before reopening in 1929 as a research-oriented institution. Despite its short tenure, the original institute produced a number of notable graduates and is generally treated by scholars as the paradigm of modern monastic education in China. The original Huayan University also produced a class of highly accomplished monks who went on to disseminate widely the knowledge of Huayan they had gained under the school's founder, Yuexia.

PART ONE

Master Yuexia

Yuexia originally hailed from Hubei Province. He was born in 1858 and married at the age of seventeen.[10] He and his wife had two children, a son and daughter, but he eventually followed an earlier desire and became a monk. It is unclear what became of his family after he left them. During his lifetime, Yuexia practiced meditation at the era's most important Chan centers, including Tianning, Jinshan 金山, and Gaomin 高旻 Temples. He spent six years living as a hermit on Mt. Zhongnan 終南, a spiritual center for Chinese Huayan and the home of several of the early Huayan patriarchs. There he studied under Chan master Faren 法忍 (1844–1905).[11] Although we do not know if Faren specialized in the study of Huayan, it is likely that Yuexia began to develop an interest in the Huayan Sutra during his time on Mt. Zhongnan. Two of his fellow students under Faren, Yuzhu 玉桂 (1861–1937) and Puchang 溥常 (1866–?), also showed a deep interest in Huayan in their later careers.[12] In 1902, Yuexia traveled with a group of Chinese monastics on a tour of major Buddhist nations in South and Southeast Asia. When he returned, he went to Tianning Temple to continue his meditation practice under Yekai 冶開 (1852–1922), who had been one of Faren's peers on Mt. Zhongnan. At Tianning Temple, Yuexia met the monk Yingci, who was fifteen years his junior.

Yingci was born in Anfeng 安豐, Jiangsu Province, in 1873 to a family that had come from Anhui Province and had made a fortune in the salt industry. His family provided him with a traditional Confucian education, and he earned the licentiate scholar (*xiucai* 秀才) degree in the government examinations when he was fifteen. At age twenty-five, he traveled to Putuoshan 普陀山 island, where he was tonsured. After his tonsure, he moved to Nanjing and received full ordination in 1900 at Tiantong 天童 Temple in Ningbo, whose abbot at the time was well known Chan master Jichan 寄禪 (1852–1912). Over the next three years, Yingci studied at the major Chan centers in Jiangnan until he finally went to Tianning Temple in 1903.[13] In 1906, Yingci joined Yuexia and two other monks in a group dharma-transmission ceremony held by Abbott Yekai, at which time they all became forty-second-generation dharma holders of the Linji lineage. This type of mass dharma transmission, in which one abbot transmits the dharma to several successors simultaneously, emerged in the nineteenth century as a tradition in some Jiangsu temples, including Tianning.[14] The goal of that mass dharma transmission was to provide a pool of candidates from which to draw abbots in the years after Yekai's passing, but Yuexia and Yingci decided not to pursue the path of becoming an abbot. The two men instead jointly committed to living out their lives as peripatetic educators.

At this point, it is necessary to consider the formal relationship Yuexia and Yingci had with one another. These two monks worked closely together during the last decade of Yuexia's life. Yingci was clearly Yuexia's junior (by fifteen years), despite the fact that they were in the same dharma generation under Yekai. It is important to remember the nature of their relationship as we consider the history of the first and subsequent iterations of the Huayan University. The two men's names are sometimes mentioned in conjunction in the history of the original school, as though they both founded and ran it equally, but Yuexia was the primary teacher and the central figure of authority. It appears that in many ways Yingci was thus Yuexia's disciple, though he often worked alongside him and held positions of authority. Yingci was Yuexia's heir apparent and owed his interest in Huayan to him. This is worth remembering as we consider how things unfolded for the Huayan network after Yuexia's death.

After receiving dharma transmission in 1906, Yuexia was invited by Gui Bohua 桂伯華 (1861–1915) to come to Tokyo for eight months to give sutra lectures for the Chinese expatriate community there. It is not clear if Yingci joined Yuexia on this trip.[15] This community included many people who became leading figures in the Republican government and in Chinese Buddhism, including Liu Shipei 劉師培 (1884–1919), Su Manshu 蘇曼殊 (1884–1918, who taught for one term at the Jetavana Hermitage), Sun Yuyun 孫毓筠 (1869–1924), and Zhang Taiyan. Yuexia lectured to them on some of the most popular Chinese sutras, including the Vimalakīrti Sutra and the Sutra of Perfect Enlightenment.[16] Gui Bohua was one of Yang Wenhui's best students, and he had gone to Japan to further his education in Buddhist studies. Gui was particularly interested in Huayan and Consciousness-Only thought, and it is possible that Yuexia's interaction with Gui heightened his desire to focus more on Huayan in his studies and teaching.[17]

In 1910, Yuexia became formally involved with monastic education in China after Yang Wenhui recommended him to be principal at the Jiangsu Monastic Normal School at Jingjie 淨戒 Temple. Yuexia brought Yingci along as his assistant. This was a crucial moment in both of their careers, and it is likely that the plans for Huayan University were first sketched out there at the Jiangsu school. During their stint at the school, the two men gained valuable experience in running modern educational institutions, and it provided them with the bona fides necessary to garner support from the laity for their later educational endeavor. While at the Normal School, Yuexia and Yingci would also have gotten to know Taixu and Zhiguang, Yang Wenhui's students who had transferred there after the Jetavana Hermitage closed.

Yuexia and Yingci's time at the Jiangsu Monastic Normal School was also crucial in another way. There Yuexia had a chance to reunite with Yuzhu, his friend and fellow student under Chan master Faren, who was a teacher at the Normal School. Yuzhu was already a strong proponent of the Huayan Sutra, and his attitude and knowledge had a deep impact on both Yuexia and Yingci. Reflecting later, Yingci stated that he was able to write and speak about the Huayan Sutra as well as he could only because of what he had learned from Yuzhu while teaching at the Normal School.[18] Yuzhu was not a lineage holder in any of the extant Huayan lineages, but he influenced those around him to take up the Huayan Sutra, and when he passed away in 1937, his refuge disciple Fu

Jinqiu 傅近秋 (n.d., dharma name Huijiang 慧江) began a ten-year project to copy the entire eighty-volume version of the Huayan Sutra by hand.[19]

Yingci and Yuexia left the Jiangsu Monastic Normal School in 1911, handing responsibility for the school over to Dixian. They then traveled to Yuexia's native Hubei Province to lecture at Baotong 寶通 Temple in Wuhan.[20] These lectures were probably attended by the monks Chisong 持松 (1894–1972), Cizhou, Jiechen 戒塵 (1878–1948), and Liaochen 了塵 (n.d.), four natives of Hubei who would follow Yuexia to Shanghai the following year to enroll at the Huayan University.[21]

The Original University

In the latter half of 1911, the Xinhai Revolution put an end to millennia of imperial rule in China and ushered in the Republic of China. That year Yuexia and Yingci returned to Shanghai at the invitation of one of their master Yekai's lay disciples, Di Chuqing 狄楚青 (c. 1873–1941). An influential figure on Shanghai's Buddhist scene, Di secured positions for Yuexia and introduced him to important lay Buddhists. He began by inviting Yuexia to lecture on the *Awakening of Faith* at the Times Building.[22] He also asked Yuexia to assist him with the publication of China's first major Buddhist periodical, the *Buddhist Journal* (*Foxue congbao* 佛學叢報), which was produced by Di's press, the Youzheng Press (Youzheng Shuju 有正書局), from 1912 to 1914. Most significantly, he introduced Yuexia to Liza Roos Hardoon (Luo Jialing 羅迦陵, 1864–1941), the French and Chinese wife of wealthy Shanghai industrialist Silas Hardoon (1851–931), who eventually invited Yuexia and Yingci to stay in the Aili 愛麗 Gardens on her estate.[23] There they joined the monk Zongyang 宗仰 (1861–1921), a revolutionary and confederate of Sun Yat-sen who already had been living there for four years. Mrs. Hardoon was an avid supporter of Buddhism, and she had invited Zongyang to stay in a Buddhist hermitage she had built in her gardens in 1904 so that he could oversee the editing and publication of the first Chinese Buddhist canon to be produced using movable type.[24] She funded the massive expense needed for this venture, and when Yuexia and Yingci arrived, they found Zongyang ready to begin publication of the first installment of the canon in the spring of 1912. Publication continued into May 1913, but by then Yuexia and Yingci had already worked with Mrs. Hardoon to realize another of her Buddhist goals: to establish an institute for monastic education on the grounds of her estate. Because this institute was organized around Yuexia's lectures on the Huayan Sutra, it was named "Huayan University."

Huayan University opened in 1912 with a student body of around sixty monks. According to the school charter published in 1914, its curriculum was much more modest than the extensive one envisioned by Yang Wenhui for the Jetavana Hermitage, and its daily schedule was modeled more closely on traditional patterns of monastic education than Yang's had been.[25] The majority of the students' time was taken up with study of commentaries and treatises from the classical Huayan tradition, with Yuexia's afternoon lectures on the Huayan Sutra serving as the university's primary curriculum. Students were also required to practice meditation for two hours each day and to follow the monastic rule. All of this meant that the university operated far more like a *conglin* than Yang's hermitage had. This insistence on correct behavior in accordance with the monastic rule was partially responsible for the university's sudden and unfortunate relocation to Hangzhou in March 1914.

Historians, especially those writing from within the Chinese Buddhist tradition, generally assert that the precipitating cause for the relocation of the Huayan University was that Liza Roos had come under the sway of a non-Buddhist, who convinced her to make demands of the student monks that Yuexia was uncomfortable with.[26] Specifically, this person convinced her that the monks of the university ought to gather regularly to prostrate to her, as their benefactor, just as they bowed to Yuexia, the university's head.[27] In the Vinaya, monks are not permitted to bow even to the emperor, let alone to a laywoman. When this requirement was announced, Zhiguang recalled that Yuexia felt a deep sense of betrayal at Roos's actions and that his "tears flowed like rain."[28] Unwilling to compromise, Yuexia was able to arrange for the university to move to Haichao 海潮 Temple in the city of Hangzhou.

It is quite possible that there were deeper issues at play than simply a disagreement about who should bow to whom. The person who convinced Mrs. Hardoon to demand the monks' obeisance was the Hardoons' estate manager, Ji Juemi 姬覺彌 (1885–1964), a Chinese Muslim and a staunch advocate of traditional Chinese education and national studies (*guoxue* 國學).[29] A year after Huayan University vacated the Aili Gardens, Ji used them to establish a new academy dedicated to the study of the classical Chinese tradition, which he called Cangsheng Mingzhi University (Cangsheng Mingzhi Daxue 倉聖明智大學) and served as its principal.[30] Notable figures of the period, including Kang Youwei 康有為 (1858–1927), Wang Guowei 王國維 (1877–1927), and Zhang Taiyan, lectured at this school. Ji Juemi's efforts to convince Liza Roos to expel Yuexia and his students from the Hardoon estate may thus have been part of his plan to have the Hardoons use their considerable wealth to support traditional Chinese education of a less Buddhist variety. Whatever the precise reason for the Huayan University's departure from Shanghai, its move to Hangzhou, some one hundred miles away, was highly disruptive. Nevertheless, Yuexia, Yingci, and their students persevered, and they were able to complete the first three-year cycle of the Huayan University's planned course of study before Haichao Temple was seized by the military for use as a base in 1916.

It is not clear exactly how many of the original students completed the full course of study, but many of those who did went on to play important roles in Chinese Buddhist education. Some of the students at the university who will appear again as major figures in the following pages were Aiting 靄亭 (1893–1947), Changxing, Chisong, Cizhou, Huizong 惠宗 (1892–1973), Jiechen, Liaochen, Muxi 幕西 (n.d.), Tikong 體空 (n.d.), and Zhiguang. They followed different career trajectories, but each of them contributed something to the teaching of Huayan Buddhism, and they often aided one another in their endeavors. Together they formed a network that might broadly be described as a "school" of Huayan studies. Most of the major teachers of Huayan today, in mainland China as well as in Taiwan, Hong Kong, and the United States, trace their educational lineages back in one way or another to the graduates of the original Huayan University.

The Second Huayan University, 1920–1921

After the first Huayan University ceased operation in 1916, Yuexia and Yingci held on to the hope that they might be able to restart it somewhere else. The following year Yuexia became abbot of Xingfu 興福 Temple in Changshu 常熟, located about sixty miles northwest of Shanghai in the heart of the Jiangnan region. He soon became ill and died before his plans to start a second Huayan University at the temple could come to fruition. On his deathbed, Yuexia asked Yingci to continue spreading Huayan teachings and remonstrated with him to never become abbot of a temple.[31] Yingci did briefly serve as abbot of Xingfu Temple, but in order to fulfill his promise he passed the abbotship to Chisong. Yingci remained committed to the idea of education, but three years passed before he was able to reestablish the Huayan University at Xingfu Temple. To staff their program, he and Chisong hired two other graduates of the original Huayan University, Huizong and Changxing (the latter freshly returned from a period of study at the Tiantai-leaning Guanzong Research Society), to serve as teachers. Unfortunately, this university lasted only until the winter of 1921, when it closed due to a lack of funds.[32] Thus ended the second Huayan University. Such closures were a common feature not only of the various

Huayan-centered programs but also of most institutes of Buddhist monastic education during the Republican period because the social and economic instability as well as the various military actions throughout the period frequently forced institutions to relocate or close entirely.

The second Huayan University may have been a failure, but it was nevertheless the start of a new network of Huayan-centered educational programs as Yuexia's students scattered across the region. Yingci, following Yuexia's last instructions to him as best he could, chose not to stay to lead their remaining students. He instead went on pilgrimage to Mt. Wutai before returning to Hangzhou to enter a period of *biguan* at Bodhi 菩提 Temple from 1922 to 1924. After 1924, he resumed teaching and became an important figure for Huayan during the period. His career is discussed in the next chapter, as are the activities of those students who stayed behind to reestablish Huayan education at Xingfu Temple. Although they faced a great deal of difficulty, over the following decade and a half they kept running courses on Huayan, albeit under the new name "Dharmadhātu Institute" (Fajie Xueyuan 法界學院 or 法界學苑).

The remainder of this chapter is devoted to a study of three schools from the 1920s, each of which called itself "Huayan University." One of them was founded by a monk who had no direct connection with the original university but who was clearly inspired by it, while the other two were founded by students of the original university who, like Yuexia, hailed from Wuhan.

The Huayan Universities of Wuhan

The metroplex comprising Wuchang, Hankou, and Hanyang, known collectively today as Wuhan, has long been a major commercial and transit center as well as an administrative hub for central China. After it was sacked during the Taiping Rebellion in the 1850s, it was rebuilt and became an early center for industrialization in the nineteenth century. As part of this process, it was one of the first Chinese cities to be electrified in 1890.[33] And because of its size, location, and continued importance, the port city of Hankou became the terminus for China's first north–south rail line in 1905, which linked it to Beijing.[34] Wuhan remained an important city throughout the Republican period.

Huayan University of Hankou, 1921–1924

When the Huayan University of Changshu closed, four of the original university's students went to teach about Huayan in the city of Hankou. The monk Liaochen[35] had moved to Guiyuan 歸元 Temple in Wuhan immediately after graduating from the original Huayan University in 1916. In 1921, he became abbot of the nearby Jiulian Hermitage (Jiulianan 九蓮庵), where he immediately began a Huayan University preparatory course (Huayan Daxue yuke 華嚴大學預科).[36] Although Liaochen wrote that he meant for his program to follow the model of the preparatory class offered at the original Huayan University, its planned curriculum more closely followed the one Yang Wenhui had designed for the Jetavana Hermitage. The university's curriculum did include more Huayan-related materials than Yang's, and it introduced a course of meditation study based on several contemplation texts from the classical Huayan tradition.[37] Liaochen invited three of his former classmates to help him run the university, two of whom were Hubei locals. One of them was Jiechen, who had been born in Hanchuan, roughly forty miles to the west of the city. Before enrolling at the Huayan University, Jiechen had spent several years practicing meditation on Mt. Zhongnan with Xuyun 虛雲 (d. 1959),[38] the era's most famous Chan master, and another three years in biguan on Mt. Jizu 雞足 in Yunnan. After graduating from Huayan University, Jiechen spent three years in biguan in Changshu before returning to his native Hubei.[39] Liaochen and Jiechen were joined by both Cizhou, another Hubei native, who had originally ordained at

Guiyuan Temple in 1912 with Chisong, and the monk Muxi (also referred to by his dharma name Xingche 性徹), though Muxi went back to his home province of Henan in 1923 to start his own program.[40] Together, these monks did their best to reproduce the scholarly atmosphere and monastic rigor they had experienced under Yuexia and Yingci at the original Huayan University. The university's first and only class, which is reported to have numbered more than thirty students, graduated in the summer of 1924 after completing the full three-year preparatory course.[41] The fact that it actually ran to its full planned term marks it as a success for its time.

The case of the Huayan University of Hankou is an interesting one in the study of Republican-era Buddhist education given that the institution shared much in common with its much more famous peer, the Wuchang Buddhist Institute. The two programs operated at the same time in the same metropolitan area, and each lasted about as long as the other. The Huayan University of Hankou started first, running from 1921 to 1924, while the Wuchang Institute, at least in its first run, operated from 1922 to 1926. The two institutions also received support from the same prominent local lay Buddhists. In the Huayan University of Hankou's charter of 1921, Liaochen listed Li Yinchen 李隱塵 (n.d.), Chen Yuanbai 陳元白 (1877–1944), and Wang Senfu 王森甫 (1881–1934) among the institute's seven lay supporters.[42] The following year Li and Chen were responsible for organizing and funding the start of the Wuchang Institute, to which Wang also contributed money.[43] With the exception of the Huayan University's emphasis on Huayan thought and practice, the two programs even shared a similar curriculum, which included study of geography, history, and language in addition to subjects in Buddhist studies such as Consciousness-Only thought. The faculty of both institutes were even involved in the same modernist activities. Liaochen knew Taixu and participated in a number of Taixu's initiatives. He represented Hubei monastics at the second of the World Buddhist Federations (Shijie Fojiao Lianhehui 世界佛教聯合會) organized by Taixu on Mt. Lu 廬,[44] and in

1924 he was also one of the signatories, along with Taixu, Chisong, and more than a dozen other monks, to a document calling for the creation of propagation teams to spread Buddhism among China's youth.[45] Despite all of these similarities, the Wuchang Institute remains quite well known in history, whereas the Huayan University of Hankou has become a mere footnote.

The Huayan University of Hankou is rarely mentioned in discussions of modern Buddhist education, though as Rongda Lai notes, "despite its short life and sporadic activity...the Wuchang [Institute] occupies a highly significant place in the collective imagination of modern Chinese Buddhists."[46] Shi Dongchu, one of the few scholars even to mention the Huayan University of Hankou, offers the following assessment: "Because [the school's] talented people did not accomplish very much, it did not have a very big impact."[47] On this score, Dongchu is probably correct in that we do not have a list of the graduates of the university and thus cannot compare their historical impact to the better-known graduates of the Wuchang Institute. The Huayan University of Hankou also had fewer graduates than the first run of the Wuchang Institute did. The graduation notice for the former mentions that there were "more than thirty," but more than fifty students from the first class at the Wuchang Institute passed the graduation exam.[48]

It might be more instructive to compare the Wuchang Institute to the original Huayan University. In this comparison, the Huayan University of Hankou is evidence of the impact of the original program in that the original Huayan University's first generation of students were already out teaching and contributing to the broadening of Buddhist education even as the students of the Wuchang Institute were still sitting in class. Furthermore, at least one of the Huayan University of Hankou's graduates, Li'an 栗庵 (d. 1929), went on to teach in two other Huayan-centered programs before his untimely death in 1929.[49] He thus represents a third generation of modern Huayan teachers, one that was at least partially cultivated at the Huayan University of Hankou.

Liaochen may have wished to begin the three-year regular course (*zhengkei* 正科) in Huayan studies for his students directly after they completed their preparatory course in 1924, but it never happened. The Huayan University of Hankou was likely dealing with many of the same challenges that the Wuchang Institute was facing on the other side of the river. Although the proximate reason for the Wuchang Institute's closure in 1926 was the military's expropriation of its buildings during the Northern Expedition, it had already been dealing with an erosion of lay support resulting from the departure of Taixu and his fund-raising star power in 1924 and from the growing popularity of esoteric Buddhism among the Wuhan laity.[50] In the end, the Huayan University of Hankou may have been outcompeted by both the Wuchang Institute and the esoteric movement for the limited amount of lay funding in the area, and it was simply not possible for Liaochen to continue. No plans were ever announced for another Huayan University at Guiyuan Temple after 1924. Faced with the arrival of the Northern Expedition, Jiechen and Cizhou returned to Changshu by 1926 to assist with a revived program there. We do not know what Liaochen did.

Huayan University of Wuchang, 1928–1930

Ironically, one of the events that led to the growth of the esoteric movement in Wuhan and thus to the demise of the Wuchang Institute also laid the foundation for a second Huayan University in the area. In February 1924, Chisong, a graduate of the original Huayan University who had ordained at Guiyuan Temple, was installed as abbot of Baotong Temple. Chisong had just returned from studying Shingon esoteric Buddhism in Japan, and he quickly turned Baotong Temple into a center for esoteric Buddhist practice.[51] Chisong had not come to the area alone, however, and on the same day that he was installed as abbot at Baotong Temple, his Huayan University classmate Tikong became abbot of Lianxi 蓮溪 Temple. The two men were welcomed to the city Wuchang and to their new positions by more than fifty representatives from the local Buddhist community, including several people from the Wuchang Institute.[52]

Four years after becoming abbot, Tikong started his own Huayan University, the second in Wuhan.[53] Prior to launching the university, Tikong wrote in 1928 to the Beijing-based lay Buddhist Liu Xianliang 劉顯亮 (n.d.) to request a copy of the "college bylaws [daxue zhangcheng 大學章程]," but Liu was unable to assist him.[54] This was probably in reference to the charter of the original Huayan University, but Tikong did not publish a charter for his program, as was usually done during the period, so we know nothing about his institute's curriculum or student body. Tikong halted the program of study suddenly in 1930, transmitting the dharma and passing the abbotship to Jingchan 淨禪 (n.d.) before leaving the temple completely and disappearing from the historical record.[55]

Dharma Transmission in the Huayan University Network

In her study of modern Buddhist education, Rongdao Lai suggests that we view the Wuchang Buddhist Institute "as the origin for not just a network of schools and graduates, but a modern lineage whose identity was constantly shaped and reshaped by its participants in responding to situations both within and outside of Buddhism."[56] In the same way, the first Huayan University served as the point of origination for a network of monastics committed to furthering Buddhist education in China. The next chapter describes the history of a number of these schools, but before we turn to them, it is necessary to reflect on the nature of this network and its implications for monastic identity. The Huayan University network should not be treated as a modern sectarian movement. Its members' identities were not focused on the promotion of Huayan exclusive of other forms of Buddhism. Identity and affiliation have been constructed within Chinese Buddhism in other ways. One is through the monastic lineages to which a monk or nun might formally belong. There are several varieties of lineages, and their usage depends in part on where and how one is brought into that lineage. However, almost none of the many lineages present in Chinese Buddhism at the start of the twentieth century were connected with Huayan, and the members of the Huayan University network were not affiliated with any of them.

Historically, most Buddhist temples in China were private temples (*zisun miao* 子孫廟). These temples were usually small and were owned and controlled by a single monastic "family" with a lineage structure mirroring that of a secular family. When aspiring monks or nuns entered one of the temples, they received tonsure and were entered into that temple's lineage, which was almost always either that of the Linji 臨濟 or Caodong 曹洞 schools of Chan.[57] This affiliation did not usually make them a holder of a Chan dharma lineage (*faxi* 法系), however, but it did make them part of the monastic "family" of that temple. After their novitiate, the aspiring monk or nun would travel from their home temple to receive full ordination at one of the larger public monasteries, which were usually associated with the Vinaya School. Ordination did not mark entry into a specific lineage, but it did represent assumption of the identity of a Buddhist monastic, which was an identity marker universally recognized in Chinese Buddhist institutions. All monastics in China undertook these two common forms of identity: entry into a temple "family" and entry into Chinese Buddhism as a whole at one of the public monasteries. A minority of monastics went on to enter one or more additional lineages by receiving dharma transmission at another of the large public monasteries (*shifang conglin* 十方叢林 or simply *conglin*). This would enter them into the lineage of that monastery, making them eligible to serve as the temple's abbot at some point in the future. Just as with the dharma lineages of the private temples, by the start of the twentieth century most of the public temples were affiliated with one of the Chan schools, and thus Chan lineages made up the vast majority of lineages in China.

PART ONE

Not all public monasteries were associated with Chan lineages, however, nor did a monastery's identification with a Chan lineage prevent it from serving as a site for the teaching and study of the doctrinal schools. This fact proved to be particularly important for the members of the Huayan University network. Public monasteries identified with one of the Chan lineages are referred to as places for "practice of the patriarchs" (zongmen 宗門).[58] There were also temples that promoted the "practice of doctrine" (jiaomen 教門), and they were associated with either a Tiantai or Huayan lineage. At the start of the modern period, the vast majority of the doctrinally focused temples belonged to a Tiantai lineage rather than a Huayan one, but at least one Huayan dharma lineage is recorded in texts from the early nineteenth century.[59] These texts have been studied extensively by the contemporary monastic scholar (and Huayan lineage holder) Xiandu 賢度 (b. 1958). Recognizing that these records do not agree, Xiandu has compiled her best guess at a master lineage chart. Her chart includes figures alive through the 1920s, but, significantly here, none of the figures discussed in the present study received dharma transmission in one of China's extant Huayan lineages.

Dharma transmission did occur between some members of the Huayan University network, but the lineages involved were always Chan ones. Yingci, who had received dharma transmission alongside Yuexia in the Linji Chan lineage from Yekai at Tianning Temple in 1906, passed this lineage on to Chisong, Huizong, and Tanyue 潭月 (1858–1932) in 1918 on behalf of Yuexia. These three individuals were students at the original Huayan University, but this transmission was done in order to create a group of monks who could serve as abbots of Xingfu Temple, a branch of Tianning Temple, which Yuexia had been asked to take over just before his death. Other important students who promoted and taught Huayan, such as Cizhou and Zhiguang, never received dharma transmission from Yuexia or Yingci. Both Zhiguang and his tonsure disciple Aiting had studied under Yekai after graduation from the original Huayan University, but neither received dharma transmission from him, either. Zhiguang did receive dharma transmission later in the Caodong Chan lineage from Dejun 德竣 (or 德峻, n.d.) at Dinghui 定慧 Temple, by which time Aiting had already received dharma transmission at Zhulin 竹林 Temple. None of these transmissions involved a Huayan lineage, but they were of pragmatic importance in the flourishing of a Huayan network because membership in these lineages allowed these men to become abbots of their respective temples, which in turn gave them the authority they needed to establish educational programs where the study of Huayan was an important part of the curriculum.

New Identities and the Construction of Yuexia's Legacy

Connections formed through dharma transmission, although important, were not the only way to create networks of like-minded monastics. In the modern period, new modes of affiliation beyond tonsure and dharma transmission appeared among Chinese monastics. Rongdao Lai has described several of these novel forms of affiliation, many of which were centered on training within specific programs or institutes. For example, she argues that the graduates of the Guanzong Research Society (where both Changxing and Keduan had studied) eventually formed a new kind of sectarian identity within the Chinese *sangha* that centered on the society's founder, the great early twentieth-century Tiantai master Dixian. This network is now widespread in Hong Kong Buddhism and in the Chinese diaspora of Southeast Asia. This new Tiantai lineage grew out of a larger contemporary phenomenon, which Lai describes as the emergence of the student monk (*xueseng* 學僧) identity.[60]

In the early twentieth century, a subset of young Chinese monastics, inspired by new ideals of political involvement and modern education, forged a new understanding of their identities as monastics. They saw themselves as part of the common project of fashioning both a new China and a new Chinese Buddhism. The student monks were in part a textual community in that they were deeply informed by the many Buddhist periodicals that appeared in the 1910s, 1920s, and 1930s. But they were also molded and shaped within the new educational institutions established during the period. Lai argues that these programs provided an education that helped the students reimagine the nature of their monastic identity. Although the vertical relationship between teacher and student remained important, it was weakened as the horizontal relationship inherent in the "collective identity" of the student monks became more important.[61] In the case of the emergent Dixian-centered Tiantai lineage, participation within the educational system overseen by Dixian was the key criteria for the first generation of disciples, who established a network of affiliation. Other programs served in the same manner as the generative points for diverse networks of affiliation with modern Chinese Buddhism. The most famous is probably the Wuchang Buddhist Institute, which Lai cites as the origin of a new kind of monastic identity and lineage. It was able to accomplish this because it "provided an ideological basis" for a new identity that served as a "discursive tool for student-monks to negotiate and redefine their place in the new social order."[62] The Wuchang Buddhist Institute and the Guanzong Research Society are well-known examples of modern monastic education programs, but the original Huayan University also served as the foundation for a network similar to the Tiantai lineage Lai describes, albeit one that was much more limited in scope.

The Huayan network described in this book lacked the central authority and stable geographic center that the modern Tiantai lineage had in Dixian and his Guanzong Temple, but its members were nevertheless able to form durable, cooperative relationships among themselves. New monastic education tended to weaken vertical relationships between teachers and students and to strengthen the horizontal ones between students. In the case of the Huayan network, it allowed students to form stronger horizontal relationships with one another. The peer relationships formed by the graduates of the original Huayan University allowed them to call on each other's assistance as they launched program after program in the 1920s and 1930s. This network of relationships became self-reproducing and did not radiate out unidirectionally from Xingfu Temple. For example, Li'an was a second-generation student under the first-generation students Cizhou, Jiechen, and Liaochen at the Huayan University of Hankou before he went on to teach a third generation of students at the inaugural Dharmadhātu Institute in Changshu. That generation included Weicheng 葦乘 (n.d.), who then became a teacher at the Dharmadhātu Institute in the 1930s and possibly again in the 1940s. The Huayan network was fluid, as one can see in the case of Nanting. Nanting first studied under Changxing at the Anhui Monastic School, where the curriculum was closely modeled after the Jetavana Hermitage, but he eventually became one of Yingci's right-hand men and a key link in the transmission of the Huayan University network to Taiwan. This fluidity of affiliation even forged connections between the Huayan University network and the unaffiliated programs when Zhenhua 振華 (also written 震華, 1908–1947), a student of Keduan at the Huayan University of Hangzhou, went to work teaching at the Zhulin Buddhist Institute (Zhulin Foxueyuan 竹林佛學院).[63]

The tendency of the Huayan network to exist within horizontal relationships was reinforced by the absence of strong vertical ones. Neither Yuexia nor Yingci served an active role in maintaining a Huayan network after the original Huayan University ceased operation, which prompted members of the second generation to set out on their own, usually with much assistance from one another. Some of the original university's students, including Zhiguang and Aiting, had become traditional disciples to Yuexia after the university closed, but his death in 1917 put an end to this. As for Yingci, he was and is still treated as merely the second-in-charge at the university. After the failure of the second Huayan University in 1921, Yingci stepped down from the abbotship of Xingfu Temple and left it to go into *biguan*. By that time, however, most of the university's Hubei student group had already departed Jiangnan to start their own Huayan University in Hankou. Some came back, but by then they had gained experience operating independently as teachers on their own.

Yuexia's death meant that he was not able to serve as a living head for a modern Huayan School, but he did come to serve as a symbolically important source of authority for the Huayan University network. Beginning in the late 1920s and continuing to the present, Yuexia has been regularly invoked in Buddhist writings as the modern master par excellence of the Huayan Sutra. I believe that he owes this reputation solely to his association with the original Huayan University and the success of its graduates. Yuexia's own emphasis on the Huayan Sutra came relatively late in his life; as a result he did not publish any major commentaries on it that we know of, and he gave only one full lecture series on the sutra before his death. I make this observation not to question Yuexia's merits as a master of the sutra, only to note that the most lasting legacy of his teaching on that text consisted of his students. In other words, Yuexia has been deemed a master of Huayan because he taught a group of students who went on to successfully teach about it in the following decades. At the same time, those students regularly relied on Yuexia's status as a master of Huayan to certify their own mastery of it. Articles published in the Buddhist press to promote the institutes and lectures run by Yingci, Cizhou, Zhiguang, and others continued to mention their tutelage under Yuexia, identified as the great modern master of Huayan, as a way of showing those teachers' bona fides. In such notices and in the later activity of the network's members, we can see the reciprocal construction of Yuexia's authority and that of his students.

The construction of religious authority in China occurs via multiple channels and can involve different types of mastery on the part of the religious figure who is being elevated. The composition and circulation of hagiography is one common way that an individual is posthumously raised to the status of holy figure. Vincent Goossaert argues that within Chinese religion the most important religious figures are deemed to be important because they operate in one or more of four "idioms of religious excellence": the idioms of self-cultivation, scholarship and knowledge, discipleship and genealogy, and morality and leadership.[64] Yuexia came to be considered an important religious figure because of his scholarship and knowledge of the Huayan Sutra, but this reputation did not spread during his lifetime; rather, it was constructed over time as his students worked to assert their own excellence through discipleship and a genealogy centered on him. To put it more simply, in order to assert their mastery of Huayan the graduates of the original Huayan University cited their tutelage under Yuexia, whom they had to identify as a master of Huayan. In true Huayan fashion, the reputation and authority of Yuexia as a Huayan master as well as the reputation and authority of the members of the Huayan University network as masters appeared in mutual dependence on each other.

THREE

Second- and Third-Generation Programs

THE ORIGINAL HUAYAN University served as the originating node for a network of graduates who took part in trends in monastic education to create more than a dozen loosely affiliated programs and institutes dedicated to teaching Huayan. The majority of these programs were located in the Jiangnan region, especially in Jiangsu Province and the city of Shanghai. The only exceptions were the two Huayan Universities in Wuhan and the Dharmadhātu Institute that Cizhou ran in the southern Fujian Province in the early 1930s. Yingci's home region, Jiangnan, along China's central east coast, is a populous area comprising parts of four different provinces centered on the lower Yangzi River. It has long held a prominent role in Chinese cultural and economic life, and this role intensified during the Republican period. It was also a major focus for Chinese Buddhism, with its Buddhist centers in Zhenjiang and Yangzhou (which, despite being north of the Yangzi, is still generally considered to be part of Jiangnan) lying halfway between the growing cosmopolis of Shanghai and Nanjing, which served as the nation's capital from 1927 on. All of the more than one dozen monastic programs dedicated to the study of Huayan that ran in Jiangnan and Wuhan were short-lived affairs, with few lasting longer than three years.

In studying Buddhist education in Republican China, one is struck both by the number of monastic schools founded in either the early 1920s or the late 1920s and by the frequent closure of schools in both the mid-1920s and the late 1930s. Of course, one of the primary contributing factors to this pattern is the national political context. The first three decades of the twentieth century were a fraught time for religious institutions and religious actors in China because of the near-total reorganization of Chinese society concomitant with the emergence of the modern Chinese state. Starting in the early 1900s, certain segments of the ruling elite, invoking the new category of "religion," called for the expropriation of the capital held by Buddhists, Daoists, and others. This was called the Use Temple Property to Advance Education (*miaochan xingxue* 廟產興學) movement in China. The monastic schools discussed at the start of chapter 2 were part of the Buddhist response to this movement. Buddhists organized these institutions to show their value to the state in promoting modern education. This pattern would repeat several times over the next several decades as Buddhists continued to plan, open, and often prematurely close a broad range of programs for the education of the Buddhist *sangha* and laity.

Scholars have been tempted to treat the short tenure of the many schools of the period as the Republican Buddhists' failure to create permanent institutions, but we should be cautious about drawing such a conclusion. Most of the new Buddhist educational programs of the Republican period were planned on three-year course cycles, and many of were never expected to serve as permanent institutions. In the case of the Huayan University network, for example, both Cizhou's Dharmadhātu Institute in Fujian (1933–1936) and Yingci's Huayan Institute (Huayan Xueyuan 華嚴學院) in Shanghai (1940–1942) were created only to support a fixed-term lecture series. Even the original Huayan University simply followed a regular course cycle to its completion. The tendency to lament these programs' short lifespans, rooted in an expectation of their permanence, may result in part from the names they were given. Some of the Huayan education programs were called *daxue* 大學, "universities," following the precedent established by Yuexia. Even

PART ONE

in Chinese, this term tends to make one think of permanent institutions, with stable staff, facilities, and budgets. I suggest that it would be better to think of most of the educational programs launched during the Republican period as institutes, not institutions. Unlike the term *institution*, the term *institute* can refer to both permanent and impermanent organizations. It is particularly appropriate for the programs run by graduates of the original Huayan University. Just like academic institutes, most of these programs were planned as fixed-term, intensive courses of study in one specific subject: the Huayan Sutra and its exegetical tradition. For this reason, I refer here to educational programs and institutes, not to schools, seminaries, or academies. I likewise translate both *foxueyuan* 佛學院 and *xueyuan* 學院 (or 學苑)—the most common terms used for Buddhist educational programs following Taixu's popularization of the terms in 1922 with the Wuchang Buddhist Institute—as "institute." Some of the era's Buddhist institutes were indeed envisioned as long-term permanent institutions, but it would be inaccurate to treat all of the Huayan study programs discussed here as though they were planned to be permanent, even if they were called *xueyuans*.

In the histories provided in this chapter, one sees again and again the pattern of a program launched with great enthusiasm and much fanfare but then forced to end earlier than hoped. In some cases, a determined monastic leader refused to let the vagaries of time and the economy stop him, and he would start institute after institute. In other cases, the leader was to blame for the closure, departing suddenly and leaving a program in the lurch before the end of a course cycle (sometimes even in the middle of a semester). The historical record for most of these programs is thin, and we do not have enough data to understand the precise causes for many a program's demise. Major historical events occurring during these years, however, likely had inescapable impacts on the founding and dissolution of the various Huayan education programs.

The year 1912 may have marked the formal establishment of the Republic of China, but in large sections of China the republic existed only in theory on account of the new government's nonexistent control over much of the country. As the Republican government struggled to unify its hold over the whole of China, it began to draft laws for the new nation. Freedom of religion was guaranteed in the Constitution of 1912 and in every subsequent Chinese Constitution, but in practice there were limits to this freedom and to the protection that the law provided religious bodies. One of the new government's goals in formulating its laws was to tame religion to serve the state and to reduce or eradicate harmful "superstition" (*mixin* 迷信). Obviously, these concepts were not neutral, nor were they entirely native to China, drawing much from post-Enlightenment discourse in Europe. Government efforts to stamp out superstition and to transform the people of China into citizens of the new secular state put pressure on temples and traditional practices that might fall under the category of "superstition." By the early 1920s, these attitudes, combined with radical ideas of social reform held by segments of China's intelligentsia, resulted in the first "antireligion" (*fei zongjiao* 非宗教) movements in China. Although the primary target of these movements at this time was Christianity, many Buddhists practices were also aimed at.[1] Under pressure from both government power and certain groups in society, some Buddhists founded educational programs both to demonstrate the value of Buddhism for modern society and to train a cohort of monastics prepared to engage in the important debates of the day. It is hardly surprising, therefore, that the Huayan University of Hankou, the Huayan University of Yangzhou (Yangzhou Huayan Daxue 揚州華嚴大學, discussed later in this chapter), and the Dharmadhātu Institute of Changshu would appear alongside the Faxiang University of Nanjing and the Wuchang Buddhist Institute in the early 1920s. Many of these programs closed or went on hiatus during the mid-1920s, however, likely as a result of the Northern Expedition.

The Northern Expedition (1926–1928) was the Nationalists' military campaign to unify China under their rule. It began in southern China and moved north. When all was said and done, the

Nationalists had gained much greater (though not absolute) control over the country. It was a difficult time for Buddhists trying to teach and study Huayan, to say nothing of everyday people trying to go about their lives. One might look, for example, to Wuhan to get a sense of what occurred. After the Northern Expedition passed through the city in October 1926, one faction of left-leaning Nationalists took power and began reorganizing the government. They also had a less than close relationship to the main Nationalist faction, led by Chiang Kai-shek 蔣介石 (1887–1975), who had taken charge earlier that year. By early 1927, however, the two factions united against the Communists in Wuhan, which led to widespread fighting and damage to all three of its constituent cities.[2] Elsewhere, fighting and its attendant economic and human costs hindered the stability of Buddhist institutions.

In 1927, the Nationalists declared Nanjing to be the new capital of the Republic of China. Although the Northern Expedition did not end until 1928, historians generally consider 1927 to mark the beginning of the Nanjing Decade. This was a period of relative peace and unity in China before the Second Sino-Japanese War began in earnest in 1937. Following closely on its military unification of the country, the Nanjing government began to pass laws and ordinances with the aim of creating a unified citizenry. Distinct spheres of life were identified and mapped to rationalize society and bring it under the government's control.[3] One type of social group the government sought to control was religious organizations. As Rebecca Nedostup has studied in great detail, from 1928 on the Republican government worked to classify and regulate religion. In this process, it also sought to claim and redirect capital held by religious organizations, which it needed to build the institutions of the modern state.[4] The biggest targets were those activities and institutions the government deemed to be superstitious. The category "superstition" as well as the category "religion" were in flux at the time as many inside and outside the government argued about what should be included in each.[5] For their part, religious groups worked to deflect the criticism that they were superstitious. One way to do this was to promote modern education in the service of the state, and it is not a coincidence that the years 1927 and 1928 witnessed the rise of another round of antireligion movements and the concomitant appearance of many new Buddhist educational programs.

This chapter describes the network of programs that sprang from the original Huayan University during the tumultuous 1920s and 1930s. Given the mercurial nature of most Buddhist educational programs during these years as well as the fairly large graduating class from the original Huayan University, it is too great a task to account for all of the programs those graduates were involved with during this period, which probably number more than two dozen. Here I focus on those that emphasized the teaching and practice of Huayan in their curricula. This chapter also includes a brief description of two other unaffiliated programs that focused on Huayan and about which we know something of their curricula. I begin by looking at the career of Yuexia's most well-known disciple, Yingci. Although he demurred from accepting a position of authority in the Huayan University network, he continued to teach about Huayan during the Republican period and ran a number of Huayan institutes.

Yingci, Student and Master

After the second Huayan University sputtered to an end in 1921, Yingci determined to enter a period of *biguan*. He first made pilgrimage to Mt. Wutai and then traveled back to Hangzhou, where he remained in confinement at Bodhi Temple from April 1922 to November 1924. During his retreat, the monk Jingbo 靜波 (n.d.), who was the abbot and modern restorer of Qingliang 清涼 Temple in Changzhou, contacted Yingci and invited him to help establish a Buddhist educational program at the temple. Upon completion of his confinement, Yingci traveled the roughly 130 miles north to Jingbo's temple. He first oversaw a meditation retreat for the students that winter before starting classes in 1925.[6]

Before Yingci's arrival, the ground was already being laid for the program, to be named the Qingliang Institute (Qingliang Xueyuan 清涼學院). Jingbo was assisted in this work by Qinghai 清海 (n.d.), who had recently become abbot of Faqi 法起 Temple. Qinghai had wanted to start a monastic educational program for some time and had even spoken with both Yingci and Yuexia about it a decade earlier. The new Qingliang Institute was to be run jointly by the Qingliang and Faqi Temples.[7] In April 1924, Qinghai submitted petitions to both the provincial government and the provincial board of education requesting permission to start a monastic institute. He received that permission in May[8] and formally opened the institute in the fall of that year.[9] By 1926, notices about the institute and its bylaws were appearing in the Buddhist press, along with congratulations from Jiang Weiqiao, a prominent lay Buddhist and member of the provincial board of education.[10]

Yingci took a guiding hand in the institute's organization and development, including writing its bylaws and curriculum. Study was organized into two classes, a three-year preparatory course (*yuke* 預科) focusing on basic Buddhist education and a specialized course (*zhuanke* 專科) in Huayan thought, which would put a special emphasis on the works of Chengguan and Li Tongxuan.[11] As was often the case for such programs during this period, these two courses ended up running consecutively rather than concurrently, probably due to a shortage of applicants who had the necessary preparation for the specialized course. Things went smoothly during the institute's first few years. The preparatory course was under way, and in 1927 the institute was even able to host a visit by a delegation of Japanese Buddhists who were in China on a fact-finding mission.[12]

Things became difficult at the institute after the graduation of the first class in the spring of 1928, when, for reasons that as usual are not clearly recorded, Jingbo and Yingci decided to move the institute to Shanghai.¹³ Yingci had traveled to Shanghai the previous year at the invitation of one Mrs. Sheng 盛 (n.d.), a wealthy lay Buddhist, who had requested he lecture on the Huayan Sutra at her Xinhai 辛亥 Gardens in the English Concession. Mrs. Sheng, perhaps inspired by the example of Liza Roos Hardoon and the Huayan University, told Yingci during his visit that she wanted to contribute to the education of monastics and promised to house a monastic institute in her gardens, which became home to the Huayan Hermitage (Huayan Jingshe 華嚴精舍). Unfortunately, Mrs. Sheng died in early 1928, but Yingci and Jingbo were still able to move the Qingliang Institute to Shanghai, and the specialized course in Huayan began in August 1928.¹⁴ They were assisted by the monk Xinyan 心嚴 (n.d.), who had grown up in Yingci's hometown.¹⁵

The curriculum of the institute's specialized course centered on Yingci's lectures on *Introductory Discourse to Commentary on the Huayan Sutra* (*Huayan shuchao xuantan* 華嚴疏鈔懸談) by Chengguan.¹⁶ This text is an introduction and summary to Chengguan's two major commentaries on the Huayan Sutra. A layman enrolled at the institute in Shanghai recalled that every day the students practiced meditation and listened to Yingci's lectures. He reported that the atmosphere around the lectures was solemn, and Yingci explained the text in great detail. This good atmosphere did not last very long, however. The institute's precarious financial situation, likely caused by the death of its benefactor, forced Jingbo to begin hiring out the monks to perform funeral rites.¹⁷ Such activities were unpopular with the new breed of student monks, who were committed to studying and practicing the dharma for the sake of Buddhism and saw such commercialized activities as beneath them. These activities also took away from the students' time for studying.

The performance of funeral rites was necessary for the financial survival of the Qingliang Institute, but Yingci eventually grew tired of the distraction it caused and suddenly stopped classes and moved the institute out of Shanghai in April 1929.¹⁸ He eventually found a new home for the program in 1930 at Yongqing 永慶

Temple, located seventy miles upriver from Shanghai. They had barely begun classes, however, when the government expropriated the temple to serve as a military base, and Yingci was forced to move everything again, this time to the Huayan Hermitage (Huayan'an 華嚴庵, not the same institute as Huayan Jingshe, named earlier) in the city of Wuxi. The hermitage hosted the institute until the successful completion of the special course in 1931.[19]

In addition to Yingci, consistent members of the Qingliang Institute faculty included Xinyan and Nanting, who went on to play an important role in the next generation of modern Huayan teachers. Nanting had studied under Yingci's student Changxing for three semesters at the Anhui Monastic School in 1923 and 1924 directly before Yingci had him as a student teacher at the Qingliang Institute. Because Nanting was not entirely prepared to teach, he spent a lot of time studying by himself while the preparatory course was running. When the Qingliang Institute went on hiatus in the fall of 1929, he used his new knowledge to assist Yingci's student Aiting by teaching a course on the Vimalakīrti Sutra at the Buddhist institute that Aiting had opened at Zhulin Temple in Zhenjiang (discussed in greater detail later in this chapter).[20] Nanting returned to the Qingliang Institute in 1930 to serve as the assistant lecturer (*pianzuo fashi* 偏座法師)[21] until its closure at the end of the semester. We do not have clear records on the identities and thus on the careers of any of the people associated with the Qingliang Institute other than Nanting and Yingci.

Through the Qingliang Institute, Yingci had been able to continue the work of the original Huayan University. It took perseverance, but Yingci was able to lead his students through both the preparatory course and the specialized course, providing them with a firm foundation in Huayan Buddhism, which made the Qingliang Institute one of the most successful of the programs in the Huayan University network. When the institute ended in 1931, Nanting went back to Zhenjiang to teach at Aiting's institute during its final semester. Yingci, for his part, continued his life as a traveling teacher of Huayan. After the graduation ceremony, he made a second pilgrimage to Mt. Wutai. (In all, he visited the mountain four times over the course of his life, in 1922, 1931, 1934, and 1937.) Upon the completion of his second pilgrimage to Mt. Wutai, he returned to Changshu to lead a meditation retreat at Xingfu Temple. Yingci had become a well-known lecturer on Huayan by the 1930s, but he was still a lineage-holding Chan master, and he led five more meditation retreats before his last one in Shanghai in 1949. He led retreats at Tianning Temple in Yangzhou, in Wuxi, and at the famous Chan center, the Tiantong Temple in Ningbo, where he had been ordained in 1900.

Over the next few decades, Yingci remained committed to teaching and training young monks and continued to focus his efforts on Huayan. He worked mostly in the Jiangnan region, leading meditation retreats, presiding over ordination ceremonies, and overseeing a much-celebrated reprinting of Chengguan's *Commentary and Subcommentary on the Huayan Sutra* (*Huayan shuchao* 華嚴疏鈔) that took place between 1939 and 1944. Yingci was most famous for his sutra lecture series. In the twenty years between 1931 and 1952, he delivered at least one such series each year and sometimes as many as four in a year. Some of the texts he favored most were the Brahmā Net (Fanwang Jing 梵網經), Lotus, and Śūraṅgama Sutras. He lectured the most on the various Huayan Sutras and other Huayan-related texts. He taught the entirety of Chengguan's *Introductory Discourse to Commentary on the Huayan Sutra* at Tiantong Temple over the course of four summer sessions from 1933 to 1936; he also lectured on this text again in Shanghai in 1945 and in Nanjing in 1947. He also lectured three times on the complete forty-volume version of the Huayan Sutra:[22] in Changshu from the fall of 1936 to the spring of 1937, again at Yufo 玉佛 Temple in Shanghai from 1938 to 1939, and again in Hangzhou in 1947.

In 1939, as Yingci was completing a lecture series on the forty-volume Huayan Sutra in Shanghai, a new printing of the sixty-volume version was nearing completion. On October 18 of that year, while in meditation, Yingci had a vision of fireworks in the sky, with the character for "sun" (*ri* 日) appearing in the east and the character for "field" (*tian* 田) appearing in the west. After the fireworks subsided, dragons flew down from the sky and gathered in front of him. Yingci took this vision as a sign that he, who had just turned sixty years old (which he referred to in his account of the dream as "the age of dragons"), should lecture on the sixty-volume Huayan Sutra. As befitting such a large undertaking, Yingci decided to rent a cluster of five halls in the city in order to establish the Huayan Institute, where he could hold the lecture series. The institute, centered on Yingci's lectures, opened in March 1940 and ran until its completion on March 22, 1942.[23] This would be the last time that Yingci completed a lecture series on either of the two larger versions of the Huayan Sutra. (He did start a series on the eighty-volume Huayan Sutra in Nanjing in 1950, but he had to stop soon after he began.[24])

It is noteworthy that the most well-known and well-connected master of Huayan doctrine in Republican China lectured on a full version of the Huayan Sutra only a couple of times and usually in the context of one of his institutes. Following the tendency that had been established in Chinese Buddhism during the Song dynasty, most of Yingci's teaching activity focused instead on Chengguan's commentaries on the text.[25] Yingci also gave talks on a few other texts written by the patriarchs of classical Huayan, but he never gave more than one series on any. He spoke on the *Method for Contemplation of the Dharmadhātu* (*Fajie guanmen* 法界觀門)[26] the year after he concluded his Huayan Institute, on Fazang's *Exploration of the Profundities of the* Huayan Sutra (*Huayanjing tanxuanji* 華嚴經探玄記) in Nanjing in 1947, and on Chengguan's *Method of Contemplation on the Complete Interfusion of the Three Sages* (*Sansheng yuanrong guanmen* 三聖圓融觀門) in 1948.[27]

Beyond lecturing, leading retreats, and serving at ordinations, Yingci remained involved in other Buddhist activities throughout his career. He is perhaps most well known for serving on the board of the Huayan Commentary and Subcommentary Publishing Committee (Huayan Shuchao Bianyin Hui 華嚴疏鈔編印會), which worked to publish a complete and carefully edited modern edition of Chengguan's *Commentary and Subcommentary on the Huayan Sutra.* Chengguan's commentary is still considered the definitive explanation of the Huayan Sutra, but the complete text had been lost in China since the ninth century and had existed only as fragments within other texts. The project to reprint it had originally been the idea of the Beijing-based lay Buddhist publisher Xu Weiru 徐蔚如 (1878–1937), but after his untimely death a group formed in Shanghai in 1939 to complete the task using texts secured from Mii-dera 御井寺 on Mt. Hiei 比叡 in Japan.[28] Yingci joined a number of others, including the laymen Jiang Weiqiao and Li Yuanjing 李圓淨 (c. 1894–1950), on the committee to produce this work. They edited the text, raised funds for its publication, and were able to complete the full printing in 1944.[29]

In 1948, Yingci went to Nanjing, where he became head of the Nanjing Huayan Society (Nanjing Huayan Hui 南京華嚴會), a position he held for several years. There in 1949, he launched one final Huayan educational program: the Huayan Normal Institute (Huayan Shifan Xueyuan 華嚴師範學院).[30] One of the student teachers for the program was Zhenchan 真襌 (1916–1995), the younger brother of one of the teacher's at Yingci's Qingliang Institute, Xinyan. Zhenchan had first heard Yingci lecture on the Śūraṅgama Sutra in Yangzhou in 1933, but after attending Yingci's lectures in 1948, he began to focus his own studies on Huayan thought. He eventually became an important figure both in the later Huayan tradition and, as discussed in the next chapter, in mainland Chinese Buddhism after the end of the Cultural Revolution.[31]

I have found no information on the curriculum or history of the Huayan Normal Institute, and with the end of the Chinese Civil War in 1949, Yingci seems to have moved back to Shanghai permanently. His teaching activities began to decline in frequency after 1949. This was likely the result of both his advancing age (he was seventy-six that year) and the gradual erosion of Buddhist activity under the policies of religious disestablishment carried out by the Communist government in the 1950s. Apart from one short trip to Hangzhou to preside over an ordination ceremony and another to lecture on the Heart Sutra in Beijing in 1955, Yingci appears to have remained in Shanghai until his death on August 31, 1965.

Passing the Lamp: The Dharmadhātu Institutes

Dharmadhātu Institutes of Changshu, 1926–1936

The second Huayan University closed in 1921, but the study and teaching of Huayan continued among Yuexia and Yingci's students at Xingfu Temple. In the mid-1920s, these activities were held under the auspices of the Dharmadhātu Institute. One contemporary writer said that this new name was needed because of the much-reduced scale of the program that succeeded the second Huayan University there.[32] Even a change of name could not prevent familiar institutional challenges from rearing their heads, however, and the new Dharmadhātu Institute was never quite on a solid organizational footing. Over the next decade, a string of different principals and teachers came and went as the institute repeatedly ceased and then resumed operation. As noted earlier, instability of this kind was not unusual during the period because the financial and institutional infrastructure to support such monastic education in Republican China was continually undermined by military adventure, economic challenges, antireligious sentiment, and government policy. Nevertheless, one must wonder if the Dharmadhātu Institute's instability did not stem at least in part from Yuexia and Yingci's personal resistance to serving as temple abbots. This choice may have set a precedent for their students, whose own constant coming and going left the Dharmadhātu Institute without consistent leadership.

Xingfu Temple is located on Mt. Yu 虞 in Changshu and dates from the Tang dynasty. It was a private residence when its owner invited Yuexia to come serve as abbot in 1917, but, as noted in the previous chapter, with Yuexia's illness and death the abbotship passed to Yingci.[33] True to his vows, Yingci did not remain long in this position. In February 1918, he transmitted the dharma to Chisong, Huizong, and a third monk who had not been a student at the original Huayan University, Tanyue, making them all forty-third-generation lineage holders in the Linji line. Chisong became abbot soon after this, but in 1922, less than a year after the closure of the second Huayan University, he left to teach with Changxing at the latter's newly formed Anhui Monastic School. Chisong stayed there for less than a year before his burgeoning interest in esoteric Buddhism led him to depart for Japan.

Back at Xingfu Temple, in the wake of Chisong's departure, Huizong ascended to become the fourth abbot in nearly as many years. Huizong had been practicing meditation at Jinshan Temple when Yingci personally invited him to enroll in the first class at the original Huayan University, and he had followed his teachers from Shanghai to Hangzhou and then to Changshu.[34] Huizong originally hailed from the same county in Hubei as Cizhou, and without the responsibility of the abbotship of Xingfu Temple he might have gone to help Jiechen run the Huayan University of Hankou. He instead worked to continue the original university's legacy in Jiangsu. It was he who decided to change the school's name to Dharmadhātu Institute, invoking the concept of the Huayan-related concept of the Dharmadhātu, or Dharma Realm.

The institute published a formal set of bylaws in 1927, but few records exist to indicate what kind of educational activities were taking place there between 1921 and 1927. Jiechen had returned from Wuhan by 1925,[35] and Cizhou returned by at least 1926, bringing with him Li'an, who had been their student at the Huayan University of Hankou.[36] It is likely that the curriculum ran something along the lines of a *conglin* training regime, with students participating in meditation, attending sutra lectures given by senior monks, and carefully observing the monastic rule. A letter sent to Taixu by the "students of the Dharmadhātu Institute [Fajie Xueyuan xuesheng 法界學苑學生]" published in *HCY* in March 1926 indicates it had some sort of institutional identity at that point. The letter, which invited Taixu to come lecture at the institute, mentioned that Cizhou, who was serving as the head of the institute, had been lecturing there on the Vinaya.[37] Observance of the Buddhist monastic rule was a core part of the institute's identity, and by January 1927 the monks there had formed the Dharmadhātu Institute Students' Association for the Observance of the Monastic Rule (Fajie Xueyuan Tongxue Pini Cejinhui 法界學院同學毘尼策進會). The association's charter lists Cizhou and Huizong as officers, as well as Jiechen, Chen Yuanbai, the monk Kuanrong 寬融 (n.d.), and others.[38]

The formation of the association proved to be a fittingly auspicious start of the year for the Dharmadhātu Institute. Throughout the year, regular funding for the institute's activities was provided by the lay members of Xingfu Temple's Huayan Assembly.[39] By September 1927, this funding allowed Huizong, Cizhou, Jiechen, and Chisong (who had just returned from a second trip to Japan) to launch a new rigorous three-year study program similar to the ones they had run elsewhere. Although the proposed curriculum for this program did include non-Buddhist subjects such as foreign languages, Western philosophy, and history, it was much more modest—one might even say more realistic—in scope than the programs proposed for the Huayan University of Hankou and the Wuchang Institute. There was also a decided emphasis on the study of basic Huayan and Consciousness-Only texts. The curriculum also included study of the Vinaya and meditation practice based on Huayan contemplation manuals.[40]

The sense of promise that came with this new curriculum and the new students it attracted to the temple was palpable at the Dharmadhātu Institute. One sees this feeling in the talk that Chisong delivered during convocation in September 1927. In his speech, he spoke of history and the current state of Buddhism in China, urging the students to study hard for the sake of Buddhism and the nation. He stated that the Qing dynasty had been a period of decline for Buddhism in China, but that this status had been reversed during the Guangxu 光緒 Era (1871–1908) due to the effort of talented people who had studied Buddhism. In the twenty years that had passed since the end of that era, Chinese monastics had continued to work hard in adapting Buddhist thought to the modern world. Chisong, who had studied in Japan twice over the previous three years, repeatedly framed his comments about Chinese Buddhism with comparisons to Japanese Buddhism. He felt that Chinese Buddhists had done well to modernize their tradition up to that point, but they were beginning to be outpaced academically by their Japanese peers. He closed his talk by encouraging the students at the institute to study deeply the wisdom of China, to aid the world, and to raise the stature of Chinese Buddhism.[41] Chisong had great hopes for what the students could accomplish, which comes across clearly in his speech, but his hopes for the institute sadly went unfulfilled.

I have not been able to determine the reason, but less than a year into the start of classes Chisong, Cizhou, Jiechen, and Kuanrong left the Dharmadhātu Institute. The loss of the teaching talent represented by these four men was significant. After their departure, Huizong was able to hire Huiting 蕙庭 (1897–1933), a friend and colleague of Changxing, to teach and to head the institute. Huiting had graduated from Ouyang Jingwu's Faxiang University in 1926 and had spent the time since then helping Changxing start the educational program that would eventually become the Minnan Buddhist Institute.[42] After arriving at Xingfu Temple, Huiting invited several new teachers to help at the Dharmadhātu Institute, including the monks Xianyue 現月 (n.d.) and Shiqing 實清 (n.d.).[43] These measures were not enough to keep Huizong around, however, and before the year was out he followed in the footsteps of both his teachers and his classmates by resigning his position as abbot and leaving the institute. To add insult to injury, he took Huiting with him to assist Changxing start yet another new program in Hangzhou. With Huizong's departure, the abbotship passed to Tanyue, who became Xingfu Temple's fifth abbot in a decade and the only remaining teacher who had been at the first Dharmadhātu Institute.[44] Despite the turnover within the leadership, classes at the institute continued, and a number of its graduates went on to have important careers at other institutions of monastic education.

In 1930, economic hardship once again forced a temporary closure of the institute, but an announcement in 1931 stated that classes would resume under the direction of Zhengdao 正道 (n.d.). Many elements of the curriculum proposed in 1931 were the same as in 1927, but the number of texts studied was reduced. The institute still included the study of Huayan, but the sutra's role within the curriculum was clearly diminishing as the institute adopted a more holistic educational model. At this point, new leaders emerged to assist the institute, including Weifang 葦舫 (c.1908–c.1969), Chengkong 乘空 (n.d.), as well as the returned Kuanrong, who had been with the institute in 1927.[45] The historical record does not tell us much about the success of this iteration of the institute. It is unclear if classes were actually held or how long this iteration lasted.

Changxing and Chisong eventually returned to Xingfu Temple to help Tanyue and Weicheng, one of the Dharmadhātu Institute's initial graduates, restart the institute in the spring of 1935. By this point, a number of modern Buddhist schools had been running in various parts of China off and on for years, and Chisong and Changxing were able to hire a number of monks who had graduated from these schools, including some of Changxing's former students at the Anhui Monastic School and the Minnan Buddhist Institute. The curriculum for the Dharmadhātu Institute published in 1935 is short on detail, though much was made of the fact that it included study of the Japanese language. What information is present in the announcement shows that although the name remained the same, students at this Dharmadhātu Institute would spend little time studying Huayan thought. The target enrollment for the institute was a fairly typical thirty, but it began with only twenty-five student monks split evenly between one basic class and a more advanced one.[46] Most of these monks came from Jiangsu and were in their late teens or early twenties.[47] They were described as the "fourth class" of the institute, and their studies were supposed to continue until the winter of 1937. Unfortunately, economic pressure forced the class to shrink to a mere eight students within the first year. Then in the summer of 1936 the Chinese military, which had begun to prepare for an all-out war with Japan, made plans to occupy Xingfu Temple. Weicheng, seeing the writing on the wall, called all of the remaining students and teachers together early on the morning of July 16 to announce that graduation would be held early and the institute would close.[48] This was probably the final semester of the last Dharmadhātu Institute at Xingfu Temple. Weicheng tried to revive the program in 1942, but it does not appear as though he was successful.[49]

The Dharmadhātu Institute of Changshu and the Zhulin Buddhist Institute (discussed later in this chapter) began as programs centered on the study of Huayan, but both eventually lost this focus as faculty turnover and institutional changes reduced the amount of time devoted to Huayan studies in their syllabi. Yingci's Qingliang Institute, which was set up more along the lines of the traditional monastic education system, centered on lectures given by one primary master, Yingci, and remained focused on Huayan until the course cycle ended in 1931. Cizhou followed in his teacher's footsteps and spent much of the 1930s running similar institutions using the name "Dharmadhātu Institute," focusing on the dual study of Huayan and Vinaya.

Cizhou's Dharmadhātu Institutes, 1933–1936, 1936–?

Cizhou's monastic biography is intimately connected to modern Huayan studies. I have mentioned him several times already in this book, but for the benefit of the reader I review that information here. Cizhou was from Sui 隨 County in Hubei. He ordained at Guiyuan Temple in Wuhan in 1912 and then enrolled at the original Huayan University. During the 1920s, he traveled around giving lectures and taught for varying lengths of time at the Huayan University of Hankou, the Dharmadhātu Institute of Changshu, and the Zhulin Buddhist Institute. From 1928 to 1933, he delivered a lecture series focusing on Vinaya and Huayan texts. Cizhou chose the path of a traveling lecturer, following in the footsteps of his teacher Yingci, who was also instrumental in helping Cizhou establish his own Dharmadhātu Institute.

During the first month of 1933, Yingci gave a lecture series on the Brahmā Net Sutra, a favorite text among Sinitic Buddhists that spells out the so-called bodhisattva precepts that are believed to reflect the essence of Buddhist moral practice. The Chan master Xuyun had invited him to come to Mt. Gu 鼓 in Fujian to lecture on this text at Yongquan 湧泉 Temple, where Xuyun was abbot. While Yingci was staying at Yongquan Temple, he was pleased to learn that it had originally been called "Huayan Temple" and that it had a long tradition of emphasizing the dual study of Chan and Huayan, just as he and his teacher Yuexia did. The temple had been the home of the Qing dynasty Huayan master Daopei 道霈 (1615–1702), and Yingci was struck by the fact that the temple's library held many Huayan texts, some of which dated as far back as the Song dynasty of the tenth through the early thirteenth centuries.[50]

Soon after his visit, Xuyun invited Yingci's student Cizhou to resurrect the Huayan tradition at Yongquan Temple by taking over the Gushan Buddhist institute (Gushan Foxueyuan 鼓山佛學院) and transforming it into a Dharmadhātu Institute using temple funds.[51] An article announcing the institute's opening, dated July 1933 and published in September of that year, states that the institute sought forty students for three separate classes. The Huayan Sutra would serve as the "primary coursework [zhuke 主課]" for the institute. In tandem with their study of this sutra, students would also study basic Buddhist texts for a year and a half before moving on to study the Vinaya for the following year and a half.[52] One of the students who attended the entire institute was Mengcan 夢參 (1915–2016), a former military-academy student from Heilongjiang who went on to serve as an important link in the revival of Huayan studies in China after the Cultural Revolution.[53]

Cizhou's Dharmadhātu Institute at Yongquan Temple successfully completed its planned three-year course cycle in 1936. Cizhou was invited afterward to run another Dharmadhātu Institute at Fahai 法海 Temple in Fuzhou Province. Funds were solicited in April,[54] and the institute's bylaws, including its planned curriculum (which closely followed the curriculum at the Dharmadhātu Institute of Yongquan Temple) were published in May.[55] Later that same year, however, Cizhou accepted an invitation from Tanxu 倓虛 (1875–1963)[56] to lecture at the Zhanshan Temple Buddhist Institute (Zhanshansi Foxueyuan 湛山寺佛學院) in Qingdao.[57] Mengcan went with Cizhou to Qingdao, where he remained to study Tiantai thought with Tanxu. It is unclear if the Dharmadhātu Institute at Fahai Temple ever opened, but it seems unlikely.[58]

By the end of 1936, Cizhou decided to start another Dharmadhātu Institute at Jinglian 淨蓮 Temple in Beijing.[59] There, he lectured on the entire Huayan Sutra (which version is not recorded) from the spring of 1937 to the fall of 1939. When the series was complete, he took two years off before starting again on March 24, 1941.[60] He taught there until poor health forced him to stop in 1944. That year Cizhou moved to Anyang Hermitage (Anyang Jingshe 安養精舍), located at number 16 Shoupa Hutong 手帕胡同 in Dongzhimen 東直門, where he restarted his program the following year.[61] Given the wars that raged in China throughout the 1940s, it is unclear how uninterrupted Cizhou's teaching activities were during those years. He remained at Anyang Hermitage until his death in 1958.[62]

An Expanding Network

Zhulin Buddhist Institute, 1928–1931

The Zhulin Buddhist Institute was the brainchild of Aiting, a tonsure disciple of one of the graduates of the original Huayan University, Zhiguang, and the abbot of Zhulin Temple in Zhenjiang. Located 150 miles northwest of Shanghai in the heart of the Jiangnan region, Zhenjiang sits on the south bank of the Yangzi, roughly equidistant between Yangzhou, Changzhou, and Nanjing. It was a major site for Chinese Buddhism in the late-imperial and Republican periods, and many important temples were located there. Aiting was local to the region as both he and his master Zhiguang hailed from Tai 泰 County just to the north.[63] After graduating from the original Huayan University, both men stayed in the southern Jiangsu area, practicing meditation first in Changzhou and then in Zhenjiang. The account of his program's history given here is taken from an article that Aiting's tonsure-brother Nanting wrote in mid-June 1931, soon after his own arrival there.

Aiting had become abbot of Zhulin Temple in the spring of 1927 and immediately started to lay the groundwork for a Buddhist institute. With the mass departure of teachers from the Dharmadhātu Institute in Changshu in 1928, Aiting was able to secure the services of Cizhou and his student Li'an (a graduate of the Huayan University in Hankou) to teach in the new Zhulin Buddhist Institute, though Cizhou left after only one semester. Classes began on August 1, 1928. In the first semester, the curriculum focused on the Vinaya. Students began Huayan studies in the second semester with a course on the *Outline of Xianshou's Five Teachings* (*Xianshou wujiaoyi* 賢首五教儀) taught by Li'an.[64] However, this class was cut short due to Li'an's sudden death from tuberculosis. Despite such difficulties, Aiting was able to keep the institute going by hiring different teachers, including in 1930 Zhenhua, who was a graduate of the unaffiliated Huayan University of Yanghzou (discussed later in this chapter). As a result of Aiting's efforts, the institute continued to flourish and had forty students by the time Nanting arrived in the spring of 1931 to teach Consciousness-Only and Buddhist logic during the final semester.

Nanting's account of the history of the Zhulin Buddhist Institute, published in 1931, ends on a sad and slightly defensive note. He closed by explaining at great length the financial difficulties they faced in running such an institute and was careful to point out that what monastic teachers the institute was able to hire were paid little more than room and board. He even directed an oblique criticism at the students, who, he said, contributed to the instability of the institute because they "come and go like sparrows."⁶⁵ Nanting likely felt he had to explain the institute in this way because the Zhulin Buddhist Institute and the Qingliang Institute had been the subject of an exposé published in 1929 in the Buddhist journal *Modern Sangha* (*Xiandai sengqie* 現代僧伽).

Modern Sangha, which ran from 1928 to 1932, was started at Minnan Buddhist Institute by monks who had been associated with the Buddhist New Youth (*Fohua xin qingnian* 佛化新青年) movement of the early and mid-1920s. This movement was composed of monks with anarchosocialist leanings and centered on the New Buddhist Youth League (Xin Fohua Qingniantuan 新佛化青年團) founded in Beijing in 1922. By 1927, the league had a membership of roughly four thousand, with branches in major cities across and outside of China. These "young monastics" sought to reform the Chinese Buddhist *sangha* using education and other means to seize control of the institutions of power from more tradition-minded teachers such as Yinguang and Dixian.⁶⁶ The educational legacy of Yuexia and Yingci, which had deep roots in the traditional educational modes, would also have been a target for these Young Turks. *Modern Sangha* served as the primary mouthpiece for the radical reformist agenda, and its editors were quick to publish stories that valorized the efforts of the young monastics and demonized their opponents. In 1929, the magazine published two reports on misdeeds at the Zhulin and Qingliang Institutes written by aggrieved students as well as a preface that summarized the two reports and stated that the journal's editors had independently checked the students' claims and found them to be true. They criticized the institutes for failing their students and issued a warning to students at other Buddhist institutes to be on the lookout for similar problems.⁶⁷

As noted earlier, the Qingliang Institute faced financial problems soon after Jingbo and Yingci moved it to Shanghai. As a result, Jingbo had to seek out lay patronage and began to hire out the students to perform funeral rites, which reformist monks considered the least-acceptable activity for young monks bent on improving themselves and the world through education. It is hardly surprising, therefore, that this move would lead to a great deal of resentment and hostility. The student writing about the institute reported that Jingbo had lost his commitment to the pursuit of pure Buddhism and was dragging the students down with him. They claimed that he had closed the Chan hall, so they had nowhere to meditate, and that he had begun to mingle with mediums and foolish laypeople, all as the money began to "pile up like snow."[68]

A student who called himself Yincun 印存 wrote a long letter about all he thought was going wrong at the Zhulin Buddhist Institute.[69] Although Yincun had been very excited when he first enrolled, he felt that everything he had been told about it was a lie. After Cizhou left, Yincun said, the entire program had gone down the drain. He criticized the students for being lazy and the teachers for being ignorant. The proctor had a feudalistic mindset and had organized a "clique" around himself to control everything, and those who did not go along with him were bullied. Nanting addressed some of these concerns in the piece he wrote in 1931, noting that after Cizhou had left, Aiting had hired the monk Lengding 楞定 (n.d.), who had experience teaching in a grammar school. Lengding had gotten into some kind of disagreement with a group of students over starting a school newspaper, and some of Lengding's words, which Nanting felt were taken out of context, had been published. Nanting was likely referring to the piece by Yincun, who in the end may have gotten his way because Lengding did eventually leave the Zhulin Buddhist Institute.[70]

It is difficult to know how to treat these reports. One can certainly understand the disappointment of idealistic young monks who had earnestly embarked on the path of education. There is likely some truth to their criticisms, but they also wrote about these issues in a certain formulaic way. One sees this approach also in the memoirs of Chen-hua 真華 (1922–2012), a younger contemporary of these monks, who had many similar criticisms of monastic education in Jiangnan.[71] In the absence of other data, we must simply take these stories as probably partially true accounts of these two Huayan-centered programs.

Jiaoshan Buddhist Institute, 1934–1937

Aiting retired as abbot of Zhulin Temple in 1932 and moved to Hong Kong, but Buddhist education continued in Zhenjiang. Two years after Aiting's departure, Zhiguang, Aiting's tonsure master and fellow student at the original Huayan University, became abbot of Dinghui Temple on Mt. Jiao 焦 in Zhenjiang. The temple was in the process of being transformed into a *conglin*, and it is clear that Zhiguang, who was often described in the Buddhist press as a master of Huayan, had big plans for the temple. He sought and received the support of the former abbot and other senior members of the temple to start a Buddhist institute there. This institute began as the Huayan Research Society (Huayan Yanjiushe 華嚴研究社), for which Zhiguang invited Nanting to serve as the chief lecturer (*zhujiang* 主講), and eventually became the Jiaoshan Buddhist Institute (Jiaoshan Foxueyuan 焦山佛學院). Nanting had likely remained in Zhenjiang after the closure of the Zhulin Buddhist Institute in 1931, probably assisting Changxing, who had become abbot of Guangxiao 光孝 Temple in Nanting's native Tai County (discussed later in this chapter). As Dinghui Temple's Huayan Research Society transformed into a full-fledged Buddhist institute in the fall of 1934, Zhiguang hired several monks to teach at the institute, including two graduates of the nearby Zhulin Institute, Xuefan 雪煩 (1909–1994) and Dongchu.[72] Both men received dharma transmission in 1936, and each served as abbot of Dinghui Temple in the 1940s. After the Chinese Civil War, both Dongchu and Nanting went to Taiwan and became important figures there,[73] while Xuefan labored to keep Chinese Buddhism alive in mainland China by working with the government in the 1960s, 1980s, and 1990s.[74]

Zhiguang wanted to create a Buddhist institute with a regular curriculum as well as transform Dinghui Temple into a center for self-study and Buddhist research. The plan for the institute published in *HCY* in December 1934 is somewhat vague regarding the curriculum, but there was a typical division of the coursework into two levels: the first class (*jiazu* 甲組) studied the three major sections of the Buddhist canon (scripture, Vinaya, and commentaries), Chinese language, and history, and the second class (*yizu* 乙組) added calligraphy, math, and Sanskrit pronunciation.[75] By that time, seventy-one students were enrolled in the institute, sixty-five of whom were from Jiangsu Province.[76] Beyond the regular classes, Zhiguang planned to turn the Huayan Research Society into the Jiaoshan Buddhist Studies Library (Jiaoshan Foxue Tushuguan 焦山佛學圖書館), probably along the lines of the similar library established three years earlier at the revived Wuchang Buddhist Institute by Taixu and his disciples.[77] In order to supplement the three sets of the Buddhist canon held at the temple, Zhiguang wanted to order for this library a broad range of historical and contemporary resources from both China and abroad, including important newspapers, magazines, and books.[78] By October 1935, the school's leadership had been able to secure the necessary funds to open the library. Zhiguang put this library to use right away by assigning extra readings to the institute's students beyond the standard curriculum. He also hired Juemin 覺民 (n.d.), a teacher from the Wuchang Buddhist Institute, to assist him.[79]

Early in the following year, Zhiguang stepped down as abbot, passing that role to Jingyan 靜嚴 (1906–1969), one of the previous abbot's students.[80] Jingyan took over running the Dinghui Temple and the institute there and began the practice (or perhaps carried on a tradition started by Zhiguang) of setting aside time in the middle of the fourth lunar month for a Huayan Assembly to chant the entire Huayan Sutra. The monks at the temple were joined by local laypeople, and several dozen people are said to have participated. A report on the event in June 1936 also mentioned that the noted Hubei layman Li Zikuan 李子寬 (1882–1973) even came to give a speech of encouragement to the institute's students.[81] Without clear details about its curriculum, it is difficult to be certain how much Huayan was being taught at the Dinghui Temple, but the presence of both Zhiguang's Huayan Research Society and Jingyan's regular Huayan Assemblies show some connection between the institute and Huayan.

The Dinghui Temple institute's first class graduated in early 1937, but before the second class could get very far into their studies, the Second Sino-Japanese War broke out, and Jingyan's efforts to maintain the temple and its institute came to a sudden and dramatic end as Japanese troops bombed the temple at the end of 1937.[82] Nevertheless, Jingyan somehow managed to restart his educational program in March 1940, with seats for thirty students.[83] Around this time, he passed the abbotship of the Dinghui Temple to Xuefan, who hired several new teachers, including Xianyue, who had taught at the Dharmadhātu Institute in Changshu in the late 1920s. The only record I have seen of the Dinghui institute's curriculum at this point is in Shi Dongchu's writings, which state that it included philosophy, physics, and math. Dongchu does not say what Buddhist subjects were taught.[84]

Guangxiao Buddhist Institute, 1935?–1937

At some point in the mid-1930s, Nanting became abbot of Guangxiao Temple in Tai County and started a Buddhist institute centered on the study of Huayan. Guangxiao Temple had already faced its share of ups and downs prior to Nanting's arrival. It was rejuvenated by several abbots, including Yucheng 玉成 (1854–1936), another native of Tai County who was Zhiguang's grandmaster. In the late 1920s, the temple's fortunes had started to wane, and there were disputes over ownership of the temple's land. Changxing became abbot in 1931 and turned things around, building up the temple property and putting it on a solid financial footing before passing the abbotship to Nanting. As with other programs, students at the Guangxiao Buddhist Institute (Guangxiao Foxueyuan 光孝佛學院) were divided into two classes. Nanting's student and disciple Chengyi 成一 (1914–2011), who joined the institute in the spring of 1936, recalled that the students in the more advanced first class (*jiaban*) studied Xufa's *Outline of Xianshou's Five Teachings* during the first year before moving on to Fazang's *Treatise on the Five Teachings* (*Wujiao zhang*) in their second year. The institute's curriculum also included the history of Buddhism in China and India, philosophy, and the correspondence of Buddhism and science.[85] Nanting was probably not the principal teacher at the institute given that he was also sometimes teaching at the Jiaoshan Buddhist Institute fifty miles away around the same time. Just as happened at Jiaoshan, the Guangxiao Institute was forced to close by the end of 1937 after the temple was bombed by the Japanese military.[86]

Programs Unaffiliated with the Huayan University Network

The majority of the programs that focused on Huayan during the Republican period were started by students and faculty from the original Huayan University, but a few programs inspired by the Huayan University were founded by monks not affiliated with the original school. The first adopted the name and much of the curriculum of Yuexia's school.

Huayan University of Yangzhou, 1923–1928?

As Yuexia's students struggled to launch their own programs to educate China's monks about Huayan, another monk with no clear affiliation to the original university opened his own Huayan University in Jiangnan to much fanfare from the local Buddhist elite. This Huayan University grew out of lecture series offered from 1919 to the early 1920s by the monk Keduan at Changsheng 長生 Temple in Yangzhou. Keduan eventually turned this lecture series into a semipermanent institute with an expanded curriculum, which he called the Huayan University of Yangzhou. Although there is not much information about Keduan, there are much more data about the program he ran than there are about most of the other Huayan institutes of the period, which makes it an excellent case study.

Keduan was born in Jiyang 暨陽 (present-day Zhuji 諸暨) in Zhejiang Province. In the first decade of the twentieth century, he joined thousands of his countrymen and women who studied abroad in Japan. Upon his return, he served as an officer in the military but quit after the failure of the Second Revolution, a coup to oust President Yuan Shikai 袁世凱 (1859–1916) from power in late 1913. Struck by the impermanence of life (and possibly needing to retreat from society to avoid retribution by Yuan's allies), Keduan ordained as a monk. After his ordination, he went into the mountains to practice at Jade Maiden Peak (Yunüfeng 玉女峰).[87] He eventually studied under Dixian at Guanzong Temple and enrolled briefly in the first class of the Guanzong Research Society.[88]

In 1919, Keduan accepted an invitation from Xinglian 性蓮 (n.d.), abbot of Changsheng Temple, located just outside of central Yangzhou on the east side of the city's central canal. There he began a three-year lecture series on the *Ten Profound Gates of the Huayan One Vehicle* (*Huayan yisheng shixuanmen* 華嚴一乘十玄門),[89] which culminated in a full ordination ceremony in 1922. At some point during this three-year period, Keduan assumed the abbotship of the temple. Inspired by the success of his first lecture series, Keduan decided to continue his teaching activities as a more formal institute centered on Chengguan's *Introductory Discourse to Commentary on the Huayan Sutra* and the Diamond Sutra. In his statement on the purpose of the institute, he said that he explicitly planned to focus his teaching on the core Huayan doctrinal concepts of the Four Dharmadhātu (*sifajie* 四法界), the Five Teachings, the Six Characteristics, and the Ten Profound Gates.[90] As in the original Huayan University, he ran the institute according to the rules of a *conglin*, which emphasized strict observance of the monastic rule and the dual practice of doctrinal study and meditation.[91] After months of planning, the university opened on January 12, 1923, with nearly fifty students.[92]

Two months after classes began, the Huayan University of Yangzhou published the first issue of its magazine *Buddha's Light*. Four issues of this magazine were published, all in 1923, and they serve as a valuable source of historical information about the institute's activities. Issues were distributed in and outside of China, including at the Wuchang Buddhist Institute.[93] Keduan asked the monk Xianyin 顯蔭 (1902–1925) to serve as the magazine's editor. Xianyin, whom Keduan likely knew from Dixian's school, was just beginning to make a name for himself in the Buddhist publishing world.[94] In addition to the university bylaws and essays on various issues of Buddhist thought and practice, roughly a third of the inaugural issue of *Buddha's Light* was taken up with greetings, calligraphy, and congratulatory verses from Chinese Buddhism's leading figures and institutions. Jiang Weiqiao, Yinguang, and Zhang Taiyan submitted something. From the Wuchang Buddhist Institute, Taixu, Tang Dayuan, and Shi Yiru 史一如 (1876–1925) sent contributions, as did Dixian's Guanzong Temple and the World Buddhist Householder Grove (Shijie Fojiao Jushilin 世界佛教居士林), a new but influential organization of Shanghai's lay Buddhist urbanites.[95] The magazine published more than seventy notices offering congratulations on the auspicious founding of the Huayan University of Yangzhou. This event was clearly notable in Jiangnan Buddhism.

Much like most Buddhist institutes of the period, Keduan's university did not go entirely to plan, but in this case not because of negative factors. After the first two semesters of class, Keduan announced in the September 1923 issue of *Buddha's Light* that classes (and publication of the magazine) would go on hiatus for three months from October to January 1924 so that the students could engage in a ninety-day meditation retreat in the temple's brand-new Huayan Hall of Great Discernment (Huayan Dache Tang 華嚴大徹堂). Keduan seems to have made winter retreats a regular occurrence, and the announcement encouraged the journal's readers to spread the word that the institute's classes would resume and that it would run annually from February 24 to July 2 and August 15 to November 11.[96] It is, however, unclear if class resumed in early 1924 as planned. Whatever the case, the university had ceased operations by early 1925, when Keduan and his longtime associate the layman Xiao Weisheng 蕭唯昇 (n.d.) announced the start of a new lecture series at Changsheng Temple. Keduan clearly saw this lecture series as a continuation of the Huayan University, however, because the announcement for it repeats much of the information about the founding of the university in the first issue of *Buddha's Light*.[97] The daily schedule still featured Keduan's lectures on the Huayan Sutra in the afternoon, but several new lecturers were hired to teach an expanded curriculum that included composition, Vinaya studies, and the Confucian classics.[98]

Once again, it is unclear how long the institute was able to operate because at some point later that year or early in the next the government took control of the Changsheng Temple for use as a military base during the Northern Expedition. The occupation did not last very long, however, and by September 1926 an undaunted Keduan was once again issuing a call for students and announcing the opening of the Huayan University. Interestingly, despite its stated name, this iteration of the university featured lectures on the *Outline of the Central Tenets of Teaching and Contemplation* (*Jiaoguan gangzong* 教觀綱宗), a Tiantai text, in the morning, and on the Nirvana Sutra (Niepan Jing 涅槃經) in the afternoon.[99] The trend toward the inclusion of Tiantai doctrine within the program's curriculum had already begun in 1925 with the inclusion of Tiantai Zhiyi's writings alongside the Huayan commentaries of Chengguan and Li Tongxuan.[100] Given that Keduan had studied under Dixian, it is not surprising that he would promote Tiantai studies in his program, an inclusion reflective of the ecumenical view toward Buddhist studies. Even in his discussion of the reasons behind founding the Huayan University of Yangzhou in 1923, Keduan emphasized that Fazang's doctrinal classification scheme was not meant to deny the validity of other Buddhist doctrines, such as the one found in Tiantai.[101] We do not know when this version of the Huayan University of Yangzhou ceased operation, but in an open letter in February 1928 addressed to all the abbots of China and calling for the reform of Chinese Buddhism, Keduan stated that he was writing "from Huayan University."[102]

Even after his Huayan University closed, Keduan displayed a continued commitment both to the reform of Chinese Buddhism in general and to Buddhist monastic education in particular. He was elected to serve as one of the executive directors of the Buddhist Association of China (Zhongguo Fojiaohui 中國佛教會) founded in Shanghai in April 1929, a position he held at least through the late 1930s. In 1930, he started yet another educational program at the Changsheng Temple focusing on Tiantai and Huayan doctrine, this time called the Jiangdu Buddhist Teaching Center (Jiangdu Fojiao Zhuanxisuo 江都佛教傳習).[103] Once again, we do not know how long this program lasted.[104]

Xiangrui's Two Programs

Little is recorded about the monk Xiangrui 祥瑞 (n.d.), who organized in succession two programs centered on the study of Huayan. There is no evidence he had any formal connection with the members of the modern Huayan network described earlier, though it is possible he did. We do know that he had a keen interest in the teaching of Huayan, though. He lectured on the *Outline of Xianshou's Five Teachings* in Taiyuan, Shanxi Province, in 1924.[105] In April 1926, he became abbot of Doushuo 兜率 Temple in Yancheng 鹽城 on the east coast in Jiangsu. The temple was in the midst of being converted from a private temple to a *conglin*, and as part of this process Xiangrui was tasked with organizing an educational institute at the temple. He chose to focus the institute on the study of Huayan doctrine, creating the Institute of the Xianshou School (Xianshouzong Xueyuan 賢首宗學院). Xiangrui was assisted by Renshan 仁山 (1887–1951), a confederate of Taixu and notable monk of the period, who agreed to serve as the head of the institute.[106] Renshan had studied at both the Jetavana Hermitage and the Jiangsu Monastic Normal School (under Yuexia and Dixian) before teaching at Dixian's Guanzong Research Society from 1918 to 1921 and briefly at his own Tiantai-leaning Sihong Institute (Sihong Xueyuan 四弘學院) in Jiangsu.[107]

Xiangrui wrote later in the formal announcement for the institute in October 1926 that its goal was to teach and research the Five Teachings,[108] a reference to Fazang's doctrinal classification scheme that also figured prominently in the brief statement of the institute's curriculum published in October 1926.[109] A fuller curriculum was published in April 1927. The plan was for the institute to run a two-year preparatory course (*yuke*) that would include common basic Buddhist texts as well as the history of Buddhism in China and India. Students in the preparatory course would also begin studying Huayan commentaries and practicing the Contemplation of the Dharmadhātu (*fajieguan* 法界觀). These studies would then be deepened in a three-year "basic course" (*benke* 本科).[110] It is likely that the students at the Institute of the Xianshou School did not get any further than the two-year preparatory course begun in 1926 because at that point Xiangrui decamped to start a new program at another temple. The exact reasons for and timing of this move are not recorded.

In January 1930, Xiangrui announced the opening of the Śūraṅgama Buddhist Institute (Lengyan Foxueyuan 楞嚴佛學院) at Huxin 湖心 Temple, located in Huaian some ninety miles west of Yancheng. Befitting the institute's name, regular study of the Śūraṅgama Sutra was central in its published three-year curriculum, but Xiangrui maintained the Huayan elements of the program, insisting that his students study the *Outline of Xianshou's Five Teachings* and practice the Contemplation of the Dharmadhātu.[111] As with the Institute of the Xianshou School, we do not know how much success Xiangrui had with the Śūraṅgama Buddhist Institute, but we do know that classes continued at least through the summer of 1931 because a photograph of the program's students in their martial arts class appeared in *HCY* in August that year.[112]

FOUR

The Huayan University Network After 1949

THE FOUNDING OF the People's Republic of China (PRC) in 1949 was a major turning point in modern world history. In China, though the new PRC did not change the status of Buddhism, it did mark the beginning of a shift in the center of gravity of Chinese Buddhism from the mainland out to the Chinese diaspora. From 1950 to the early 1980s, the story of Huayan mirrors the story of Chinese Buddhism as a whole. As Buddhism declined in mainland China in the face of ever-increasing government pressure, Chinese Buddhists in Hong Kong, Southeast Asia, the United States, and especially Taiwan preserved and strengthened the tradition in the context of increasingly globalized Chinese diaspora networks. The teachers and institutions of Huayan Buddhism in the second half of the century followed the precedent set during the Republican period by continuing to promote the teaching and practice of Huayan. They created programs for monastic education and emphasized the study of Huayan doctrine by both monastics and the laity. Teachers lectured on the Huayan Sutra and hosted Huayan Dharma Assemblies to chant it. After the Cultural Revolution (1966–1976) subsided and Buddhism was revived in the 1980s, masters who had gone abroad as well as those who had never left once again disseminated Huayan in mainland China, usually with self-conscious reference to the legacies of Yuexia and Yingci.

THE HUAYAN UNIVERSITY NETWORK AFTER 1949

Although this book focuses primarily on the first half of the twentieth century, there is now enough historical distance for us to consider the extent to which the figures and activities of this first half influenced Chinese Buddhism in the second half. This chapter briefly describes the impact of the Huayan network after the close of the Chinese Civil War in 1949. It shows a few of the ongoing influences that events and activities from the early twentieth century continued to exert at century's end. It is not meant to be a comprehensive study of late twentieth-century Huayan, nor does it claim to cover all of the important Huayan teachers of the second half of the century. This chapter focuses instead on the stories of a few key individuals who carried the legacy of Republican-era Huayan to the year 2000.

The Huayan Network in the Early PRC

The Second Sino-Japanese War (1937–1945) wrought tremendous devastation and suffering upon the Chinese people and was very disruptive for China's Buddhists. Although Yingci and Cizhou somehow managed to continue teaching Huayan Buddhism in Jiangnan and Beijing, most of the era's Huayan educational programs halted as temples were bombed or occupied by one or another army. Even those temples that escaped the predations of military adventurers saw their economic bases reduced drastically, forcing them to cut their expenses. Buddhism did thrive in Sichuan and Chongqing, the wartime center of the Chinese Republic, but there was little Huayan-specific activity recorded in those areas during the war years.

After the end of World War II, Japanese forces surrendered and eventually retreated from China. The hoped-for period of peace and reconstruction in China never happened, however, as the long-simmering conflict between the Nationalists and the Communists escalated into an all-out civil war that raged for three years before the Communists emerged as the victors in 1949. The Communists' victory posed a challenge to many in Chinese society, especially landlords, intellectuals, and clergy, all of whom were targeted by Communist ideology. Those who had the means had to decide for themselves if it were safer to leave China or to stay. Most stayed, including the majority of Buddhist monks and nuns. The latter experienced a steady erosion of religion's economic, social, and legal status, culminating in the outright destruction of religious institutions and persecution of religious actors during the Cultural Revolution.

In the early years, the policy of the Chinese Communist Party (CCP) toward religion was ambiguous. Freedom of religion was guaranteed in the Constitution, but it was not always respected in real life. In 1951, the CCP set up the Religious Affairs Bureau (Zongjiao Shiwu Ju 宗教事務局), which was run by party members and was charged with overseeing the activities of the country's various religious groups. Secondary organizations that fell under the authority of the Religious Affairs Bureau were organized to oversee each individual religion. Buddhism was represented by the Chinese Buddhist Association (Zhongguo Fojiao Xiehui 中國佛教協會, CBA), which had authority over all types of Buddhist activities, including the ordination of new monastics and the appointment of abbots. One of the CBA's major responsibilities was to enforce the central government's policies within the Buddhist sphere, which served to reduce the size and power of Buddhism. The land reforms of 1950 deprived many monasteries of their land holdings and the rental income they produced. There was also a decline in the performance of funerary rites, deemed superstitious by the CCP, especially after the mid-1950s, and this decline removed another one of the important revenue streams that temples depended on for their operations. Holmes Welch argues that the CCP used psychological and economic pressure to reduce the size of the Buddhist clergy in China by 90 percent even before the start of the Great Leap Forward in 1958.[1]

Many of the monastics affiliated with the Republican Huayan network left mainland China in 1948 or 1949, but some stayed.

THE HUAYAN UNIVERSITY NETWORK AFTER 1949

After the Civil War ended, Yingci returned to Yufo Temple in Shanghai. His lectures became increasingly less frequent, and he focused on shorter, more generic Chinese Buddhist texts such as the Heart Sutra. Zhenchan, who had become a favored attendant and assistant lecturer to Yingci in the master's later years, returned with him to Shanghai, where he continued to live throughout the 1950s, participating as local delegate to national meetings of the CBA. As far as I have been able to determine, Zhenchan did not lecture or teach about Huayan during this period. Another of Yingci's students, Cizhou, remained at his hermitage in Beijing until his death in 1958. Apart from some lectures in the late 1940s, it is unclear how much he was able to teach during the last decade of his life. Mengcan, who had studied under Cizhou at the first Dharmadhātu Institute in Fujian, spent most of the 1940s at Sera Monastery in Tibet, studying Tibetan Buddhism under several different lamas. The entry of the People's Liberation Army into Tibet prompted him to return to Sichuan in 1951, where he was soon thrown in jail by the government. He remained imprisoned into the 1960s.[2]

A difficult situation became dire as first the Great Leap Forward (1958–1962) and then the Cultural Revolution multiplied the economic, social, and political pressures on Buddhism. The economic hardships and famine of the Great Leap Forward are well known, and these conditions drove many monastics to leave the monasteries. But it was the Cultural Revolution, a decade of paranoia and persecution inaugurated by infighting within the CCP and spilling out across the nation, that finally brought all religious activity to a halt. Temples were looted and destroyed, and those monastics who did not return to lay life were publicly denounced by their own communities, thrown in jail, or worse. Yingci remained in Shanghai during this entire period, dying in 1965 at the age of ninety-two on the eve of the Cultural Revolution. Although the status of Shanghai's Yufo Temple appears to have afforded his student Zhenchan some protection in the early 1960s, Zhenchan was eventually arrested and spent the entire decade of the Cultural

Revolution in prison.³ Mengcan, who had already been in prison for more than a decade by the time the Cultural Revolution began, was sent to a forced-labor camp, where he remained until 1982. All told, Mengcan spent more than thirty years as a PRC prisoner.⁴ Regarding the teaching and practice of Huayan in mainland China, therefore, one can say that there was little activity during the 1950s and no activity during the twenty years between the early 1960s and the 1980s. The situation was quite different outside of the PRC, however.

Huayan was carried out of China in the middle of the twentieth century by the flow of Chinese emigration. There was a chance for the modern Huayan network to spread to areas not controlled by the Chinese government in the 1930s when Aiting, a student of Yuexia, Yingci, and Zhiguang, accepted the invitation by Clara Lin Kok Ho Tung (He Dong Lianjue 何東蓮覺, 1875–1937) to go to Hong Kong to help her establish a nunnery, which was eventually named Tung Lin Kok Monastery (Tung Lin Kok Yuen 東蓮覺苑). Aiting arrived in 1932 to help oversee the construction of the temple, which was completed in 1934. It is unclear if Aiting, who had compiled an extensive commentary on Fazang's *Treatise on the Five Teachings*,⁵ emphasized Huayan within the curriculum. Regardless of what his plans for the temple were, he did not have much time to carry out them out as the arrival of Japanese forces in Hong Kong in 1941 forced him into hiding in Kowloon. After the war ended, Aiting returned to Jiangnan to pay his respects to his teachers, both living and deceased. In 1947, he boarded a Hong Kong-bound steamship in Shanghai but died onboard before reaching his destination.⁶ The Tung Lin Kok Yuen remains an influential institution with links to the powerful Robert N. Ho Family Foundation. Further research may illuminate what impact, if any, Huayan teachings have had on either. The most obvious point of continuity for the Huayan University network outside of mainland China in the latter half of the twentieth century developed in Taiwan.

Mainlander Buddhism in Taiwan

In 1949, the Nationalist government retreated from mainland China to Taiwan, bringing its armies, family members, and other refugees. Altogether, around 1.5 million mainlanders, mostly Mandarin speakers from the central east coast provinces, fled to Taiwan. They immediately began to assume control of the island, which was populated by Hokkien-speaking Chinese and a smaller number of Polynesian aboriginals, all of whom had been until 1945 citizens of the Japanese Empire. Linguistic and cultural differences between the newcomers and the island's long-term residents as well as the heavy-handed approach to control taken by the Republican government (which arrived in a state of martial law) led to tension and conflicts around the island. Internal problems were exacerbated by the precarious situation in which the Republic of China found itself externally in the early 1950s, with unclear commitments from its international allies and a constant fear of invasion by the PRC.

Buddhist monks and nuns from the mainland came with the Nationalist migration of 1949. Some had been drafted into the army and came with it to Taiwan, whereas others, fearing the effects of the Communist regime, made their own way to the island. Many lay Buddhists came as well. The Buddhism they found on the island was typical of traditional Chinese religiosity in many ways; few distinctions were made between practices and deities that educated mainland monastics would have labeled as specifically Buddhist or Daoist or folk religious in origin. Taiwanese Buddhism had also been heavily influenced by Japanese Buddhism, so that it lacked a celibate clergy as well as *conglin* monasteries and regular monastic ordinations. One result of the absence of monasteries was that there were few suitable places for the monastics from the mainland to stay after they first arrived, especially the younger monastics who lacked the reputation or the connections necessary to smooth the way for them. Some even had to spend nights in jail after being picked up by the police for sleeping outdoors.[7]

As in other sectors of Taiwanese society, mainlanders began to exert their control over local Buddhist affairs as they worked to recreate the associations and institutions they had operated before they arrived on the island. The Buddhist Association of China (BAC), which had run in China from 1929 to 1937, was reconstituted in 1952 and headquartered at Shandao 善導 Temple in Taipei. Monks from this organization traveled around the island first on fact-finding tours and then on propagation tours in the 1950s. The goal was to maintain Buddhism among those recently arrived as well as to refashion Taiwanese Buddhism according to the BAC's ideals. The BAC assumed a government-backed monopoly over several aspects of Buddhist life in Taiwan, including the organization of ordinations, which it began holding in 1952 (for nuns) and 1953 (for monks). The BAC was dominated by monks from the mainland, and it was able to monopolize aspects of Buddhism because under the laws of the Republic of China each sector or niche in society could be overseen by only one organization, which in turn reported to the central government. Despite ongoing complaints that the BAC was not particularly effective, it remained de jure the central authority over Buddhism in Taiwan until the 1980s, when revisions to the legal codes allowed greater diversity within Taiwanese civil society.[8]

Alongside attempts to enforce orthodox ordinations and monastic behavior, mainland Buddhists also sold or distributed free copies of Buddhist scriptures and worked to spread the teaching of Buddhism in other ways. One example of this proselytization was the promotion of Buddhist education within Taiwan's growing number of colleges. One of the most important figures in these efforts was Zhou Xuande 周宣德 (1899–1989), a disciple of Zhiguang and colleague of Nanting whom the Nationalists had sent to Taiwan before 1949 to take charge of the lucrative Taiwan Sugar Company. By the late 1950s, he had begun to organize Buddhist scholarships and essay competitions for college students. Buddhist educational activities aimed at college students grew in scope as the Taiwanese economy boomed during the 1960s and 1970s.[9]

THE HUAYAN UNIVERSITY NETWORK AFTER 1949

As the PRC descended into the social chaos of the Cultural Revolution, the economy and the society of the Republic of China grew in strength. One result of this growth for Buddhism was the increasing availability of funds to support the maintenance of older Buddhist institutions and the creation of new ones. The two largest and most influential Chinese Buddhist organizations in the world today were founded in Taiwan during the 1960s. Foguangshan 佛光山, which became the world's largest global monastic order by the end of the twentieth century, with nearly one hundred overseas temples on five continents, was founded in 1967 by the mainland monk Xingyun 星雲 (b. 1927).[10] The other, the Tzu Chi 慈濟 Foundation, a global charitable and relief organization, was started by the Taiwanese nun Zhengyan 證嚴 (b. 1937). Both Foguangshan and Tzu Chi grew slowly in Taiwan during the 1970s and more quickly in the 1980s. And both followed a wave of emigration of the Taiwanese in the early 1990s to establish themselves in Chinese diaspora communities around the world.[11]

These trends—the arrival and dominance of mainland monks in Taiwanese Buddhism in the 1950s, domestic growth in the 1960s and 1970s, and the external flow of Buddhism with emigration in the 1980s and 1990s—affected the creation and development of Huayan-centered institutions in Taiwan that inherited the legacy of Yuexia and Yingci. Just as happened during the Republican period when the students of the original Huayan University went off to found a second generation of Buddhist educational programs, students of these second-generation programs (as well as of some third-generation ones) set about building their own institutions in Taiwan. Whereas members of the second generation were able to establish their programs at existing temples in the 1920s and 1930s, those who came to Taiwan often had to build the temples that they needed to host their Huayan activities. One of the monks who did this was Longquan 隆泉 (1902–1973), who was from the same county in Jiangsu as Yingci and was one of Yingci's longtime students. He also briefly studied under Chisong and Huizong in 1945. Longquan came to Taiwan with the Nationalists and eventually established the short-lived Huayan Temple in Taipei's northern Shilin District (it was later demolished during a road-widening project). Another promoter of Huayan in Taiwan was Jiede 戒德 (1909–2011), who originally came from Wuhan, Hubei. He studied under Cizhou at the Dharmadhātu Institute of Changshu in the late 1920s before teaching at the Minnan Buddhist Institute in the early 1930s. After Jiede came to Taiwan, he established the Miaofa 妙法 Temple southwest of Taipei in the Daxi District. There he held two Huayan Dharma Assemblies each year, one in the spring and one in the fall.[12] Another of Cizhou's students, Lingyuan 靈源 (1902–1988), who had studied under the Huayan master in Fujian in the early 1930s alongside Mengcan, established Dajue 大覺 Temple in Keelung after he came to Taiwan in 1953. Although the temple focused primarily on Chan, Lingyuan also taught Huayan studies there.[13]

The Huayan Lotus Society

The largest and oldest of the Huayan-centered organizations in Taiwan is the Huayan Lotus Society (Huayan Lianshe 華嚴蓮社), which was founded in 1952 as the brainchild of Zhiguang and his disciple Nanting. The society should be seen as a continuation of Zhiguang's Jiaoshan Buddhist Institute, which he had started as the Huayan Research Society in 1934. In launching the Huayan Lotus Society, Zhiguang appointed his student Nanting to be the chief lecturer. Zhiguang and Nanting arrived in Taiwan on May 1, 1949, on what was reportedly the last flight out of Shanghai. Unlike many younger, less-established monks, Zhiguang and Nanting had little difficulty finding a place to stay when they arrived because one of Nanting's former students from the Guangxiao Institute invited them to stay at Shipu 十普 Temple. The two monks' reputation grew within the mainland lay Buddhist population in Taiwan owing to their connections with the prominent lay Buddhist Zhang Qingyang 張清揚 (1913–1992), the wife of the Guomindang general Sun Liren 孫立人 (1900–1990). Zhiguang, who had already passed his sixtieth year, was respected enough by the burgeoning Buddhist community in Taiwan that Li Zikuan asked him to oversee Shandao Temple after its renovation to serve as the headquarters for the BAC.[14] This was the same Li Zikuan who had visited Jiaoshan Buddhist Institute in 1936 to give his encouragement to the student monks studying there.

While Zhiguang was busy with his duties at Shandao Temple, Nanting was able to gather enough funds to rent an apartment in 1952, where he declared the start of the Huayan Lotus Society. Although the society would grow into an important force within Taiwanese Buddhism, like other Buddhist activities it faced many challenges during the 1950s, in particular a lack of funds, followers, and even basic Buddhist materials. The society owned a copy of Chengguan's commentaries, which a disciple of Yingci had been able to bring over from the mainland, but it had only a single section of the Huayan Sutra that Nanting had brought with him from Shanghai until he was able to buy a copy that had been printed in Thailand by the Longhua Buddhist Association (Longhua Fojiaoshe 龍華佛教社).[15] In order to run the new society, Nanting brought in his disciple Chengyi, a student from the Guangxiao Institute. Chengyi had arrived in Taipei in 1948, where with lay assistance he established the Jueshi Book and Stationery Company (Jueshi Shuju Wenju She 覺世書局文具社) to disseminate Buddhist texts and Buddhist teaching. By 1951, the company had sold all of the Buddhist books it had brought over from the mainland (totaling around half a million New Taiwan dollars), initiated its own printing activities, and started a radio program called *The Voice of Buddhism* (*Fojiao zhi sheng* 佛教之聲). Chengyi left the Jueshi Company to help Nanting, though he also continued to participate in a variety of propagation activities around the island.[16]

The Huayan Lotus Society grew slowly. In 1954, Nanting moved it out of its original apartment on South Xinsheng 新生 Road to a bigger space of land on Ji'nan 濟南 Road. Renovations of existing structures and construction of a new building followed in the 1960s and 1970s, and the construction of one of the main halls was finished in 1974 with the installation of a statue of Vairocana Buddha that had been purchased from Hong Kong.[17] Even from its first days, the Huayan Lotus Society was centered on the study and practice of the Huayan Sutra. It hosted a full recitation of the sutra twice each year, during the third and tenth months of the lunar calendar. This practice has continued unbroken for more than sixty years. Each year during the eleventh lunar month, the society also hosts a seven-day Huayan Buddha retreat (*Huayan foqi* 華嚴佛七), during which participants chant the names of the buddhas and bodhisattvas in the text. The society emphasizes the study of the Huayan Sutra by hosting regular lectures on it. In recent decades, these lectures have occurred on a weekly basis.

As with other Buddhist organizations in Taiwan, the Huayan Lotus Society has diversified its propagation and educational activities over the years. It produces its own periodical and runs its own press. It also now runs a variety of educational programs, including a kindergarten, a vocational college, and short-term courses in Buddhism for college and primary-school students, and offers scholarships.[18] The most well known of its educational activities are those that operate under the auspices of the Huayan Buddhist College (Huayan Zhuanzong Xueyuan 華嚴專宗學院).[19] The college was founded in 1975, with Nanting inviting Chengyi to supervise its operation. The first class had only eighteen students, but this number quickly grew to thirty. The college offers the equivalent of a four-year undergraduate degree. Graduate studies were added in 1983 with a three-year master's degree course. The curriculum of the undergraduate degree showed the clear influence of Nanting's experience of Buddhist educational programs in the mainland during the 1930s. He lectured on the Huayan Sutra as the main course (*zhuke*) and sometimes taught a class on Gyōnen's *Essentials of the Eight Sects*. Chengyi lectured on the *Awakening of Faith*, and there were also courses in Chinese Buddhist history, Vinaya, Chan, history, philosophy, and foreign languages. Courses on computers, music, and composition were added later. Sometimes there were also lectures on Fazang's *Treatise on the Five Teachings* and Xufa's *Outline of Xianshou's Five Teachings*. In addition to the regular courses, many famous lay and ordained Buddhists lectured at the college over the years, including Shengyan (Sheng Yen) 聖嚴, Zhenhua, Jingkong 淨空 (b. 1927), and Xuanhua 宣化 (1918–1995).[20]

In their approach to Huayan, Nanting and Chengyi promoted a view of the tradition that matched the general understanding expounded in the Republican period, as described here in chapters 1 and 5. Chengyi, who sometimes adopted his teacher Nanting's language,[21] began his summaries of Huayan with the usual discussion of the proper names for the school, mentioning the names "Xianshou School," "Qingliang School," and "Huayan School."[22] Both men attributed the school's founding to the five patriarchs, but neither of them included Li Tongxuan as an important figure in the school's history. Nanting did not emphasize the Song dynasty masters Changshui Zixuan and Jinshui Jingyuan, but Chengyi mentioned them as important in the continuation of the Huayan tradition.[23] Both men linked the identity of Huayan to the Five Teachings doctrinal classification scheme finalized by Fazang and focused on the teachings of the Six Characteristics and the Ten Profound Gates as essential points of Huayan doctrine. Like those before them, they did not draw a strong distinction between the Huayan Sutra and Huayan doctrine, claiming that the central doctrinal goal of both is to elucidate the "one true Dharmadhātu [*yi zhen fajie* 一真法界]."[24] Finally, although I have not been able to determine if the Contemplation of the Dharmadhātu was practiced formally at the Huayan Lotus Society the way that it was in a number of the earlier Huayan institutes, Chengyi identified it as the heart of Huayan practice[25] and as the best among all of the methods of contemplation promoted by the various schools of Chinese Buddhism.[26]

Major changes occurred in the Huayan Lotus Society in the 1980s as leadership passed from a generation of male monastics who came from central Jiangsu Province to a new generation of nuns who had been born in Taiwan and trained at the Huayan College. Chengyi, who had taken over from Nanting in 1972 as the third abbot of the society (Zhiguang is considered the first abbot), stepped down in 1984, and Liaozhong 了中 (b. 1932) became the fourth abbot. Liaozhong was succeeded by Jinghai 淨海 (b. 1931) in 1988. Like Nanting and Chengyi, Liaozhong and Jinghai hailed from Tai County in Jiangsu, not far from Yingci's birthplace.[27] In 1994, with the encouragement of her teacher Chengyi, the nun Xiandu became the sixth abbot of the Huayan Lotus Society. Xiandu was born in Taiwan in 1958 to devout Buddhist parents from Jiangxi. She eventually became a tonsure disciple of Chengyi and a star pupil at the Huayan Buddhist College before serving as the Huayan Lotus Society's sixth abbot for seven years.[28] She has been succeeded as abbot by two more nuns from the school. Since the start of the twenty-first century, Xiandu has furthered her education and written a number of excellent books on Huayan, but this chapter aims to deal with events that occurred before 2000, so I will not go into the details of these publications.

It is certainly a positive thing to see nuns promoted into positions of leadership, and I am well aware that this is the first time women have appeared in anything but a supporting role in this book. The assumption of authority in the Huayan Lotus Society by nuns from its own college is also indicative of both the demographics of the society and of Buddhism in Taiwan more generally. Nanting had originally planned for the Huayan Buddhist College to serve a male student body, but only two or three of the monastics who applied were male. Because it was necessary to separate monks and nuns, Nanting and Chengyi eventually saw that it was too difficult to be equitable when the ratio of female to male students was nine to one, so they decided that the Huayan Buddhist College would be for nuns only.[29] The gender disparity that Nanting and Chengyi saw among the initial applicants to their college reflects a broader reality within Taiwanese Buddhism. Since regular ordinations began under the auspices of the BAC in the early

1950s, the number of women taking monastic ordination in Taiwan has been triple the number of men.[30] As a result, the ratio of nuns to monks in Taiwan today might be as high as nine to one. Taiwan's nuns have been successful practitioners, teachers, and writers and are highly engaged in social issues. One reason for their success has been the fact that beginning in the late 1970s many of the women who entered the nunneries were already well educated.[31] In the case of the Huayan Buddhist College, its instructors have been able to expect their students to possess a higher level of education than what Zhiguang and Nanting could have hoped to see among the monks they taught in their monastic educational programs on the mainland in the 1930s.

This overall high level of education among Taiwan's nuns also meant that students from the Huayan Buddhist College were able to have a large impact on Buddhism both on the island and abroad before the end of the twentieth century. Following the pattern of the students of the original Huayan University half a century earlier, many of the early graduates of the Huayan Buddhist College went on to run or teach in other Buddhist educational programs around Taiwan. Graduates also lectured on the Huayan Sutra in Taiwan as well as in the PRC, the United States, Germany, and other countries.[32] They have also established branch temples overseas, perhaps most notably in California's San Francisco Bay Area. Chengyi first visited the Chinese immigrant communities in San Jose, California, in 1984 and 1985. After his visit, a group of laypeople formed a Buddhist studies center there, which they invited him to oversee. By April 1989, they registered with the state government and formally established the Huayan Lotus Society of the United States (Meiguo Huayan Lianshe 美國華嚴蓮社).[33] Like the parent organization in Taiwan, this branch holds weekly lectures on the Huayan Sutra and several annual Huayan Dharma Assemblies where it is chanted. It also holds monthly memorial services for the society's spiritual forebears Yucheng, Zhiguang, Nanting, and Chengyi.[34]

PART ONE

Reviving Huayan in Mainland China

After the Cultural Revolution subsided in the mid-1970s, the Communist Party began reforming its economic and social policies. Starting at the end of that decade, the government introduced measures and changed laws with the aim of easing restrictions on economic and other activities, including religious ones. As the 1980s began in China, religious actors cautiously started to take advantage of the loosening of state control to resume their practices and to rebuild the institutions that had been destroyed over the previous decades. Nuns, monks, pastors, and priests who had been jailed during the Cultural Revolution were released, and buildings and some lands were gradually returned to the control of newly revived religious organizations. The Religious Affairs Bureau retained its oversight over the growing number of religious activities, but there was a clear, if slow, softening of government policy over the final two decades of the twentieth century.

For Buddhism, as with other religious traditions in China, the rupture caused by the Cultural Revolution was not total. Although many of the country's most learned and senior monks and nuns had died during those dark years, the period of state suppression did not last long enough to erase living memory. Monastics such as Zhenchan and Mengcan, who had been old enough to receive good training and guidance in the tradition during the 1930s and 1940s, were only in their midsixties in 1980 and still vigorous enough to renew the rituals and begin training a new generation of monks and nuns in the practices and teachings of Buddhism.

Zhenchan was released from prison in 1976 and returned to Yufo Temple in Shanghai. Three years later he presided over a ceremonial bathing of the Buddha, a rite performed annually on the Buddha's birthday in the spring and the first religious ritual held at the temple in more than a decade. This highly symbolic act, which commemorates one sort of beginning for the Buddhist tradition, also marked the rebirth of Buddhism in China. Zhenchan became abbot of Yufo Temple later that year, and by 1981 the temple had begun to host a full range of Buddhist activities as more than one hundred monks returned to ordained life there.[35] Zhenchan felt that it was important to support the revival of the Buddhist *sangha* with educational programs for monks and nuns. He led the creation of a Vinaya studies hall (a traditional venue for instruction in monastic life) at the temple in 1982, which was followed by the opening of a Buddhist institute (*foxueyuan*) for monks in 1983 and another for nuns in 1984. Zhenchan also lent his expertise to help others establish similar programs in Nanjing and elsewhere.[36] Like his coreligionists in Taiwan, Zhenchan did not limit his teaching activities to mainland China. He traveled around the United States in 1984, visiting, among other places, Los Angeles, San Francisco, and Dasheng Temple in New York City. He returned to Los Angeles in 1988 to participate in the ceremonial opening of Xilai 西來 Temple, the U.S. headquarters of Taiwan's Buddhist organization Foguangshan. He also went to Taiwan in early 1993, visiting dozens of temples while on the island.[37]

Zhenchan was a lineage holder in the Linji school of Chan as well as a favored student of Yingci. In his lectures and writings, Zhenchan focused equally on Chan and Huayan, echoing the approach taken by his own teacher. He gave two major lecture series each year during the 1980s, one in the spring and another in the fall. He often lectured on Huayan-related topics, taking one chapter of the Huayan Sutra as the primary subject of several series. The "Chapter on the Practice and Vows of Samantabhadra" was a favorite topic for him, as it was for many others monastic lecturers. He also wrote and lectured on the history and teachings of the Huayan School. In addition to these efforts to preserve the broader Huayan School, Zhenchan also sought to preserve Yingci's legacy. In 1985, he established a memorial hall dedicated to Yingci, and he spent many years collecting and editing Yingci's writings for publication.[38] Zhenchan passed away on December 1, 1995.

Another student from the Republican Huayan network who was important in reestablishing the Huayan tradition in mainland China during the 1980s and 1990s was Mengcan. Unlike Zhenchan,

Mengcan was not released from prison until 1982, but despite the toll that the many years of forced labor must have taken on him, he proved to be an energetic promoter of Buddhism. Having studied Chan under Xuyun, Tiantai under Tanxu, and Vinaya under Hongyi (each considered a modern master of his respective tradition), he was in high demand as a teacher by the reformed Chinese Buddhist *sangha*.[39] He lectured at the Chinese Buddhist Institute (Zhongguo Foxueyuan 中國佛學院) in Beijing, the first Buddhist educational center to be revived after 1980, as well as at the Minnan Buddhist Institute.[40] Mengcan was also like Zhenchan in that he went abroad to spread Chinese Buddhism in the Chinese diaspora. In 1987, he traveled to North America to give lectures on the Huayan, Lotus, and other sutras, including one lecture series at Xuanhua's City of Ten Thousand Buddhas (Wanfo Shengcheng 萬佛聖城) monastery complex in Talmage, California.

Despite Mengcan's ecumenism, his teaching and practice remained closely associated with Huayan. He lectured on a variety of sutras, such as the Heart, Lotus, and Diamond Sutras, but his primary specialty was the Huayan Sutra. He also wrote several books on Huayan and worked to spread the tradition in China and abroad. He returned to Canada in 1992 for another lecture series on the eighty-volume Huayan Sutra.[41] In 2001, he took up permanent residence at Pushou 普壽 Temple on Mt. Wutai and became the spiritual master for a neighboring nunnery that had some five hundred monastics in residence. He lectured regularly there on the Huayan Sutra, and in early 2007 at the age of ninety-two he completed a full lecture series on the eighty-volume Huayan Sutra.[42]

* * *

In the late twentieth century, the flow of economic resources between Taiwan and the PRC was unidirectional, from Taiwan to the mainland. But the flow of religious resources moved in both directions. It is well known that the revival of Buddhism in mainland China was also aided by monks who had gone abroad in 1949, and this was true for members of the Huayan University network. Chengyi took a direct and ongoing approach to rebuilding Buddhism there. In 1988, one year after the government in Taiwan lifted its travel ban to mainland China, Chengyi traveled to Jiangsu to see the state of temples there. He was particularly affected when he saw that Guangxiao Temple had been mostly destroyed. From 1990 to 1993, he raised funds and worked to get the main temple rebuilt. Chengyi visited the mainland many times and contributed much to the revival of Buddhism there during the 1990s and the 2000s.[43]

Elder monks in the Huayan University network came from the mainland to Taiwan on several occasions in the 1990s, and with them they brought lineage and knowledge. As noted earlier, Zhenchan made a lengthy tour of Taiwan in 1993. Mengcan had come to Taiwan the previous year, and while there he accepted a number of tonsure disciples, including one who ordained in 1994 under the name Jimeng 繼夢 (b. 1950). In 1996, Jimeng, also known as Haiyun 海雲, founded the Huayan Studies Association (Huayan Xuehui 華嚴學會) in Taipei, which was followed in 1999 by the founding of the larger Caotangshan Great Huayan Temple (Caotangshan Da Huayansi 草堂山大華嚴寺). This temple hosts many Huayan-related activities, including a weekly Huayan Assembly. Since 2000, the association has grown internationally, with branches in Australia, Canada, and the United States.[44] It has thus become an important institution of modern Chinese Huayan, but because this chapter focuses on the twentieth century, it is not entirely relevant here. It is interesting to note that Haiyun Jimeng's dharma lineages[45] and thus his authority as a teacher derive from a mainland monk in the Huayan University network who came to Taiwan after the Cultural Revolution. All of the other major Buddhist organizations in Taiwan can be traced to monks and nuns who came to the island around 1949. This line of descent illustrates, among other things, the fact that the authority of senior mainland monastics and the living connection they had to the pre-1949 tradition were still worth something in Taiwanese Buddhism at the end of the twentieth century.

PART TWO

FIVE

Huayan Doctrine in Republican China

HAVING INTRODUCED THE people and programs that conducted Huayan education during the Republican period, I now turn to a study of the doctrinal and practical content of that education. As we have seen, the Huayan School generally lacked a strong institutional identity in Chinese history, but it was widely regarded as a coherent school of thought with a distinctive body of doctrine. Just as part I framed the emergence of the modern Huayan University network in the context of the general history of the Huayan School in China, this chapter draws from journal articles, textbooks, and general histories of Buddhism to outline the general emic understanding of Huayan doctrine that was prevalent during the Republican period. These sources describe Huayan thought as comprising several key concepts: the Six Characteristics, the Ten Profound Gates, and the Four Dharmadhātu, along with the doctrinal classification scheme created by Fazang to explain the relationship between the doctrines of the Huayan Sutra and the other teachings of Chinese Buddhism. Modern specialists include a greater range of concepts in their definitions of Huayan, but the popular understanding of Huayan Buddhism in the Republic of China was focused on only a few central doctrines. In the same way, examination of mass media from the Republican period shows us that Huayan teaching was likewise focused on a few traditional texts, usually the Huayan Sutra itself, and it did not generally concern itself with either the newly recovered texts of the Huayan tradition or any of the other less-well-known ones. This pattern is also seen when we compare the deeper courses of study offered in the various Huayan-centered educational programs, which are analyzed in chapter 6.

Sources of Modern Huayan Thought

Several premodern texts exerted a significant influence on how people understood Huayan in modern China. Gyōnen's *Essentials of the Eight Sects* provided the general model for sectarian histories of Sinitic Buddhism as a whole. This work also had some influence on how Chinese people discussed Huayan specifically. However, few of the works studied here copied Gyōnen's specific treatment of Huayan in its entirety. For example, the Huayan chapter of *Essentials of the Eight Sects* closes with extensive discussion of the stages of spiritual practice (*xingbu* 行布) as well as the nature of buddhas and Buddha lands (*fotu* 佛土). The stages of practice accepted within Huayan are discussed in some modern texts but not in the majority of them, and even fewer works discuss the status of buddhas and Buddha lands within Huayan. In addition to the *Essentials of the Eight Sects*, Gyōnen wrote another work devoted specifically to the Huayan School titled *Essential Meaning of the Huayan School* (*Kegonshū yogi* 華嚴宗要義). This work contains a treatment of the major elements of the school that is similar in both content and sequence to the treatment in *Essentials of the Eight Sects*, so it is not always entirely clear which text inspired modern writers. *Essentials of the Eight Sects* was, however, more widely available in China, which could indicate a greater influence.[1]

Several premodern Chinese works also had an influence on how Huayan was understood during the modern period. One was the thirteenth-century Chinese work *Chronicle of the Buddhist Patriarchs*, which included a section on the Huayan School, and multiple authors drew from its description of the activities of the Song dynasty Huayan monks Zixuan and Jingyuan. The information from the *Chronicle* was further popularized after appearing in one of the first modern histories of Sinitic Buddhism to come out of Japan, Shimaji Mokurai and Oda Tokunō's *A Brief History of Buddhism of the Three Nations* (1890).[2] Neither of these two works is organized by sect or school, as many later works were, but both are written as year-by-year chronologies. The *Chronicle of the Buddhist Patriarchs*, which was written by a Tiantai partisan, was also a common source for the Tiantai critique that although Huayan does express a philosophy, it teaches no form of meditation (*youjiao wuguan* 有教無觀).[3] Proponents of Huayan were well aware of this popular critique, and it affected how they promoted Huayan and taught it in their programs.

Two other premodern Chinese texts had a major impact on how modern Chinese Buddhists described Huayan: Xufa's *Clarification of the* Outline of Xianshou's Five Teachings (*Xianshou wujiaoyi kaimeng* 賢首五教儀開蒙) and the longer work on which it was based, *Outline of Xianshou's Five Teachings*.[4] Xufa is often cited as the leading figure of Huayan during the early Qing dynasty (1644–1911), and his contributions to Huayan also include a history of its five founding patriarchs, which Yang Wenhui reprinted in 1896. Xufa remains best known for these two studies of the doctrinal classification system outlined by Fazang, the Huayan School's third patriarch. Xufa wrote these texts in part as a defense against Tiantai criticisms of the Huayan School.[5] Although the titles of Xufa's two texts are reminiscent of *Outline of the Four Teachings of Tiantai* (*Tiantai sijiao yi* 天台四教儀) by the Korean monk Che'gwan 諦觀 (d. 970), Xufa adopted a different five-category organizational schema for his works: the three time periods (*sanshi* 三時) of Buddha's preaching; Ten Meanings (*shiyi* 十儀); Five Teachings (*wujiao*); Six Schools (*liuzong* 六宗); and Three Contemplations (*sanguan* 三觀).[6] Xufa's inclusion of the fifth category, which focused on meditation techniques outlined in classical texts of the Huayan tradition, was a direct response to the Tiantai critique that Huayan lacked a form of mediation. Several modern writers adopted Xufa's specific schema for discussing Huayan in their summaries of Hauayan.[7] Xufa began, however, by locating Huayan in relation to other forms of Buddhist discourse using the traditional practice of doctrinal classification.

Huayan Thought in Relation to Other Buddhist Doctrines

When Buddhism first began to appear in China near the start of the first millennium CE, local thinkers had to come to terms with both its alien ideas from Central and South Asia and its unwieldy number of texts representing a wide range of historical, cultural, and doctrinal perspectives. Faced with the overwhelming diversity of Buddhist texts translated into Chinese, Chinese Buddhists in the fifth through eighth centuries organized the Buddhist scriptures by ranking them according to a number of criteria, including chronology (when the Buddha taught each text during his lifetime), the method the Buddha used to teach, and the relative superiority of the doctrine in each text.[8] There were many such schemes for ranking the scriptures, even within the Huayan tradition. The most famous Huayan doctrinal classification scheme is that of the Five Teachings as defined by Fazang. Even in the twentieth century, this schema was considered fundamental to the identity of the Huayan School and was cited near the beginning of all of the modern texts examined here. In other words, aside from its association with the Huayan Sutra, the most defining feature of the Huayan School is its doctrinal classification scheme. Even when the specific *content* of Huayan doctrine was not discussed at all, authors were sure to mention the Five Teachings, a model that demonstrates the superiority of that doctrine over those of other schools.

One way that Chinese Buddhists conceptualized the relationship between the various scriptures of their tradition was by dividing them according to when they were believed to have been taught by Śākyamuni Buddha. One common scheme, which Fazang adopted, was to divide the Buddha's preaching into three time periods (*sanshi*). By the modern period, most Chinese Buddhists believed that immediately after his enlightenment, the Buddha's first teaching was the Huayan Sutra but that owing to its great profundity he decided to begin again with the most basic doctrines. He first taught the doctrines of early mainstream Buddhism (Hīnayāna Buddhism), before proceeding to Mahāyāna Buddhist ones. Different doctrinal classification schemes further subdivide the various major types of Mahāyāna thought, such as Madhyamaka, Yogācāra, and Tathāgathagarbha within this category. With the exception of the Huayan Sutra, the Chinese chronological model considers later texts to reflect more accurately the content of the Buddha's enlightenment, making them both more difficult to understand and "better" than earlier texts.

Despite these modern texts' insistence on identifying the Five Teachings as *the* doctrinal classification scheme of the Huayan School, the school's founders in fact used a variety of such schemes in their writings. These schemes developed in multiple stages prior to and after the life of Fazang, and even Fazang put forward at least eight different versions of the Five Teachings in his writings.[9] In constructing these schemes, Huayan and pre-Huayan thinkers used all of the criteria—chronology, method of teaching, and doctrinal content. Zhiyan, Fazang's immediate predecessor, drew from existing traditions and took several different approaches to organizing Buddhist doctrine.[10] The tradition claims that he eventually settled on the basic Five Teachings model that Fazang inherited and refined. Scholars, however, generally disagree with this strictly teleological view, noting that Zhiyan most often used a tripartite model made up of the Lesser Vehicle (*xiaosheng* 小乘; i.e., Hīnayāna), the Three Vehicles (*sansheng* 三乘; i.e., early Mahāyāna), and the One Vehicle (*yisheng*; i.e., final Mahāyāna).[11] In addition, he occasionally employed several Five Teachings models in his corpus, and the one he put forth in *Treatise on Topics in the Huayan Sutra* (*Huayanjing kongmu zhang* 華嚴經孔目章) appears to have been particularly influential on Fazang.[12]

In constructing his Five Teachings scheme, Fazang was influenced by a number of sources, including both the writings of Zhiyan and those of the rival Tiantai School. Fazang probably first began to formulate his ideas about the Five Teachings while he was in his thirties, but he continued to work on them through his fifties.[13] Different versions of the Five Teachings appear in his *Exploration of the Profundities of the Huayan Sutra* and *Treatise on the Five Teachings*, with the most mature form appearing in his *Treatise on the Golden Lion* (*Jin shizi zhang* 金獅子章).[14] Modern texts generally treat as definitive the Five Teachings model that he put forth in the *Treatise on the Five Teachings*. This text was studied in most of the educational programs of the Huayan University network, unlike the *Treatise on the Golden Lion*, which was not.[15]

Fazang's most typical Five Teachings scheme ranks Buddhist doctrine from the least to most profound: from those that teach only the most basic truths about the universe to those that completely and accurately teach the nature of reality and existence. The first and lowest is the Teachings of the Lesser Vehicle (*xiaoshengjiao* 小乘教), which refers to the texts and teaching of early mainstream Buddhism. It includes doctrines such as the Four Noble Truths (Ch. *sidi* 四諦, Sk. *catur-ārya-satya*) and dependent origination (Ch. *yuanqi* 緣起, Sk. *pratītya-samutpāda*). Fazang places the texts of the Āgamas and the Abhidharmakośa in this category. Fazang felt that although the Lesser Vehicle teaches about the impermanence of self, it does not fully teach about the emptiness of dharmas. This is done in the second teaching, Initial Mahāyāna Teachings (*dasheng shijiao* 大乘始教), which at its most basic is the teaching that all phenomena are empty because they arise only because of causes and conditions and thus lack permanent identity. The various Prajñāparamitā Sutras as well as the commentaries of the Madhyamaka school are included here. The category of Initial Mahāyāna Teachings also includes those texts, such as those of the Yogācāra, that describe *how* phenomena and ignorance arise. Fazang considered these explanations of emptiness to be provisional because they deal only with negation and not with the simultaneous truth of both emptiness and existence. The latter truth is contained in the Final Mahāyāna Teachings (*dasheng zhongjiao* 大乘終教). This category includes various texts associated with Tathāgathagarbha theory, such as the apocryphal yet highly influential *Awakening of Faith in the Mahāyāna*. The fourth of the Five Teachings poses some difficulty because it is not really a doctrine but a method of teaching, one that does not rely on words. The Sudden Teaching (*dunjiao*) nevertheless contains certain texts that purport to demonstrate this type of teaching, including the Vimalakīrti and Laṅkāvatāra Sutras. Later commentators generally locate the teachings of the Chan School within this category.

The most complete teachings are found, fittingly, within the Perfect Teaching of the One Vehicle (*yisheng yuanjiao*). The term *yuan* 圓 in the term *yisheng yuanjiao* here literally means "round" but carries the connotation of perfection and completion. The fifth teaching is thus the one that completes the circle, closes the circuit, and expresses most directly the ultimate truth that is the content of the enlightenment of all the buddhas. It is referred to as the "One Vehicle" because at this level one realizes that all of the other teachings, those belonging to other vehicles, are merely expedients and do not contradict the fundamental truth contained within this teaching. Given that Fazang formulated his Five Teachings models at a time when he was trying to garner and maintain imperial patronage, it should not be surprising that his scheme was sectarian in nature. Fazang took direct aim at the followers of the nascent Tiantai School, who also held that the Perfect Teaching was the teaching of One Vehicle Buddhism. Tiantai thinkers, however, following the scheme of Four Teachings laid out by Zhiyi, held that the Lotus Sutra contained the epitome of Buddhist teachings. Fazang thus had to differentiate between his version of the One Vehicle and the Tiantai version. He placed the teachings of the Lotus Sutra (and thus Tiantai) within the Final Mahāyāna Teachings, referring to the doctrine of that text as the One Vehicle of the Teachings Held in Common (*tongjiao yisheng* 同教一乘). In other words, although the Lotus Sutra did teach that all Buddhism was the same, it did not advance the content of this Buddhism beyond the ideas contained in the other sutras of that level. For Fazang, the Huayan Sutra, in contrast, expressed the highest truth, a special truth. For this reason, he referred to teachings put forth in this sutra, which was the basis for his own thought, as the One Vehicle of the Special Teaching (*biejiao yisheng* 別教一乘). Thus, we can see that Fazang's scheme had a clear sectarian function in that it placed his favored sutra and the doctrines derived from it in a position of greater status than all other Buddhist texts.

Fazang's Five Teachings scheme eventually became more closely associated with the identity of the Huayan School than any other, but it was not unchallenged in the years immediately after his death. As was often repeated by Republican-era writers, Fazang's own immediate disciple Huiyuan was highly critical of Fazang's model and revised it by removing the Sudden Teaching. This was likely the reason why Huiyuan was not included within the Huayan lineage constructed by Jingyuan, who chose to include Chengguan instead. Though Chengguan had been born decades after Fazang's death, he supported Fazang's Five Teachings model. Ironically, Zongmi, whom Jingyuan *did* identify as the fifth Huayan patriarch, also took the knife to Fazang's scheme by removing the Perfect Teaching, the very basis for the distinctiveness of the Huayan School.[16] Zongmi's model did retain five levels in that he added the Teaching of Humans and Gods (*rentianjiao* 人天教), which included Daoism and Confucianism, as the new lowest level. Zongmi laid out his scheme in *Inquiry Into the Origin of Humanity*.[17] his text was widely printed and sold during the Republican Period as an introduction to Buddhism and was used as a basic textbook in many of the Huayan institutes of the day.

Zongmi's scheme as well as certain ideas put forth by Chengguan explained later in this chapter became standard within Huayan, probably eclipsing Fazang's scheme for a time. By the Song dynasty, a number of Fazang's important texts had even been lost, but after the monk Yihe 義和 (n.d.) was able to reprint Fazang's Five Teachings, they ascended to prominence within the Huayan

School.[18] Since the Song dynasty, Fazang's Five Teachings scheme as described here has been one of the defining features of the Huayan School. This makes a great deal of sense given that the whole purpose of such schemes was to explain the relationship between the different doctrines and practices within Sinitic Buddhism. By focusing on the Five Teachings scheme, modern authors treated Huayan as a school concerned primarily with doctrine. Their emphasis on doctrinal classification further reinforced the identity of the Huayan School with the Huayan Sutra, which was the zenith of the Buddha's teachings and the sole repository of the One Vehicle of the Special Teaching.

The Five Teachings are mentioned in virtually all of the texts (both premodern and modern) I have examined. Two other doctrinal classification schemes also appear in some of these texts, but each appears in only some of the texts. The first was the Ten Schools (*shizong* 十宗) model, which had also been created by Fazang. Originally based on an Eight Schools (*bazong* 八宗) model created by Kuiji 窺基 (632–682), Fzang's Ten Schools model was really just an expanded version of his Five Teachings model in which the Teaching of the Lesser Vehicle is divided into six different "schools." Schools seven through ten correspond to the second through fifth teachings of the Five Teachings model.[19] In the present study, it should be noted that the eight or ten "schools" referred to in these models are not the same as the schools described by Gyōnen. The Ten Schools, as used by Fazang, is mentioned as a key part of Huayan thought in Sakaino Kōyō's 境野黄洋 *Outline of Chinese Buddhism* (*Shina Bukkyō shikō* 印度支那佛教史綱) and in those texts derived from it (e.g., Jiang Weiqiao's 蔣維喬 *A History of Chinese Buddhism* [*Zhongguo fojiao shi* 中國佛教史] and Huang Chanhua's 黃懺華 *Major Ideas of the Buddhist Schools* [*Fojiao gezong dayi* 佛教各宗大意]).[20] It does not appear in any of the other Japanese histories of Buddhism I have examined, nor does it appear in those texts that were based largely on Xufa's *Outline of Xianshou's Five Teachings*.

In their discussions of Huayan, many writers of the period also divided Buddhist schools into those that focused on examining the phenomenal world and those that focused on expressing its fundamental nature. They referred to the former as *faxiang*, the teaching of Dharma Characteristics, a term that Fazang had coined as a pejorative for the Yogācāra thought promoted by Xuanzang 玄奘 (602–664), who was one of his primary philosophical opponents during his lifetime. Fazang contrasted the teaching of Dharma Characteristics with the teaching of the Madhyamaka School, which he called *wuxiang* 無相, the teaching of no characteristics. The fourth Huayan patriarch Chengguan eventually began to refer to these two as schools (*zong*), positing a dichotomy between the Dharma Characteristics School (Faxiangzong 法相宗) and the Dharma Nature School (Faxingzong 法性宗).[21] This dichotomy was important in Japanese and Chinese Buddhism in the modern period, both in how Buddhist curricula were organized and in how Buddhists talked about the totality of Buddhist doctrine.[22] As many have noted, the Yogācāra School reached unprecedented levels of popularity within Chinese Buddhism during the early decades of the twentieth century, and it was commonly referred to in a nonpejorative manner as the Dharma Characteristics School. Because Chinese Buddhist thought tends to favor the synthesis of dichotomies into wholes, it was easy to refer to Buddhist doctrine as a synthesis of the two schools of Dharma Characteristics and Dharma Nature. The latter included not only Chan and Tiantai but also Huayan. This dichotomy was mentioned in conjunction with Huayan thought in about half of the modern texts examined here, including those by Taixu and Changxing.

The Most Commonly Cited Huayan Doctrines

Premodern and modern writers have been more or less unanimous in their belief that the Huayan School was defined by its distinctive doctrine and the relationship that this doctrine had to the doctrines of other branches of Buddhism. This belief does not mean that those who defined the Huayan School using the Five Teachings held to the idea that the doctrines of that school were superior to those of Tiantai. As a school of doctrine, Huayan contained philosophical positions and described a perspective on reality. Much can be said about Huayan doctrine because the five classical patriarchs and their heirs left behind many works. Our concern here, however, is not to catalog all of Huayan thought but to determine what those modern Buddhists thought are the most definitive aspects of Huayan. They overwhelmingly followed a precedent that can be seen in Huayan writings as far back as Gyōnen that focuses on two concepts: the Six Characteristics and the Ten Profound Gates, both of which Fazang had articulated clearly in *Treatise on the Five Teachings*. Many modern Chinese writers, especially those who were not directly copying Japanese scholars, also included a third concept: the Four Dharmadhātu.

In order to understand these doctrines, it is important to be aware of the larger Huayan concept of the Origination of the Dharmadhātu (*fajie yuanqi* 法界緣起). Although this concept is not mentioned by name in many of the early-modern writings I have examined, scholars today generally agree that it was central to the thought of the second, third, fourth, and fifth Huayan patriarchs.[23] This term refers to the sum total of all reality, known as the Dharma Realm or Dharmadhātu, as it exists at the present moment,[24] a grand profusion of phenomena in an interdependent flux of arising and passing away. Building on the early Buddhist concept of dependent arising or origination (*yuanqi*), Huayan concerns itself with explaining the nature of this interdependent arising. Drawing from the Huayan Sutra's claim that the realm of perfect enlightenment is none other than the realm of ordinary unenlightened beings, Huayan thinkers developed an elaborate discourse about the relationships between the realm of the ideal and the realm of the phenomenal as well as between all of the specific elements within the phenomenal world.

In attempting to explain the nature of reality, Huayan thinkers, especially Fazang and Chengguan, devoted much of their energy to mereology, the study of the relationships of parts and their wholes.

The Huayan Sutra was inspirational in this regard. The sutra talks about the identity of each specific bodhisattva practice with all bodhisattva practices. It claims that when one performs even a single form of spiritual cultivation on the path to enlightenment, such as charity or faithfulness, one is actually practicing *all* of those practices. This is how the doctrine of the Origination of the Dharmadhātu was understood by Zhiyan, the second patriarch, who placed much emphasis on the idea of the identity of one bodhisattva with all bodhisattva practices.[25] In Fazang's hands, this concept was expanded to describe the relationship between phenomena. For him, the doctrine of the Origination of the Dharmadhātu was the very essence of the Perfect Teaching,[26] and his explorations of this doctrine led him to discuss the concepts of the Six Characteristics and the Ten Profound Gates in great detail.

The Six Characteristics

The doctrine of the Six Characteristics was originally drawn from the Chinese translation of an Indian text by Vasubhandu known as the *Commentary on the Ten Stages [of the Bodhisattva Path]* (*Daśabhūmika-bhāṣya*). It refers to the six types of teachings that bodhisattvas used to save sentient beings.[27] Within the Huayan context, the doctrine of the Six Characteristics is first explained in the *Record of Investigation into the Profound* (*Souxuan ji* 搜玄記) by Zhiyan, who was influenced by the pre-Huayan thought of the monks Huiguang 慧光 (468–537) and Jingying Huiyuan 淨影慧遠 (523–592).[28] Zhiyan's *Record* also contains an early version of the Ten Profound Gates.[29] Fazang expanded on both of these concepts in his writings, especially in *Treatise on the Five Teachings*,[30] and later generations of Buddhists have generally considered his versions of these doctrines definitive. Whereas the Ten Profound Gates is concerned more with issues of the mutual causality of phenomena, the Six Characteristics is used to explain the mutuality that exists between phenomena at the present moment.[31] This is done by breaking the relationship between phenomena into three pairs of opposing qualities that characterize each such relationship: unity (*zongxiang* 總相) and separateness (*biexiang* 別相); identity (*tongxiang* 同相) and difference (*yixiang* 異相); integration (*chengxiang* 成相) and disintegration (*huaixiang* 壞相). Because this doctrine is fairly abstract, it is usually best to explain it using concrete examples, as Fazang did.

Fazang's most detailed explanation of the Six Characteristics is found within *Treatise on the Five Teachings*, but his most famous explanation of the doctrine is the one he gave to Empress Wu Zetian 武則天 (624–705) using the example of a golden lion, which is recorded in outline form in the *Treatise on the Golden Lion*. In this analogy, the golden lion represents the Dharmadhātu, the sum total of reality. Because this reality is made up of all phenomena taken together, they are characterized by their unity, but this does not negate their individuality, so phenomena are also characterized by their separateness. In terms of our analogy, the parts of the lion are all part of the unity that is the lion, but each part retains its identity as an eye, ear, foot, and so on. Because all phenomena share in their participation in reality, they are characterized by sameness, but each participates in a different way, leading to their difference. For the lion, eyes, ears, and feet share the common identity of being part of the lion and being composed of gold, but each has a different shape. Finally, the phenomena that compose reality have the dual tendency of working together to compose reality and of remaining separate from it. In the case of the lion, the foot really makes sense only if it is the foot *of* a lion, but it always remains separable from the whole. Much more can be and has been said about the Six Characteristics beyond the brief explanation I have offered here,[32] but the basic argument that this doctrine is meant to support is that reality is, to use Fazang's term, nothing other than the "complete harmonious interfusion [*yuanrong* 圓融]" of the totality of phenomena within it. The lion is none other than the harmonious whole of its many parts, which are distinct yet unified.

PART TWO

The Ten Profound Gates

Unlike the Six Characteristics, the concept of the Ten Profound Gates seem to have originated in China among the Huayan patriarchs. Adopting the symbolism of the number ten, which runs throughout the entire Huayan Sutra,[33] they outlined a series of different perspectives by which one could view the process of dependent origination. These perspectives are detailed in a number of different texts, including one titled *Ten Profound Gates of the One Vehicle of the Huayan*.[34] According to a tradition that dates to the eighth century, this text was written by Zhiyan based on oral teachings he had received from the first patriarch, Dushun. Nowadays most scholars believe that Dushun contributed very little to either the concept or that text.[35] They are less skeptical about Zhiyan's role in forming this doctrine, given its compatibility with other ideas he lays out in *Record of Investigation Into the Profound*.[36] After Zhiyan, both Fazang and Chengguan included the Ten Profound Gates in their writings. Contrary to the popular understanding, Fazang outlined two different versions of the Ten Profound Gates in his works, one based on the *Ten Profound Gates of the One Vehicle of the Huayan* (the so-called old ten profundities, *jiu shixuan* 舊十玄) and another that appears in his *Exploration of the Profundities of the Huayan Sutra* (the so-called new ten profundities, *xin shixuan* 新十玄).[37] Chengguan included the latter version in his influential commentaries on the Huayan Sutra, and it thus became the standard list used by modern writers, despite the fact that the fifth patriarch, Zongmi, did not talk about them at all.[38]

Like the Six Characteristics, the doctrine of the Ten Profound Gates expresses ideas about the relationship between wholes and their parts as well as between parts and other parts, but it treats these two issues with greater depth than the concept of the Six Characteristics. First, it does so with the idea of causal dependence, that each thing depends entirely for its existence on both every other individual thing and the entire whole of which they are all equally a part. Second, it does so with the idea of nonobstruction (*wuai* 無礙), the idea that the identity and activity that characterize a phenomenon at a given moment is not hindered by those of other phenomena. The Ten Profound Gates teaches these truths by outlining ten perspectives from which one can view phenomenal reality. They are called "gates" (*men* 門) because each affords a specific and limited aperture for conceptualization of the universe, a single viewpoint on reality. Just as the scenery one sees outside a large building will change depending on the window through which one looks at it, each of the Ten Profound Gates offers a different perspective on reality, and all of them are true. The Ten Profound Gates are, in effect, not so much an exhaustive inventory of accurate statements about reality as an exercise in perspective taking. One might see a mountain range out one's back door but a street scene from the front window. Neither of these perspectives negates the other; they are simply different pieces of the same total reality. Huayan Buddhists argue that enlightened beings, unlike ordinary beings, perceive all these perspectives simultaneously in a type of awareness referred to as the Ocean Seal Samādhi (*haiyin sanmei* 海印三昧), a meditative state that reflects the totality of reality just as the waters of a calm ocean reflect everything above it. As one studies and reflects upon the Ten Profound Gates, one draws closer to the awareness that the apparent contradictions in the identity of a thing (as both a cause *and* an effect, for example) are only apparent, that no one aspect of a thing's identity can ever describe completely all the contributions it makes to reality as it is.

As in the discussion of the Six Characteristics, it is helpful to use a concrete example to explain the concept of the Ten Profound Gates. I chose earlier to use Fazang's own analogy of the golden lion, but here I can employ one that I use to teach my students: a grass lawn on a hillside. In this explanation, I confine myself to discussing only a few of the Ten Profound Gates (all ten are listed in note 39).[39] First, we must accept that the identities of things arise entirely from their causal dependence on other things. This is none other than the standard Mahāyāna idea that all things are empty of individuality or permanence and that they exist only because of the causes and conditions that have come together to form them. In our analogy, the lawn exists only because of the water, soil, and sunlight that help it grow. It is also dependent on each single blade of grass because these blades "cause" the lawn by being its constituent parts. The individual blades of grass and thus the entire lawn are also dependent on the seeds from which they sprouted. This is a simplistic version of the explanation of the lawn offered by Buddhist emptiness philosophy.

Huayan thought agrees with this but builds on it by emphasizing that a cause does not lose its own identity just by being a cause. This is highlighted in the second of the Ten Profound Gates, which is "freedom and [nonobstruction] of extension and restriction or breadth and narrowness" (*guangxia zizai wuai men* 廣狹自在無礙). What this somewhat unwieldy phrase means is that from one perspective a thing can be a cause for other things, but this does not stop it from being itself. The participation of a single phenomenon in the great dance of reality, which is its activity of causing other things, does not obstruct or hinder its individual existence. A single blade of grass serves as a cause for the existence of whole lawn, but the fact that it is busy being part of the whole lawn does not mean it cannot still be a single blade of grass. What matters here is the perspective: seen from one viewpoint, there is only a lawn, but if one shifts one's perspective, one sees instead the individual blades of grass. This is also spelled out in the fifth gate, both concealment and revelation are completely attained (*mimi yinxian jucheng* 秘密隱顯俱成). When you focus on the lawn, the blades of grass are "concealed" because you are thinking of the whole. When you focus on one blade of grass you "reveal" it and forget for a moment about the whole lawn, which is thus "concealed." Or, to use the English proverb, when you focus on the individual blades of grass, you "can't see the forest for the trees."

The majority of the ten gates are structured in similar ways in that they say that even though a thing is functioning in a certain way in relation to other things or to the whole, it retains its singular identity. The point of these exercises is not to show that one perspective is right and another wrong but to show that the identities of a phenomenon are multiple and that how a given thing, situation, or aspect of reality appears at a given moment is a function of one's point of view. This is summarized in the tenth and final gate, each pair of subject ("lord") and object ("servant") completely illuminates the whole and contains all qualities (*zhuban yuanming jude* 主伴圓明具德). When you look at the world from the perspective of one thing, that one thing becomes the subject, and everything else in the universe becomes its objects. If you look at the lawn, then water, sunlight, and the blades of grass are simply causes. They exist only to make the lawn happen. But if you focus on the blade of grass, the lawn becomes a cause because it provides stability on the hillside. If you focus on a single grass seed, you see that the lawn and the blades of grass are just the causes for that seed, but if you shift your perspective and make the blade of grass your focus again, then the seed becomes either a mere cause for the blade or one of its product. This notion of perspective applies to human beings as well: we tend to think of ourselves as the star of the movie of our lives, but although this is true, it does not mean we are not also simply extras playing walk-on roles in the movies of others' lives. One thinks of the meme that reminds the driver, "You are not stuck in traffic; you *are* traffic." This points to the idea that in my unenlightened view traffic has only one reality: it is a problem created by others and inflicted upon me, the subject. The doctrine of the Ten Profound Gates says that although this viewpoint is true, it is also extremely limited. The point of the Ten Profound Gates is to see that none of these perspectives is true in an absolute sense, but all are valid.

The Four Dharmadhātu

All premodern and modern historians of Buddhism identify the Six Characteristics and the Ten Profound Gates as central tenets of Huayan thought. A third concept discussed by many but not all[40] is the Four Dharmadhātu (*sifajie*), which the philosopher and scholar Jin Y. Park has argued represents the very culmination of Huayan thought.[41] The concept of the Four Dharmadhātu was developed by the fourth patriarch Chengguan. He used several different Dharmadhātu models in his writings, including threefold, fourfold, and fivefold ones, but since the time of Zongmi the tradition has held the fourfold model to be definitive.[42] The Four Dharmadhātu model discusses the two key Chinese philosophical concepts of principle (*li* 理) and phenomenon/a (*shi* 事). *Shi* is fairly straightforward, effectively referring to the concrete things and events in the universe. *Li*, however, is more complex owing in part to its long history within the Chinese philosophical tradition and the wide range of meanings the character itself can take.[43] In the context of Buddhist thought, *li* generally refers to the fundamental nature of reality, which is emptiness. To be more precise, as Robert Gimello notes in his well-known discussion of emptiness in Huayan Buddhism, *li* is not the principle *of* emptiness, but the principle *that* things are fundamentally empty, empty of permanence, essence, and autonomous existence.[44] There has been a tendency both inside and outside the Sinitic Buddhist tradition to reify the category of *li* by treating it as the really existing substrate of reality. This tendency is reflected in some scholars' translation of *li* as "noumenon." I believe neither the idea nor this translation is an accurate reflection of the term in Huayan and choose to follow those scholars who translate *li* as "principle."

The pair "principle and phenomena" is elaborated to a great extent within Huayan Buddhist thought. These discussions are focused on the same central concerns as those that define the Ten Profound Gates—namely, the nature of the relationships between phenomena and the underlying emptiness of those phenomena. Chengguan's Four Dharmadhātu model is the most common framework within Huayan for discussing the relationship of principle and phenomena.

In both of his major commentaries on the Huayan Sutra, Chengguan shows a clear interest in articulating Huayan thought in terms of the relationship between principle and phenomena. In his thinking, he drew much inspiration from the *Method for Contemplation of the Dharmadhātu*.⁴⁵ This text is of singular importance as a source of thought and practice within the Huayan tradition. I outline the history and content of this text in chapter 6 in a discussion of its adoption as a meditation manual in several modern Huayan institutes. For the present, it is important to note that the *Method for Contemplation of the Dharmadhātu* develops a basic discussion of emptiness into one on the relationship between principle and phenomena.⁴⁶ It describes three contemplations or views of reality that one should practice in succession: (1) Contemplation of True Emptiness (*zhenkong guan* 眞空觀), (2) Contemplation of the Nonobstruction of Principle and Phenomena (*lishi wuai guan* 理事無礙觀), and (3) Contemplation of Universal Pervasion and Inclusion (*zhoubian hanrong guan* 周遍含容觀). Fazang and his disciple Huiyuan built on the concept of the "nonobstruction of principle and phenomena" by adding a new phrase, "the nonobstruction of phenomena" (*shishi wuai* 事事無礙), which they used to refer to the third contemplation in the *Method for Contemplation of the Dharmadhātu*.⁴⁷ Chengguan systematized these two concepts in the Four Dharmadhātu model, and they have since become of a kind of slogan for Huayan thought.

Like the Ten Profound Gates, the Four Dharmadhātu are meant to summarize different perspectives on reality. The first is the conventional view we all have of reality, which is called the "realm of phenomena" (*shi fajie* 事法界). In this view, the universe is made up of really existing independent phenomena. The second viewpoint is the same as the one offered by Buddhist emptiness philosophy, which is called here the "realm of principle" (*li fajie* 理法界). In this view, all phenomena are void of inherent existence. The third view, as laid out first in the *Method for Contemplation of the Dharmadhātu*, is that of the nonobstruction between these two realities of principle and of phenomena (*lishi wuai fajie* 理事無礙法界). Here we begin to see inklings of the specifically Huayan nature of the model. From this viewpoint, one sees that the fact of the emptiness of

[143]

phenomena, the principle *that* they are empty of permanence and autonomy, in no way prevents them from acting as phenomena. This idea is, of course, akin to the conventional truth/ultimate truth dichotomy within emptiness philosophy, but it lays the foundation for the final viewpoint, which contains Huayan philosophy's unique contribution to Sinitic Buddhist ontology. This view is that of the realm of nonobstruction between phenomena (*shishi wuai fajie* 事事無礙法界). The content of this idea is the same as that described in detail in the Ten Profound Gates. The activity and conventional existence of one phenomenon in no way hinders the activity and existence of any other phenomenon. From this viewpoint, one sees the entirety of reality as a grand profusion of interrelated and interdependent phenomena, a wholeness wheeling in a cosmic dance of arising and passing away. This vision of reality affirms the Buddhist truth of emptiness but in a way that is, as Gimello argues, deeply "kataphatic."[48]

Doctrines Downplayed in Modern Summaries of Huayan

The contemporary reader familiar with Huayan may take for granted that the Six Characteristics, Ten Profound Gates, and Four Dharmadhātu are indeed the central concepts of the Huayan School, but one should consider if our familiarity with these concepts is not in part the result of the impact of early twentieth-century discourses about the Huayan School in Japan and China. The list of doctrines given here represent a summary of the ones most commonly seen in works on general Buddhism from the 1920s and 1930s. This summary has included data from works that were primarily religious in nature as well as from those that were more reflective of the emerging field of academic Buddhist studies. These data tell us which doctrines were most popularly associated with the Huayan School in the early twentieth century. To put these doctrines into greater relief, we should also consider those doctrines of classical Huayan thought that were never or only rarely mentioned in the basic definitions of Huayan offered in these texts. Assessing these doctrines can help us understand what elements were *not* considered central to the Huayan School. Certainly, all of these doctrines are discussed in more specialized Huayan texts, but my goal here is to discuss what the popular, common image of the Huayan School was at the time.

Fazang's thought was highly influential in establishing the core identity of the Huayan School. His formulations of the Five Teachings, Six Characteristics, and Ten Profound Gates in the *Treatise on the Five Teachings* were definitive. That work, however, also contains lengthy and specific discussions of cause and effect (*yinguo* 因果) as well as Fazang's idiosyncratic reinterpretation of the Three Natures (*sanxing* 三性) paradigm, which is more commonly associated with the Yogācāra School.[49] Cause and effect is a general Buddhist concept, but it is closely tied with the Huayan doctrines discussed earlier. Fazang inherited these doctrines from his predecessors, but his treatment of the concept of Three Natures in the *Treatise on the Five Teachings* was a new addition to Huayan thought.[50] It was of considerable importance for Fazang, who disagreed with the Yogācāra School on a number of issues, but it does not make an appearance in the short or medium-length treatments of Huayan I have examined from the Republican period.

As noted in chapter 1, Gyōnen's sect-centric histories of Sinitic Buddhism had a large impact on how Chinese Buddhists understood the organization of their tradition. With regard to Huayan in particular, the school to which Gyōnen himself belonged, we can see that Gyōnen's influence on modern treatments was mixed. Writers in China focused on some of the same elements as Gyōnen and ignored some of the same elements he ignored, but this approach was not universal, and there were some elements that Gyōnen singled out as central to the Huayan School that modern Chinese writers did not feel it was important to discuss.

Most modern Chinese writers followed Gyōnen in ignoring or downplaying the importance of the Tang dynasty layman Li Tongxuan. Scholars today have recognized the importance that

Li's thought held in the Chinese Huayan tradition and beyond. His writings played an important role within Korean Buddhism, where his thoughts on spiritual practice influenced the Sŏn (Ch. Chan) master Chinul 知訥 (1158–1210).[51] Li's writings also influenced the Japanese monk Myōe 明惠 (1173–1232), who was something of a rival to Gyōnen within the Kegon Sect in Japan.[52] Despite Li's importance, of all the modern texts examined here he is mentioned only in Shimaji and Oda's *A Brief History of Buddhism of the Three Nations*. As in other things, they follow the thirteenth-century *Record of the Buddhist Patriarchs*, which mentions Li Tongxuan in connection with the Huayan School. Apart from this one work, all the other modern Chinese writers of the early twentieth century ignored Li Tongxuan's connection with the Huayan School.

In other cases, modern treatments of the Huayan School ignored issues that Gyōnen felt were important. Although most modern studies of Huayan follow the general list of topics found in Gyōnen's influential work *Essentials of the Eight Sects*, the majority of them omit the final entry in his list of topics, which is a discussion of buddhas and Buddha lands (*fotu*). Modern texts generally also eschew mention or discussion of the Huayan attitudes toward the stages of spiritual practice (*xingbu*), which occupy the final part of Gyōnen's text. The issues of spiritual practice and its fruit—Buddhahood—are of importance within the classical Huayan tradition, but they do not figure prominently within modern summaries of the school. It is possible that in this, as in other things, modern writers succumbed to the popularity of the Tiantai polemic that Huayan contained doctrinal teachings but no form of meditation (*youjiao wuguan*). This opinion was not universal, however, and writers such as Yang Wenhui, Taixu, and Changxing emphasized the presence of meditative practices within the Huayan tradition. As will be seen in the next chapter, many of the monks who ran Huayan educational programs shared the desire to promote these and other forms of Huayan meditation, and they incorporated the study and practice of Huayan meditative texts and techniques into their curricula. The same cannot be said of newly recovered Huayan scriptures.

Recovered Huayan Texts in the Republic

This analysis of the presentation of Huayan doctrine within the popular but serious literature on Buddhism shows that there was something of a common definition of the Huayan School during the Republican period. Growing literacy and innovations in printing technology made its dissemination more possible. Modern transnational connections and printing also made possible the reintroduction of Huayan texts in China that had long been lost. Scholars point to the recovery of lost Chinese Buddhist texts from Japan as one of the contributions of the modern Chinese Buddhist press, but it is worth considering if these texts actually had a noticeable impact on the development of Chinese Buddhism. Based on an analysis of popular sources, the answer, at least in the case of Huayan, would be a definitive "no."

The historical record in China is filled with the titles of texts that have been lost to disaster or the inevitable march of time. Buddhist texts, Huayan Buddhist texts in particular, are no exception. By the start of the nineteenth century a number of well-known canonical texts had been lost in China, including several of Fazang's important works, such as *Exploration of the Profundities of the Huayan Sutra* and his commentaries on the *Awakening of Faith*. By the end of that century, however, the slow disappearance of texts had been reversed as new scriptural presses, founded in the wake of the disastrous Taiping Rebellion (1850–1864), used traditional technology and methods, such as xylography, to print copies of Buddhist texts. Increased international connection in the latter part of the century also led to the renewed availability of titles lost in China that had been preserved in Japan. Yang Wenhui was particularly keen to recover such texts, and beginning in the 1870s his press in Nanjing brought more of them back into circulation than any other. In the early twentieth century, these traditional scriptural printing houses were joined by new ones, centered in the urban hub of Shanghai, that used modern mechanized presses and moveable type. These new publishers were able to produce Buddhist texts in higher volumes and at greater speeds than the traditional presses, but they did not replace them.[53] Together, these presses made Buddhist texts of all types more widely available than they had ever been before. For example, if one compares the list of Huayan texts included in the last Chinese Buddhist canon printed before the twentieth century, the Qianlong Canon (Long Zangjing 龍藏經, completed in 1669), with a catalog put out in 1937 by the largest Chinese Buddhist publishing house, Buddhist Books (Foxue Shuju 佛學書局), one finds that nearly three dozen "lost" Huayan works were returned to circulation in the modern period.

Historians of modern Chinese Buddhism regularly talk about the expansion of the Buddhist press in twentieth-century China, but how exactly did this activity affect the shape of a modernizing Chinese Buddhism? To answer this question it is necessary to have a general sense of what texts were available, when, and to whom. In most cases, it is not possible to say with complete certainty that a given Buddhist text was not extant *anywhere* in China at a certain time. The lists of the texts included in the various major canons give us a rough sense of what was available at a given time period, but the absence of a text from such lists does not mean that it was not available in some temples or local libraries. Absence of evidence is not evidence of absence. Likewise, the presence of a text in one of the major canons does not mean it was widely available to lay and monastic Buddhists in China. Nevertheless, the canon catalogs are still a useful source for rough data on the availability of a given text at a certain point in time.[54] In the discussion that follows, I use the Qianlong Canon as a reference point to determine which Huayan texts were most likely extant and in circulation at the start of the nineteenth century. For the availability of texts in the early modern period, I have used several sources, including two catalogs published by printing houses in 1914 and 1937[55] as well as the *Digital Catalogue of Chinese Buddhism*, maintained by Gregory Adam Scott, which gathers publication data on Buddhist texts printed between 1860 and 1949 as given in several studies by modern Chinese scholars.[56]

Yang Wenhui was the leading Chinese figure in recovering and printing Buddhist texts in the latter half of the nineteenth century. With the assistance of his friend Nanjō Bunyū, Yang was able to secure from Japan copies of many texts that had been lost in China. He was ecumenical in his desire to return these texts to circulation, but it is widely recognized that he was particularly attracted to Huayan and worked hard to make available texts from that school, especially lost texts written by Fazang,[57] and he published two collections of classical Huayan works before the end of the late nineteenth century. In 1876, his press, the Jinling Scriptural Press, finished printing the *Essential Collected Writings on the Huayan Sutra* (*Dafang guangfo huayanjing zhushu jiyao* 大方廣佛華嚴經著述集要) in thirteen volumes.[58] This anthology contains twenty-three different works[59] written by the latter four Huayan patriarchs as well as one text by Li Tongxuan, Xufa's *Abbreviated Record of the Five Patriarchs of the Dharmadhātu School* (*Fajiezong wuzu lüeji* 法界宗五祖略記),[60] and Xufa's *Clarification of the* Outline of Xianshou's Five Teachings. All of the works in this collection are short, and larger commentaries by Zhiyan, Chengguan, Fazang, and Li Tongxuan are not included. The collection does include a few texts that had not been preserved in the Qianlong Canon; notable among them are Fazang's *One Hundred Entrances Into the Ocean of Meanings in the Huayan Sutra* (*Huayanjing yihai baimen* 華嚴經義海百門), which Yang notes had been lost in China since the Yuan dynasty (1271–1368),[61] as well as Chengguan's *Method of Contemplation on the Complete Interfusion of the Three Sages*.[62] Yang's *Essential Collected Writings on the Huayan Sutra* made all of these shorter texts available in one place. Data on how many copies of this collection were printed are not available, but it remained in circulation through the first half of the twentieth century. It was listed as a key reference text in the curriculum of the original Huayan University in the 1910s, and Buddhist Books advertised it as one of the many Huayan works it sold in 1937.[63]

Yang's press also produced the *Xianshou Dharma Collection*, which was meant to make available in one place all of Fazang's important writings. This collection included nineteen of his works (not all of which were on the subject of Huayan) as well as an important biography of Fazang written by the Korean scholar Ch'oe Ch'i-wǒn 崔致遠 (c. 857–tenth century). Of these texts, only seven had been available in the Qianlong Canon, and Yang noted in his preface that the Canon's versions of some of those texts (such as *Record of the Transmission of the Huayan Sutra*) were not as complete as the versions in his *Dharma Collection*, which were based on texts he had received from Japan.[64] The two Huayan collections produced by Yang's press had different purposes, and there was little overlap between them. (Only seven titles appeared in both collections.) Unlike the *Essential Collected Writings*, the *Xianshou Dharma Collection* contained Fazang's lengthier major works, such as the *Treatise on the Five Teachings* and his commentary on the sixty-volume Huayan Sutra known as *Exploration of the Profundities of the Huayan Sutra*, which had been lost in China.

Yang wanted the *Xianshou Dharma Collection* to reestablish Fazang as the most important figure in Huayan Buddhism. In the preface he wrote for the collection, he explained that he wished to produce this collection because a number of Fazang's important commentaries had been lost and because people in China had not had access to all of Fazang's works they thought that Chengguan had created many of the central ideas of the Huayan School. As a result, they had turned it into the School of Qingliang (Chengguan), when it should rightly be considered the School of Xianshou. In particular, Yang mentioned several times in the preface that in studying the recently recovered *Exploration of the Profundities of the Huayan Sutra*, he discovered that many of the ideas in Chengguan's influential commentaries had their basis in Fazang's work. He cited as one example the fact that the most prevalent version of the Ten Profound Gates in Huayan can be found in that text, even though they had long been considered Chengguan's creation.

Due largely to Yang's efforts, a number of Huayan texts were returned to circulation in China, and many of them were available at the time of the founding of the original Huayan University. A catalog put out in 1914 by Youzheng Press, established by Yuexia's associate Di Chuqing in Shanghai in the early 1900s, listed twenty-nine Huayan texts for sale, including some texts not available in the Qianlong Canon. As Gregory Adam Scott has noted, the Buddhist publishing houses of Republican China not only sold those books that they produced but also served as distributors for books produced by other publishers.[65] Because of this, one can look at later catalogs, such as the one published in 1937 by Buddhist Books, to get a fairly good sense of what texts were available for purchase at that time. The catalog was organized according to the "three times," the order in which the Buddha supposedly preached the various sutras in the canon and Huayan texts are found in two places in the catalog. The very first section of the catalog is devoted to the Huayan Sutra, and this comes before the section containing the Āgamas, which belong to early mainstream Buddhism.[66] The first section contains a listing of the various available editions of the Huayan Sutra, along with editions of single chapters from it that one could buy, including three editions of the "Chapter on Pure Conduct" ("Jingxing pin" 淨行品), three editions of the "Chapter on the Ten Stages Chapter" ("Shidi pin" 十地品), and six different editions of the very popular "Chapter on the Practice and Vows of Samantabhadra." Editions of the shorter sutras that went into creating the Huayan Sutra are also included in this section. Interestingly, this section of the catalog also includes the Sutra of Perfect Enlightenment, which is a rather general (and likely apocryphal) East Asian Buddhist text. Doctrinally, this text is not particularly "Huayan-istic" in nature, and it was probably included in this section because it was favored by the fifth Huayan patriarch, Zongmi. Zongmi's *Inquiry Into the Origin of Humanity* as well as various commentaries upon it are also listed in this section. The *Inquiry* is the only nonsutra text to be included in this section. All of the other treatises and commentaries on the Huayan Sutra as well as other miscellaneous writings belonging to the Huayan School are given much later in the catalog, in a section specifically devoted to the school.[67]

In addition to publishers' catalogs, Chinese Buddhists could learn about what texts were available for purchase through ads placed by presses in the various Buddhist magazines as well as through notices written by those magazines' editors in celebration of the printing of important texts. From such notices, one sees that the publishing of Huayan-related texts continued through the war years, with a notable flurry of activity in the early 1940s. The most important of these publications was the revised and edited version of Chengguan's *Commentary and Subcommentary on the Huayan Sutra*, discussed in chapter 3. In 1944, an association led by Yingci and a group of Shanghai-based laymen finished their publication of this important text, which was a significant religious and academic achievement.[68] Based on available Chinese and Japanese versions, updates on the production of this text appeared regularly across the Buddhist periodical press in the early 1940s, and it was marked as a major event in the modern history of Chinese Huayan.

We may be tempted to assume this publishing activity and the concomitant availability of a wide range of Huayan texts led to a new vitality in the study of Huayan. But this assumption would imply that these texts were actually being recited, studied, or lectured upon. If we look primarily at the notices of lectures given, commentaries written, and texts reprinted, we find that Yang's efforts to recover the lost patrimony of the Huayan tradition did not have a particularly significant impact during the republic. For example, of the many Huayan texts Yang's press printed that had not been in the Qianlong Canon, I have found evidence of only two of them being reprinted later by other publishers.[69] Yang's *Collected Essentials Writings* was still available for purchase in 1937, but the availability of copies of this work some sixty years after its initial printing might mean that it was not especially popular. Multiple editions of the "Chapter on the Practice and Vows of Samantabhadra" were produced by a wide range of presses, but I have not found any press that printed its own version of Fazang's formerly lost work *Exploration of the Profundities of the Huayan Sutra*. Zongmi's *Inquiry Into the Origin of Humanity*, which was used as a general introduction to Buddhism, was reprinted with and without commentaries many times and was even serialized in the magazine *Great Cloud* (Dayun 大雲) from 1926 to 1927, but Fazang's *One Hundred Entrances Into the Ocean of Meanings in the Huayan Sutra* was generally ignored.

We can gauge the popularity of a text in part through the number of presses willing to reproduce it, but we can also look to the notices of lectures and study groups that appeared in Buddhist magazines. As with other forms of evidence discussed earlier, we cannot assume that all lectures and teaching events were recorded in such notices, but they do give us a general sense of what was happening, which reinforces the argument made here. Lectures on the "Chapter on the Practice and Vows of Samantabhadra" given by both monastics and laypeople were common in the Republican period. Beyond this, however, only two Huayan texts were the subject of public lectures announced in the press, and neither of these texts was written by Fazang; in fact, both were written in the Qing dynasty. The first lecture was by the lay Buddhist educator Jiang Yiyuan 江易園 (1876–1942) on the *Treatise on the Huayan Buddha Recollection Samādhi* (*Huayan nianfo sanmei lun* 華嚴念佛三昧論), written by the scholar Peng Shaosheng 彭紹升 (Jiqing 際清, 1740–1796), which Jiang delivered at the World Buddhist Householder Grove in Shanghai in 1929.[70] Jiang's lectures were serialized in the association's journal. The second was a lecture on *Outline of the Five Teachings* given in 1943 by Taixu at the Sino-Tibetan Teaching Institute (Han Zang Jiaoliyuan 漢藏教理院) in Chengdu.[71]

Besides these two examples, I found no other notices of lectures on a Huayan text that were not on the Huayan Sutra itself. Even then, public lectures on the Huayan Sutra were few and far between during the Republican period, and the vast majority of them occurred in the context of one of the Huayan institutes discussed in chapters 2 and 3. There is one example of a layman giving a lecture series on the Huayan Sutra. From May to October 1935, the publisher and scholar Xu Weiru gave evening lectures on the text as a supplement to a group recitation of the entire Huayan Sutra carried out at the Tianjin Buddhist Grove of Virtue (Tianjin Fojiao Gongdelin 天津佛教功德林), which was located in the French Concession in Shanghai.[72] A photograph taken on October 12 at the end of the recitation period shows twenty-one participants, some of whom appear to have been monastics.[73] These lectures were part of Xu's growing commitment to Huayan studies, which led to his initiation of the project to publish an edited version of Chengguan's *Commentary and Subcommentary on the Huayan Sutra*, a project that Yingci took over when Xu died in 1937.

Apart from a few lectures by Jiang and Xu, most of the teaching that did happen around Huayan thought and the Huayan Sutra during the period under discussion occurred within the context of the network of educational programs associated with the original Huayan University. The Huayan texts that Yang Wenhui recovered did not feature largely at any of these programs. For example, despite the importance that Yang attached to Fazang's *Exploration of the Profundities of the Huayan Sutra*, it appeared in the curricula of only two programs: as a third-year text in Xiangrui's Institute of the Xianshou School in 1927 and in the revised curriculum of the Zhulin Buddhist Institute when it was relaunched in 1931. The same situation occurred with two other, much shorter texts, Fazang's *One Hundred Entrances Into the Ocean of Meanings in the Huayan Sutra* and Chengguan's *Method of Contemplation on the Complete Interfusion of the Three Sages*. Chengguan's text does not appear in any curriculum after 1922, and Fazang's work, despite being recently recovered from Japan, was not studied formally in any of the Huayan educational programs. In the end, the recovery of lost texts did not affect the study of Huayan at even the most specialized institutions. Instead, the long-standing Huayan tradition continued much as it had. In the Republic of China, Huayan remained a set of core doctrines and texts that the Chinese Buddhist tradition had been successful at preserving and transmitting for centuries.

SIX

A Common Curriculum

HISTORIANS OF MODERN Chinese Buddhism are fortunate to have a fairly large body of data to draw on to understand the curricula of Republican-era Buddhist educational programs. The founding of most programs during the period are recorded in announcements published in the Buddhist press. On occasion, these announcements were simply brief notices with the program's name, location, and the names of a few of its faculty. More often, however, a program's founders would publish a complete set of bylaws (*zhangcheng* 章程 or *jianzhang* 簡章) in either the program's own in-house journal or in one of the major national Buddhist magazines. These bylaws were often preceded by a section or separate article called "Conditioned Origination" ("Yuanqi 緣起"), which described the reasons behind the founding of the program and gave a summary of the sources of support that made it possible. These documents provide a great deal of information about monastic education during the modern period, and I have used many of them in the current study, but one must exercise some caution when using them as historical sources. In most cases, bylaws and curricula were published before the program actually started, so they cannot be considered records of what was actually taught. In a few cases, we do have articles written by students or visitors after a program's commencement, which allow us to confirm the nature of the curriculum.¹ In the majority of cases, however, we do not. These documents should thus be treated as aspirational and promotional texts created to serve a variety of functions. As aspirational documents, they reflect the founders' ideal image of what a monastic educational program *ought* to be. These can be read, for example, in the first article of the bylaws, which always outlined the "main principle" (*zongzhi* 宗旨) of the program. This first article almost always included a statement to the effect that the purpose of the program is to "help oneself and help others [*zili lita* 自利利他]."

Program bylaws also served an important role as promotional texts. As discussed, Buddhist educational programs faced a number of challenges in the Republican period. They were usually short of money, but they also often had shortages of both well-prepared students and qualified faculty. Announcing a program's organizational structure and curriculum was one way to signal that it was a serious enterprise and thereby to gather both donations and students. It was also a way of gaining other kinds of support from members of the Buddhist community, such as powerful or wealthy lay Buddhists or influential abbots. Both Keduan and Aiting announced their institutes in the midst of efforts to transform the temples where they had recently become abbots from private institutions into public *conglin*. Running a modern educational program would have needed support from both the Buddhist community and the government. Announcing the founding of a modern institute was also a way to protect a temple from criticism and even confiscation by governmental and nongovernment actors in society, which were especially acute during the 1920s.

An analysis of program bylaws shows that the Huayan schools descending from the original Huayan University shared a number of curricular elements. At these schools, studies generally centered on three things: the interpretation of the Huayan Sutra found in the writings of Chengguan (and occasionally of Li Tongxuan), Fazang's doctrinal classification, and the study and practice of a uniquely Huayan form of meditation called the Contemplation of

A COMMON CURRICULUM

the Dharmadhātu. These elements represent the educational identity shared by the schools formed by members of the Huayan University network. Before discussing these elements in greater detail, it is important to place the curricula of the various Huayan institutes within the larger context of modern Buddhist education. Among other things, this will allow us to see the debt that all of the Huayan education programs owed to earlier programs, especially Yang Wenhui's Jetavana Hermitage.

The Influence of Yang Wenhui

In discussing the Buddhist educational programs of the late Qing and Republican periods, scholars identify certain elements as definitive of "modern" education. These elements include the use of blackboards, regular examinations, and graduation diplomas as well as the insertion of secular subjects such as foreign languages, law, and especially science into the curriculum. Many of the programs studied here did not teach such subjects, but this is not unusual. As Stefania Travagnin points out, even the study of science in monastic education programs did not begin until the early 1920s, and by the 1930s it had mostly disappeared.[2] As the purpose of this book is to assess the teaching of Huayan, the discussion here focuses on the Buddhist-studies elements of program curricula; for the most part, I do not look at the non-Buddhist subjects included in the curricula.

Shi Dongchu argues that "modern" Buddhist education in China began with the Hundred Days Reform in 1898,[3] but because we do not have enough data to know what was taught in the monastic schools of the 1900s, we must look to the curriculum of Yang Wenhui's Jetavana Hermitage, which had been influenced by the modern Buddhist schools of Japan. The hermitage had a concrete influence on the Huayan institutes of the Republic. Yuexia and Yingci were certainly aware of that program when they founded the original Huayan University. Their students Changxing and

Zhiguang had studied at the hermitage, which gave them firsthand experience of Yang's curricular ideas, which they reproduced elsewhere. Yang's program of study was also symbolically important for those who had not been enrolled in it. It was widely praised in the Buddhist press as a model for modern Buddhist education, especially in the 1920s, when many of the programs discussed here were founded, and the curriculum Yang created for his school in the first decade of the twentieth century continued to serve as a model for schools that opened in the 1930s. This was true even of schools not among the more commonly studied ones derived from Taixu's influential school of the 1920s, the Wuchang Buddhist Institute.[4]

Yang laid out his program of study in "Curriculum for Inner Classes at Buddhist Schools" ("Shishi xuetang neiban kecheng 釋氏學堂內班課程").[5] There he divided the course of study into three years, which became the standard length for a curricular cycle in all later Buddhist education programs. First-year students were assigned fifteen sutras, commentaries, and liturgical texts. In the second year, they focused their studies entirely on the Śūraṅgama Sutra. Four sutras and six collections of devotional verses were added in the final year. In addition to the assigned material, Yang also listed eight texts as recommended reading. Large portions of this curriculum were adopted in later programs. Changxing used the Jetavana Hermitage curriculum as the basis for the Anhui Monastic School, which he ran from 1922 to 1924, including fifteen of the nineteen sutras and commentaries in Yang's list. The Anqing School's faculty and staff eventually formed the founding core of the highly successful Minnan Buddhist Institute, so that its curriculum was also heavily influenced by Yang. His curriculum was also a model for several of the other programs discussed here. The Huayan University of Hankou based its curriculum on Yang's during its run from 1921 to 1924, and the Zhulin Buddhist Institute's published curricula from both 1928 and 1931 used many of the texts on Yang's list. Even the three-year preparatory class at Yingci's Qingliang Institute was based closely on Yang's course plan.

A COMMON CURRICULUM

Although there was variation in which texts were taught and in what order, all of these programs shared several curricular components relating to non-Huayan texts. During the first year, students in most of the programs studied the *Awakening of Faith* and the *Sutra of Bequeathed Teachings* (Yijiaojing 遺教經),[6] as well as two Consciousness-Only texts, Xuanzang's *Verses on the Structure of the Eight Consciousnesses* (Bashi guiju song 八識規矩頌) and Vasubandhu's *Clear Explanation of the One Hundred Dharmas* (Baifa mingmen lun 百法明門論).[7] They also studied the Śūraṅgama Sutra during the second year and the *Sutra of Perfect Enlightenment* during the third year.

Aside from the two texts on Consciousness-Only, Yang's introductory curriculum is composed entirely of works that scholars now believe to have been originally composed in China, the so-called apocryphal texts. These texts are central to general Sinitic Buddhist thought, so their inclusion in the curriculum is not entirely surprising. Since the Song dynasty, they were among the most popular of those texts not associated with any particular school. Their inclusion in the Jetavana Hermitage's curriculum was due to Yang's desire that his program provide a solid foundation in nonsectarian Buddhist studies, and he imagined that students would go on to specialize in the study of one of the Chinese Buddhist schools after completing that initial course.

Although the hermitage closed before any of its students could move on to specialized study, Yang did list the texts that they would have studied if they had been able to move on. For Huayan studies, he recommended six works, including Chengguan's *Commentary and Subcommentary*, the "Chapter on the Practice and Vows of Samantabhadra" in the Huayan Sutra, and Yang's own *Essential Collected Writings on the Huayan Sutra*. His list also included Fazang's *Commentary on the Treatise on the Nondistinction of the Dharmadhātu* (Fajie wuchabie lunshu 法界無差別論疏)[8] and the unusual Buddho-Daoist apocryphal text *Foundational Treatise on the Mysteries of the Stages of the Great Lineage* (Dazong dixuan wenben lun 大宗地玄文本論),[9] which Yang was partial to. Neither of these two texts was incorporated into the curriculum of any of the later Huayan institutes.

PART TWO

Centrality of the Huayan Sutra

Yang designed his curriculum so that students would build a broad foundation in the study of general Sinitic Buddhism. The various Huayan institutes generally adhered to this same commitment in their own curricula, though they did place the greatest emphasis on sustained study of the Huayan Sutra. The original Huayan University was so called because the main class every day was based on Yuexia's lectures on that sutra, and this emphasis continued in the various programs run by Cizhou, Yingci, Keduan, and others. Most of the programs described in this study focused on the study of the Huayan Sutra and its commentaries, though the Dharmadhātu Institute at Changshu did eventually move away from this model.

The format for sutra lectures in Chinese Buddhism took several forms based on where they were given. In the case of both the Huayan Sutra and its major commentaries, its length tended to encourage longer, more intensive periods of study. These series often followed a common traditional format, especially when they occurred at a temple. Holmes Welch outlines this format in *The Practice of Chinese Buddhism*.[10] For less-intensive sutra lectures, monasteries would host one two-hour lecture each day at midday. "At other monasteries, which placed less emphasis on meditation and more on teaching, there would be a round-the-clock program of lectures and study that turned the premises virtually into a school."[11] These monasteries would invite an eminent master with expertise in a specific sutra to come to their temples. Ads for such lecture series would be distributed and posted near the temple and in the Buddhist press in the modern period. The daily schedule for one of these intensive study periods would have four parts. The central focus would be the main lecture (*dazuo* 大座), which would be given for two hours each day by the master, amid much ritual, usually at midday or in the early afternoon. Later that evening, one of the master's senior students would give a supplemental lecture (*pianzuo* 偏座) on the same passage from the text. The supplemental lecture would be a chance for the students to receive clarification on harder parts of the text. It was also a training opportunity for the master's senior students to practice their lecturing skills. Yingci got practice with delivering supplemental lectures on the Huayan Sutra when he was an assistant for Yuexia. And when Yingci later gave the main lectures during his own Huayan Sutra lecture series, both Nanting and Zhenchan delivered supplemental lectures. The final two parts of the daily schedule gave the attendees the chance to deepen their own engagement with the material. Each day there was at least one (and perhaps more) periods of self-study, with the master's senior students present to act as teaching assistants. Finally, on the morning of the day after the main lecture, one of the junior students would be drawn by lot to give yet another lecture on the same passage, this time reflecting what he had learned the previous day.

Most of the monastic educational programs of the Republican period followed this daily structure with greater or lesser degrees of modification. Welch notes that some masters chose to forgo the pomp of the traditional *dazuo*, and rather than give the lecture from the high seat they came down and used the equipment of modern education, such as blackboards.[12] Many of the Huayan institutes described here had expanded and diverse curricula that went far beyond one text, and they modified their schedules to accommodate a range of lectures. Several of the Huayan institutes of the Republican period followed fairly closely to the traditional lecture series format, however, and their curriculum was centered on the intensive study of a single text, the Huayan Sutra. The original Huayan University listed a number of texts within the curriculum, especially for the preparatory course, but daily activity for both groups of students centered on Yuexia's lectures on the eighty-volume Huayan Sutra, which took place from one to three o'clock every afternoon. This was supplemented by other lectures and self-study of commentarial texts as well as by three to four hours of review time set aside for students each day.[13]

As noted in chapter 3, Yingci became an active lecturer after the closure of the second Huayan University, and he gave lectures on the Huayan Sutra and its major commentaries both at monasteries and to mixed groups of lay and monastic Buddhists in Shanghai and Nanjing. We do not have detailed information on the exact schedule he used for these series, but it is safe to assume they followed a fairly traditional format. During the preparatory course at his Qingliang Institute, students studied a broad list of texts that was influenced by the curriculum from Yang Wenhui's Jetavana Hermitage. In the specialized course, which began in Shanghai in 1928 and ended in Wuxi in 1931, Yingci had his students focus their studies on the eighty-volume Huayan Sutra, which they supplemented with Chengguan's and Li Tongxuan's major commentaries.[14] Yingci particularly favored Chengguan's *Introductory Discourse to Commentary on the Huayan Sutra*,[15] and he lectured on it at Tiantong Monastery every summer from 1933 to 1937, in Shanghai in 1945, and in Nanjing in 1947.[16] Chenggaun's text has been and remains both an essential summary of Huayan School doctrine and a common outline for lectures on the Huayan Sutra.

Although not formally affiliated with Yingci or the original Huayan University, Keduan's Huayan University of Yangzhou followed a similarly traditional model, at least during its first year in 1923. A report from August of that year describes the daily schedule at the Yangzhou university. Mornings were set aside for sutra study as well as for classes on Huayan doctrine (*Huayan jiaoyi* 華嚴教義) and Chinese language. Just as at the original Huayan University, at Yangzhou the daily schedule centered on Keduan's main lecture (*dazuo*) on the eighty-volume Huayan Sutra. This main lecture was followed by individual research on the day's section of the text, for which students were to make use of Chengguan's *Commentary and Subcommentary on the Huayan Sutra*. The afternoon included study of Consciousness-Only thought and a supplemental lecture (*pianzuo*) on the day's main lecture.[17] The format of the Huayan University of Yangzhou was thus roughly the same as a traditional sutra lecture series at a public monastery as well as at the original Huayan University. An earlier version of the curriculum from 1923 even lists a morning study session for which monks would draw lots.[18] When Keduan restarted the university in 1925, he gave equal time in the curriculum to the study of the Huayan Sutra and the Lotus Sutra, and both lectures were moved to the morning. The curriculum continued to include periods of self-study on those sutras as well as daily supplemental lectures, with one given by a student chosen by lots. As Yingci did later at the Qingliang Institute, Keduan also added Li Tongxuan's *Combined Commentary on the Huayan Sutra* (*Huayanjing helun* 華嚴經合論) to the list of commentaries approved for study.[19]

Outside of Yingci and Keduan, there are few examples of Buddhists, monastic or lay, who put in the tremendous effort required to lecture on the Huayan Sutra, the longest sutra in the Chinese canon. The only other monk to lecture on the Huayan Sutra more than once during the Republican period was Yingci's student Cizhou. Available data suggest that Cizhou also ran his institutes following the format of traditional intensive sutra lecture series. In September 1933 the published announcement for the Dharmdhatū Institute, which ran from 1933 to 1936 at Yongquan Temple, stated that after one and a half years of studying the Buddhist canon, the "primary coursework [*zhuke* 主課]" would be study of the Huayan Sutra.[20]

Common Curricula of Huayan Educational Programs

The various Huayan programs of the Republican period focused on the Huayan Sutra, but they required that their students also study broadly in both Huayan thought and Chinese Buddhism. The curricula of the Jetavana Hermitage and the original Huayan University served as the two primary models for these programs. None of the later programs followed the curriculum of either model exactly, but they all drew inspiration from the two as they established their own approaches to monastic education.

Compared to the Jetavana Hermitage, the original Huayan University had a much more focused, one might almost say sectarian, curriculum. Even the curriculum in its preparatory course was heavily weighted toward Huayan studies, eschewing most of the general Sinitic Buddhist texts studied at Yang's hermitage. Yuexia did insist students in the preparatory course study the *Awakening of Faith* and the *Verses on the Structure of the Eight Consciousnesses*, but the central focus of the university remained the writings of the Huayan patriarchs. Yuexia and Yingci added two texts to the curriculum at the Huayan University that would become common in some later programs: Fazang's *Treatise on the Five Teachings* and Chengguan's *Contemplation of the Five Skandha* (*Wuyunguan* 五蘊觀).[21]

The *Contemplation of the Five Skandha* is an interesting case in that it serves as evidence of the influence of the original Huayan University on the Wuchang Buddhist Institute. The *Contemplation* is a short text that encourages people to seek liberation through the twin contemplation of the emptiness of persons (*renkongguan* 人空觀) and the emptiness of dharmas (*fakongguan* 法空觀). Although it was written by Chengguan, it is a general text and is devoid of Huayan terminology or concepts. Its relative simplicity and short length make it very well suited for use as an introductory text, but it was not widely taught in later Huayan-centered programs. Nevertheless, its inclusion in the curriculum of the original Huayan University may have led to its popularity in monastic educational programs not centered on Huayan. The text was assigned in the first year at the Huayan University of Hankou, the slightly older but much less well-known neighbor of the Wuchang Buddhist Institute. As discussed in chapter 2, there are clear indications of links between these two programs, such as through the group of laymen who were responsible for funding both. When the Wuchang Institute opened, it appears to have adopted some of the curricular elements of its older sibling. In addition to Chengguan's *Contemplation of the Five Skandha* and Fazang's *Treatise on the Five Teachings*, students in both programs studied the seminal Huayan meditation manual the *Method for Contemplation of the Dharmadhātu*, Chengguan's *Method of Contemplation on the Complete Interfusion of the Three Sages*, and Fazang's *Contemplation for Practicing the Huayan's*

Mysterious Teaching for Eliminating Delusions and Returning to the Origin (*Xiu huayan aozhi wangjin huanyuan guan* 修華嚴奧旨妄盡還源觀).²² In comparing the bylaws of the Wuchang Institute to those of the Huayan University of Hankou, one gets the strong sense that the drafters of the former had consulted the latter. The *Contemplation of the Five Skandha* also went on to feature in the curriculum of the Minnan Buddhist Institute, one of the most important monastic educational programs of the period.

As already noted, most of the Huayan programs that came after the original university, including all of those that followed the format of traditional intensive sutra study periods, used the commentaries of Chengguan and Li Tongxuan as basic reference texts. These programs included not only the original Huayan University but also Keduan's Huayan University of Yangzhou and Xiangrui's Institute of the Xianshou School as well as the regular course of Yingci's Qingliang Institute and the specialized class on Huayan offered for advanced students at the Minnan Buddhist Institute. Other programs, those based on the more expansive general curriculum of the Jetavana Hermitage, such as the programs at the Huayan University of Hankou and the Zhulin Buddhist Institute, did not include these core commentarial texts of the Huayan tradition. Students in those programs did study several texts that had loose connections to the Huayan tradition, such as the *Awakening of Faith*, the Sutra of Perfect Enlightenment, and the *Huayan Inquiry Into the Origin of Humanity*, but these texts do not teach the doctrines most specifically associated with the classical Huayan that were tradition discussed in chapter 5.

The two texts most commonly used to study Huayan doctrine in Republican monastic educational programs had been available in China before Yang began his work reviving the Huayan textual tradition. The first was Fazang's *Treatise on the Five Teachings*, which was taught at almost all of the programs mentioned earlier, often in the third year.²³ The other text was *Outline of Xianshou's Five Teachings*, Xufa's summary of Fazang's work, which was assigned as a first-year text in most of the programs.²⁴ Because Xufa's full summary was about the same length as the work it was meant to summarize, I suspect that in many cases students were assigned the shorter "summary of the summary" that Xufa wrote of his own work. The full title of this smaller text is *Clarification of the Outline of Xianshou's Five Teachings*, but it was often referred to using the same title as Xufa's longer summary.

Fazang wrote the *Treatise on the Five Teachings* fairly early in his career. Most of this work consists of an extensive delineation of his doctrinal classification system, which includes both his fivefold and tenfold schemas.[25] As noted in the previous chapter, the doctrinal classification scheme of the Five Teachings is considered the foundation for the identity and doctrine of the Huayan School, and this work remains the most authoritative statement of it. In studying this text, modern students would have encountered the line of reasoning Fazang used to support his Five Teachings scheme. They would have also been introduced to the key Huayan doctrines of the Ten Profound Gates and the Six Characteristics, which Fazang lays out in the tenth and final chapter of the work. As discussed in the previous chapter, these two doctrines were widely considered to be among the most central ideas of the Huayan School. The tenth chapter of the *Treatise on the Five Teachings* actually begins with Fazang's idiosyncratic interpretation of the Consciousness-Only doctrine of the Three Natures, but, as noted, this interpretation was not commonly mentioned in discussions of the Huayan School during the Republican period.

Fazang's work is daunting in its complexity, and it is reasonable that programs would wait until the third year of instruction to introduce it. By contrast, Xufa's two works are much simpler because he wrote them for the express purpose of serving as accessible introductions to Fazang's thought, and the two works had commonly served in this role even before the modern period. The contemporary scholars Chen Bing and Deng Zimei note that during the Qing dynasty, apart from a few exceptional temples, most of the monasteries dedicated to teaching Buddhist doctrine lacked complete sets of the Buddhist canon. Because of this, most monks studied Tiantai and Huayan doctrine only through the *Outline of the Four Teachings of Tiantai* and the *Outline of Xianshou's Five Teachings*, respectively. Although Chen Bing and Deng Zimei feel that reliance on these two texts meant that the level of education among doctrinal monks was not very deep,[26] I would observe that even when the full range of surviving Huayan texts was available, as they were in the early twentieth century, instructors continued to assign Xufa's text as an introduction to the Huayan tradition. Even in programs where the host temple held at least one complete edition of the Buddhist canon, such as the Guangxiao Buddhist Institute and the Huayan University of Yangzhou, Xufa's work served as the primary introduction to Huayan thought. Just as the commentaries of Chengguan and Li Tongxuan served as the heart of the interpretive tradition around the Huayan Sutra, Xufa's writings were the heart of the interpretive tradition around Huayan School doctrine throughout the Republican period.

Xufa was born in 1641 in Hangzhou. He entered the Buddhist community when he was nine and received full ordination at Ciyun 慈雲 Temple under Mingyuan 明源 (n.d.) when he was sixteen. Xufa earned a reputation for the depth of his learning, and he was given the nickname "Doctrinal Tiger of the Southeast" (Dongnan Yihu 東南義虎). He was a partisan of the Huayan tradition, so much of his scholastic work focused on comparing Huayan and Tiantai doctrine. Like Yang Wenhui, Xufa treated Fazang's writings as the foundation of the Huayan tradition,[27] and he began studying the *Treatise on the Five Teachings* in earnest in 1666, when he was twenty-five years old. In 1675, he felt he had made sufficient progress in his studies to lecture publicly on the entire text. These lectures formed the basis for *Outline of Xianshou's Five Teachings*. When Xufa lectured again on Fazang's text again in 1681, he realized that people needed a briefer and clearer introduction to the work, which prompted him to write *Clarification of the* Outline of Xianshou's Five Teachings, which was carved into wood blocks for its first printing the following year.[28] The longer of Xufa's two works includes expanded explanations of certain ideas, several introductory charts, and pronunciation guides to technical terms at the end of each chapter, but the two texts share the same structure. Both works are divided into five sections: the three time periods (*sanshi*) of Buddha's teaching, the Ten Meanings (*shiyi*), the Five Teachings (*wujiao*), the Six Schools (*liuzong*), and the Three Contemplations (*sanguan*). As far as I have been able to determine, this schema was Xufa's own creation. Fazang does not mention the three time periods specifically in *Treatise*, nor are the Six Schools a major category for him there. It is clear that Xufa meant his writings not merely as a commentary on Fazang's *Treatise* but also as a general introduction to the entire Huayan tradition, and they were used in exactly this way in many monastic education programs during the first half of the twentieth century.

Alongside classes devoted to the study of Buddhist texts and secular subjects, regular meditation was also included in the daily schedules of virtually all of the Republic's Huayan programs. Holmes Welch notes that Yingci insisted that his students take part in seven weeks of intensive Chan practice every year.[29] Keduan's university in Yangzhou followed a similar pattern, at least in its first year. Given the widespread notion at the time that the Huayan School lacks meditative practices, it would be fruitful to ask if the Huayan programs of the period required their students to practice some specifically Huayan form of meditation or if they simply prescribed modes of meditation common to Chinese Buddhism as a whole. Welch claims that "with respect to religious practice, there was a tendency for students of Avatamsaka to employ Ch'an [*sic*] system of meditation."[30] There is some truth to this statement, but it is not the whole story.

Almost all of the programs whose syllabi I have examined (both the specifically Huayan-centered programs and the more general ones) set time aside each day for some form of meditative praxis. Such practice was of three types: *chan*, recollection of the name of Amitābha Buddha (*nianfo* 念佛), and contemplation (*guan* 觀). Some programs included only one form of meditation within their curricula, while others included multiple types. Keduan's Huayan

University of Yangzhou and the first incarnation of the Zhulin Buddhist Institute were the only programs I have seen that included all three. The original Huayan University included both *chan* and contemplation, as did Yingci's Qingliang Institute. Cizhou's Dharmadhātu Institutes included both contemplation and *nianfo*. Of the programs with the clearest focus on teaching Huayan, only two assigned *chan* meditation as the sole practice, as Welch claims: the Dharmadhātu Institute in Changshu (in its 1927 incarnation) and Xiangrui's Xianshou Institute. All of the others included some form of contemplation. Each of these three major types of Chinese Buddhist meditation—*chan*, *nianfo*, and *guan*—can be practiced in multiple ways, but program syllabi are usually brief, and they do not explain the exact *chan* or *nianfo* methods the programs taught. There is often more information available regarding contemplation, which is important here because the specifically Huayan forms of meditation fall into this category.

Huayan Meditation

The Sinitic Buddhist tradition holds that the distinctive form of Huayan meditation is the Contemplation of the Dharmadhātu, which is named after the text that outlines it, *Method for Contemplation of the Dharmadhātu*. This text is attributed to Dushun, the first Huayan patriarch, and has been so foundational for the Huayan School that it would be fair to say that it is second only to the Huayan Sutra for its importance within the school. This status is striking given the fact that no independent version of the text actually existed within the canon. Rather, we find the text embedded within commentaries on it written by patriarchs Fazang, Chengguan, and Zongmi[31] as well as in Xufa's much later *Outline of Xianshou's Five Teachings*. The lack of an independently circulating version of the *Method for Contemplation* has led many scholars to question the text's provenance. Since at least the seventeenth century, scholars in Japan have argued about whether the text was actually written by Dushun or was perhaps the work of Fazang instead. Since the twentieth century, most scholars have agreed that the *Method for Contemplation* is not the work of Dushun. Some suspect that Fazang's commentary, which exists in several versions under two different titles,[32] was not actually a commentary but the base text from which the *Method for Contemplation* was created. Others have argued that Fazang's work was indeed based on another text, but that text had to have been written much later than Dushun's lifetime owing to its content.[33] In particular, some have noted that *Method* includes a far more involved discussion of the relationship between principle (*li*) and phenomena (*shi*) than one finds even in the work of the second Huayan patriarch, Zhiyan.[34]

The Contemplation of the Dharmadhātu outlined in *Method for Contemplation* is composed of three successive contemplations, each of which is explained from ten different perspectives. The three contemplations (*sanguan*),[35] as they are known, represent a successive progression through increasingly correct ways of looking at the world, culminating in the Huayan vision of a world comprising a multitude of phenomena existing in complete interpenetrative harmony. The first contemplation is Contemplation of True Emptiness (*zhenkong guan*). This is none other than the emptiness philosophy foundational to Mahāyāna Buddhism, and as such it does not depart from general Mahāyāna thought. The specifically Huayan nature of the practice emerges in the second and third contemplations. The second is the Contemplation of the Nonobstruction of Phenomena and Principle (*lishi wuai guan*). While the first contemplation invites the meditator to reflect on the relationship between emptiness (*kong* 空) and forms (*se* 色), or dharmas, the second contemplation reframes that relationship as one between principle and phenomena. As Robert Gimello notes in his extensive study of this text, the move from *se* to *shi* is an expansion of the discourse to encompass things beyond the usual lists of dharmas, including events. Likewise, the move from *kong* to *li* represents an expansion as *li* reveals the true function of emptiness more clearly than *kong*. Chengguan and Zongmi understood that the move from *kong/se* to li/shi was a major shift in perspective that emphasizes the real activity of principle in the world, the entire phenomenal reality, in a positive rather than a negative sense. This movement is completed, both philosophically and for the contemplator, in the third contemplation, Contemplation of Universal Pervasion and Inclusion (zhoubian hanrong guan). In this, the final shift in perspective, principle drops out entirely as the focus becomes the relationship *between* phenomena. Contemplation of phenomena becomes a sufficient means to apprehend the realm of total phenomenal interpenetration, which is none other than the dharmadhātu. This is the zenith of Huayan ontology, which is described in the text as "one within one, one within all, all within one, and all within all [yi zhong yi, yiqie zhong yi, yi zhong yiqie, yiqie zhong yiqie 一中一, 一切中一, 一中一切, 一切中一切]."[36]

Although modern scholars have doubts about who actually wrote the *Method for Contemplation*, by the 780s Chengguan had already started to identify Dushun as the text's author. This attribution became widespread in the early 800s, appearing in sutra catalogs and other writings.[37] Although Chengguan is known primarily for his commentarial writings on the Huayan Sutra, he also emphasized meditation, which he based on the *Method for Contemplation*.[38] Under his influence, there was a shift in the object of Huayan meditation. This shift had already begun in Fazang's *Contemplation for Practicing the Huayan's Mysterious Teaching for Eliminating Delusions and Returning to the Origin* but becomes clearer in the writings of Chengguan and Zongmi. Contemplation of the Dharmadhātu was originally practiced as a form of Contemplation of Origination (yuanqi guan 緣起觀). In this, the goal was to observe the myriad phenomena of the universe in their totality and in their absolute interdependence with one another. In this view, one should see the entire universe in a mote of dust. Fazang maintained this interpretation of the Contemplation of Origination but under the influence of the *Awakening of Faith* also saw it as Contemplation of Nature Origination (xingqi guan 性起觀). In this mode, the goal of the meditation is increasing awareness of the pure One

Mind that is the original basis for reality.[39] Chengguan and Zongmi favored the latter interpretation, which brought the Contemplation of the Dharmadhātu in line with the dominant understandings of meditation within the Chan tradition.

The Contemplation of the Dharmadhātu as Meditative Praxis

Regardless of its changing interpretation, the Contemplation of the Dharmadhātu has been central to Huayan from the Tang dynasty to the present. Nevertheless, it has been widely accepted in Chinese Buddhism since the Song dynasty that Huayan teaches no form of meditation. This view has everything to do with how meditation is defined. The extensive discussion of the Contemplation of the Dharmadhātu that Xufa included in his two *Outlines* were clearly meant to rebut the widespread criticism that Huayan taught no form of meditation. In this rebuttal, Xufa joined a long line of Huayan thinkers who had made that argument since this critique had first appeared in the Song dynasty. All of them pointed to the Contemplation of the Dharmadhātu as the paradigmatic method of Huayan meditation, though some thinkers also pointed to other texts by Fazang and Chengguan that had the word *contemplation* in the title (including the *Contemplation for Practicing the Huayan's Mysterious Teaching for Eliminating Delusions and Returning to the Origin* and *Method of Contemplation on the Complete Interfusion of the Three Sages*, both mentioned earlier). In Japan, Gyōnen, who was well aware of the Tiantai criticism, collected all of these techniques and eventually created a list of ten different Huayan contemplation methods (*kegon kanpō* 華嚴觀法) that continues to influence the scholarly understanding of Huayan meditation.[40]

The argument that Huayan lacks a specific form of meditation is generally based on the fact that the tradition does not have a text analogous to Zhiyi's *Great Calming and Contemplation* (*Mohe zhiguan* 摩訶止觀), which is the basis for meditation in the Tiantai School.[41] This text contains highly specific instructions for how to practice meditation that gives specific instructions about how to position one's body, how to breathe, and other aspects of meditative practice. But despite a later and narrower interpretation of his work, Zhiyi himself understood meditation in a fairly expansive manner. He considered meditation to include not only formal techniques of concentration but also the practice of moral restraint and the cultivation of wisdom. The meditation he taught was also highly ritualized and directed, not based on a freeform cultivation of empty states of mind. Beyond the *Great Calming and Contemplation*, Zhiyi also wrote many smaller works on meditation, and some of them are similar to the contemplation texts written by the later Huayan patriarchs discussed earlier in this chapter.[42]

In assessing the status of meditative practices within the Huayan tradition, it is important to be clear what we mean by the term *meditation*. Given the ambiguity of the concept of meditation within Zhiyi's own writings, these writings should not serve as the model against which Huayan meditation is judged. Popular contemporary notions of meditation, at least in the West, often treat meditation as a nonrational practice that is designed to facilitate the attainment of transcendent experiences by its practitioners. These experiences are most often treated as occurring beyond the realm of thought and are thus indescribable. Robert Sharf points out in his critique of the use of "experience" as a category of scholarly inquiry that the notion that unmediated, nonrational experience is the essential goal of Asian religious traditions is a relatively recent idea, which was popularized in the early twentieth century.[43] Halvor Eifring proposes that in place of the idea that meditation is about removing rational thought or all mental activity, we define meditation etically as "an attention-based technique for inner transformation." This definition moves away from the emphasis on experience for its own sake and recognizes that the goal of any such transitory experience is the long-term change of an individual in intellectual, spiritual, emotional, or other ways, which differ by tradition.[44]

Eifring proposes a taxonomy of meditation practices that divide them into "directive" and "nondirective" forms: "directive techniques seek to lead the mind and body toward preset goals embedded in culturally determined webs of meaning, while nondirective techniques are based on universal psychological working mechanisms bringing about reflexive effects on body and mind."[45] This taxonomy differs from the emic Buddhist one of śamatha and vipaśyanā, which Eifring argues has come to serve as the de facto taxonomy for most scholars of meditation. The problem with the emic taxonomy is that it ignores a number of practices that are common, even within the Buddhist tradition itself. Ignored practices most often fall into Eifring's category of "directive" meditation techniques, which are suggestive, concentrative, and thematic. He describes these techniques as "outside-in" because the religious and institutional context in which they are practiced provides the direction for the meditator.[46] Contemplative meditation (guan), the type of meditation explained in the Huayan tradition, is usually a form of directive meditation.

Contemplation has a long history in East Asia. The term guan was used in Daoism to refer to certain visualization practices.[47] It was also used as the most common way to render the Buddhist term vipaśyanā, analytical or observational meditation, as opposed to śamatha, or concentration meditation (Ch. zhi 止).[48] In East Asia, calming and contemplation taken together as zhiguan 止觀 were considered to encompass the full range of traditional Indic Buddhist meditative practices and are often used generally to simply mean meditation. The term chan is also used generically in this fashion, though it also came to be associated with the specific techniques of the Chan School. Depending on the context, zhiguan and chan can be used interchangeably. Zhiyi initially favored the term chan in his writings but by his later writings preferred zhiguan, which he felt was more comprehensive than chan.[49] Within Sinitic Buddhism, the term guan also came to refer to specific practices. Writing a century after Zhiyi, both the famous seventh-century monastic traveler and translator Xuanzang and his disciple Kuiji used the term *guan* to refer to two kinds of practices. As Alan Sponberg writes, "The first involves a technique of eidetic visualization whereby one enters into a different level of existence. In contrast to that highly specific technique, the second practice involves a set of 'discernments' or 'contemplations' presenting successive steps by which one gains insight into the nature of existence as understood by the Yogacarins."[50] Both monks were proponents of Consciousness-Only thought, and the former was something of a rival to Fazang. Like Huayan, Consciousness-Only is not known for having a system of meditation, but Sponberg argues that it does contain exercises designed to change "the overall manner in which one views the world." Writing thirty years before Eifring, Sponberg also cautions against a narrow definition of meditation that focuses solely on transitory mental states. The goal of contemplation, as understood by Xuanzang and Kuiji, is "the realization of a distinctively Buddhist view of the world, toward a particular insight into the nature of existence."[51] In the same fashion, the Huayan tradition developed, transmitted, and expanded on its own methods of contemplation, which were presented in a stepwise fashion, revealing successive insights into the nature of reality as understood in that school. Although the texts that taught these insights lack the detail of Zhiyi's *Great Calming and Contemplation*, they nevertheless lay out a directive meditative structure, designed to lead the practitioner's mind "toward preset goals embedded in culturally determined webs of meaning," as Eifring puts it.

The Contemplation of the Dharmadhātu—the paradigm of Huayan meditation—leads the meditator through successive perspectives on the world. Beginning with the general Mahāyāna notion of emptiness, it invites contemplators to change their viewpoint by examining the nature of the relationship between phenomena and emptiness and then between phenomena themselves. The goal is the cultivation of an enlightened view of the world, which is none other than enlightenment itself. The *Method for Contemplation the Dharmadhātu*, in Sponberg's words, prescribes "a set of 'discernments' or 'contemplations' presenting successive steps by which one gains insight into the nature of existence." The text is short on specific details, such as how often one should undertake this practice or how long one should spend on the first contemplation before moving to the second, but it is likely that this form of contemplation was meant to be practiced with the guidance of a learned teacher, just as other forms of Buddhist meditation are. What is clear is that the text fulfills Eifring's definition of meditation as it describes "an attention-based technique" whose ultimate goal is the "inner transformation" of the practitioner. This transformation occurs by following the directive techniques laid out in the text, which "lead the mind ... toward preset goals embedded in culturally determined webs of meaning." In this case, the "culturally determined web of meaning" is the supreme vision of Huayan, which sees the entirety of phenomenal reality— the Dharmadhātu—as nothing more than a web of interconnecting relationships.

Huayan Meditation in the Monastic Curriculum

The Contemplation of the Dharmadhātu was a central feature of Xufa's two *Outlines*, which were studied widely in Huayan programs during the Republican period, but it was also included explicitly on its own within many program's curricula. It is listed by name as the program's meditative practice in the curricula of the Huayan University of Hankou, the Qingliang Institute, the Institute of the Xianshou School, and the Śūraṅgama Buddhist Institute. There is also a good chance that it was the system of meditation taught at the Huayan University of Yangzhou and the Dharmadhātu Institute in Fujian, where contemplation was prescribed but no specific system was named. As aspirational documents, program curricula can tell us only so much, but in a few cases we do have a record of what was actually being taught in the programs, and these records reinforce the importance of the Contemplation of the Dharmadhātu within the programs. The best example of this kind of evidence comes from the four issues of *Buddha's Light* (*Foguang*), produced at the Huayan University of Yangzhou.

The second, third, and fourth issues of *Buddha's Light* carried essays by students, many of which were answers to exam questions. In order to get some sense of how Huayan was being taught at the Huayan University of Yangzhou, these essays can be compared with the many articles by Keduan that also appeared in the journal, which often consisted of the notes or records of lectures he gave at the university. We find that Huayan meditation was a central focus in his students' studies. The second issue of *Buddha's Light*, published in June 1923, carried a section of Keduan's lectures on Chengguan's commentary on the Huayan Sutra. It also contained an article in which Keduan commented on the Tiantai understanding of the "three contemplations [*sanguan*]" as outlined by his master, Dixian. Keduan argued that the central tenet of Huayan is the idea of "universal inclusion [*zhoubian hanrong*]," which is a term derived from the Contemplation of the Dharmadhātu.[52] Throughout his essay, Keduan maintained an ecumenical position regarding the relative effectiveness of Tiantai and Huayan forms of meditation. This attitude clearly affected his students: two student essays in the same issue made roughly the same point, arguing that although the methods of Tiantai, Huayan, and Chan meditation differ, their goals are ultimately the same.[53]

Huayan meditation was one of the central topics of study for students at Keduan's university. The August issue of *Buddha's Light* began with another of his lectures on the topic.[54] This issue also featured two articles by students and twenty-two student exam essays. Both of the student articles dealt with the Contemplation of the Dharmadhātu, as did four of the exam essays. Among the students' writings, several authors invoked the Ten Profound Gates, which Chengguan used to explain the contemplation. Another student chose to cite the Four Dharmadhātu, and another made reference to the Perfect Teaching of the One Vehicle (*yisheng yuanjiao*). An additional five exam essays focused specifically on the idea of universal inclusion within the Contemplation. Other students wrote about studying Buddhism in general (five essays), the nature of the Perfect Teaching as outlined in both Huayan and Tiantai doctrinal classification (four essays), *nianfo* (two essays), and the origination of phenomena as described in the doctrine of Consciousness-Only (two essays).[55] The final issue of *Buddha's Light*, published in September 1923, included another ten student exam essays, covering roughly the same range of topics.[56]

From these essays, it is clear that by the end of their first year at the Huayan University of Yangzhou, students had begun to master basic Huayan concepts and had learned enough that they were able to formulate their own ways of linking these concepts to one another. In other words, it does not seem they were engaging in mere rote learning. Although the five exam essays on the Contemplation of the Dharmadhātu that appeared in issues three and four of *Buddha's Light* were written by classmates at the same university, each used different Huayan ideas to explain it. These students were clearly influenced by their teacher, Keduan, especially in their ecumenism, but it is also clear that there was some room for creativity within the curriculum. The students' scholastic study of Huayan meditation was bolstered by the fact that it was a regular part of the university's daily schedule, as it was at several other programs during the period.

* * *

Looking at the shared Huayan curriculum of the Republican period, the modern scholar might be surprised at the omission of Fazang's *Treatise on the Golden Lion*. That treatise is a clear and brief introduction to many of the core ideas of Huayan thought and is one of the writings most popularly associated with Fazang's legacy today. Yet it does not appear in the curricula of the various Huayan programs. One sees instead three elements regularly included in program syllabi. The first is the extended study of the Huayan Sutra using the commentaries of Chengguan and, to a lesser degree, Li Tongxuan. These sutra studies were coupled with training in classical Huayan doctrines of the Five Teachings, Six Characteristics, and Ten Profound Gates, which were accessed first using Xufa's summaries and then Fazang's *Treatise on the Five Teachings*. Finally, programs often included the specifically Huayan form of meditation known as the Contemplation of the Dharmadhātu, which was also studied using Xufa's texts. Even with the work Yang Wenhui and others had done in the late Qing to recover the rich resources of the Huayan textual tradition, the teaching and study of Huayan in the Republican period thus followed a traditional, tried-and-true model that had been common in China since the late-imperial period.

Since the Song dynasty, it has been widely accepted that the Contemplation of the Dharmadhātu is the very foundation of Huayan thought.[57] Commentary on the contemplation comprised a third of each of Xufa's popular Qing dynasty summaries of Huayan thought, and, as shown in this chapter, the Contemplation of the Dharmadhātu maintained a central place in the study of Huayan in the Republican period, either through the study of Xufa's summaries or through its practice as a form of meditation. In other words, the Contemplation of the Dharmadhātu is not just tangential to the Huayan tradition, it is fundamental, and the twentieth-century emphasis on teaching and practicing this contemplation represents a continuation of the Chinese Huayan tradition.

Conclusion

HUAYAN HAS PLAYED an integral but understudied role in Chinese Buddhist history. There are several reasons why it has received less scholarly attention than some other traditions, such as Chan and Pure Land, one being that as a polyvalent sign "Huayan" refers to a wide range of phenomena, which can make its identity difficult to pin down. Nevertheless, its influence is everywhere. If one looks deeply enough into any corner of the Chinese Buddhist tradition, one can find traces of Huayan. Passages from the Huayan Sutra appear all over, carved on columns in temples, in the calligraphy adorning the walls of Buddhists' studies, and in the daily services (*zaowanke* 早晚課) performed by monastics. Huayan teachings embed the Emei, Wutai, and Zhongnan mountain ranges in sacred geographies that call to earthly pilgrims. Pure Land devotees have embraced the Huayan Sutra's "Chapter on the Practice and Vows of Samantabhadra" as one of the key texts of their praxis, and many Chinese Buddhists use it as a guide to the Buddhist path. Huayan doctrine tries to unify competing strands of Yogācāra and Tathāgathgarbha thought, and it continues to serve as the philosophical foundation for Chan. Scholars often try to draw hard lines between these different manifestations of Huayan, but the Huayanist would contend that there is actually no obstruction between them because they are but different facets of the same unity.

CONCLUSION

The subtle and diffused existence of Huayan within Chinese Buddhism makes it difficult to grasp completely, but this diffusion does make it an excellent case for the study of modern Chinese Buddhism. Huayan itself teaches that we can understand an entire thing or situation simply by investigating one of its elements. The complete story of a lawn on a hillside can be understood by describing the causal network in which one blade of grass is embedded: to understand the presence of a single blade of grass, we must talk about sunlight and rainwater, flowers and seeds, earthworms, nitrogen, and erosion. In the same way, telling the story of the Huayan University network has been an opportunity to tell the whole story of twentieth-century Chinese Buddhism. The history presented here, that of the teaching and practice of Huayan, has touched on most of the important issues in the study of Buddhism in China and the Chinese diaspora during the twentieth century: varieties of lay and monastic practice; changing ideas about sect and lineage in China from the 1900s to the 1930s; the Buddhist press's recovery of lost scriptures in the late nineteenth century and its production of texts and periodicals in the 1920s and 1930s; the creation and development of networks of monastic education in the 1920s and 1930s; the effect of war on the fortunes of Buddhist institutions from the 1920s through the 1940s; the revival of Buddhism in the PRC after the Cultural Revolution; and the internationalization of Chinese Buddhism in the latter part of the twentieth century. All of these issues have been touched on here. In the midst of the great upheavals of the twentieth century, people tried to maintain the continuity of Chinese Buddhism, relying on texts and traditions from both its early days and the late-imperial period. If I have done my job, I have shown how Huayan was affected by all of these events and trends.

Spurred by a (misplaced) sense of the decadence of their tradition, Chinese Buddhists in the late nineteenth and early twentieth centuries emphasized the importance of reviving their tradition's lost schools through publication of each school's key texts and through educational initiatives. Huayan, which carried the prestige of its popular association—one could even say identity—with the Huayan Sutra, was one such school. It was explained and taught in introductory textbooks, journal articles, and public lectures, which presented the unified claim that the Huayan Sutra was taught first by the Buddha and contains his highest teachings. These teachings were then explained in the Huayan School, a school founded in China in the Sui and Tang dynasties by five patriarchs who organized them by means of the Contemplation of the Dharmadhātu and the doctrines of the Five Teachings, the Six Characteristics, and the Ten Profound Gates. The Huayan Sutra, the king of sutras, was also the subject of much devotional activity by monastics and laity alike. Huayan, as both a school and a sutra, was chosen as the focus for a number of monastic educational programs started during the Republican period.

I suspect one of the reasons why Huayan, Tiantai, and Yogācāra were chosen so often to serve as the central subjects in these programs' curricula is that these traditions are highly teachable. This is not to say that they are easy to understand, far from it, but each of these three traditions contains enough richness and complexity of thought to support a lifetime of study by the philosophically inclined. Although one might study the intricacies of monastic regulations in one of the traditional Vinaya Halls, the most complex modes of thought of Chinese Buddhism are found in the analytical convolutions of Yogācāra, the endless retreat from determinacy offered in Tiantai, and the vast, holographic imagination of Huayan. Chinese Buddhists claim that the Huayan Sutra contains all of the teachings of Buddhism. Indeed, this sutra does touch on all of the important teachings of Mahāyāna, including the nature of reality, the majesty of the Pure Lands, the importance of faith, and the practices and stages that make up the path to enlightenment. It also offers the basis for the reconciliation of Tatāgathagarbha and emptiness thought that the Huayan patriarchs read into it later. A lecture series on the full Huayan Sutra is thus a course in the entirety of Mahāyāna Buddhism. And because the sutra was rarely studied without the guidance of Chengguan and Fazang's writings, it also allowed lecturers to discuss the *Awakening of Faith*, whose doctrines are central to East Asian Buddhism. Educational programs centered on the Huayan Sutra, such as those offered by the Huayan University and the programs it inspired, were thus courses in the totality of Chinese Buddhism. The students who matriculated through these programs would have been exposed to all of the major ideas of the Chinese Buddhist tradition.

The graduating class of the original Huayan University established and ran a number of Huayan-centered educational programs during the Republican period, and their educational heirs continue this legacy today. Although their programs were not unified by a single curriculum, they did share some similarities in their approaches to teaching about Huayan. The activities and identities of the graduates of the first Huayan University were unified in some ways, but they did not constitute a new Huayan School. The Huayan University network was neither a sectarian movement nor a traditional monastic lineage; instead, it is a clear example of a modern form of monastic affiliation. Graduates and their students formed a cooperative network characterized by horizontal relationships and founded on their shared experience at the university. Through their work, they also contributed to the posthumous elevation of Yuexia to a position of religious authority within modern Chinese Buddhism. From the Republic of China to the present, historians as well as monastic teachers of Huayan cite Yuexia as the originator of authoritative knowledge about Huayan for the modern period. Although not a religious lineage of the type found in Chan, monastics in this network continue to trace themselves back through educational relationships to Yuexia in order to invoke and assume some of his authority, and both his and the original Huayan University's influence are still felt today.

List of Chinese Characters

Aili	愛麗
Aiting	藹亭
Anfeng	安豐
Anhui Seng Xuexiao	安徽僧學校
Anyang Jingshe	安養精舍
Baifa mingmen lun	百法明門論
Bailin Jiaoliyuan	柏林教理院
Baohuashan	寶華山
Baotong	寶通
Bashi guiju song	八識規矩頌
bazong	八宗
benke	本科
biejiao yisheng	別教一乘
biexiang	別相
biguan	閉關
Bishan	碧山
Cangsheng Mingzhi Daxue	倉聖明智大學
Caodong	曹洞
Cao Songqiao	曹崧喬
Caotangshan Da Huayansi	草堂山大華嚴寺
chan	禪
Changguan	常觀

LIST OF CHINESE CHARACTERS

Changsheng	長生
Changshu	常熟
Changshui Zixuan	長水子璿
Changxing	常惺
Chanzong	禪宗
Che'gwan	諦觀
Chengguan	澄觀
Chengkong	乘空
Chengqian	承遷
Chengshizong	成實宗
chengxiang	成相
Chen Yuanbai	陳元白
Chinul	知訥
Chisong	持松
Ch'oe Ch'i-wŏn	崔致遠
chuxue	初學
Cienzong	慈恩宗
Ciji	慈濟
Ciyun	慈雲
Cizhou	慈舟
conglin	叢林
Dafang guangfo huayanjing zhushu jiyao	大方廣佛華嚴經著述集要
Da foxuebao	大佛學報
Dajue	大覺
Daopei	道霈
dasheng	大乘
Dasheng qixinlun	大乘起信論
dasheng shijiao	大乘始教
dasheng zhongjiao	大乘終教
Daxi	大溪
daxue	大學
daxue zhangcheng	大學章程
Dazong dixuan wenben lun	大宗地玄文本論
dazuo	大座
Dejun	德竣

Di Chuqing	狄楚青
Dilunzong	地論宗
Dinghui	定慧
Dixian	諦閑
Dongnan Yihu	東南義虎
Dongzhimen	東直門
Doushuo	兜率
duilian	對聯
Du Jiwen	杜繼文
dunjiao	頓教
Dushun	杜順
Fafang	法舫
Fahai	法海
fajieguan	法界觀
Fajie guanmen	法界觀門
Fajie wuchabie lunshu	法界無差別論疏
fajiexing	法界性
Fajie Xueyuan	法界學苑 or 法界學院
Fajie Xueyuan Tongxue Pini Cejinhui	法界學院同學毗尼策進會
Fajie Xueyuan xuesheng	法界學苑學生
fajie yuanqi	法界緣起
fakongguan	法空觀
Fan Gunong	范古農
Fanwang Jing	梵網經
Faqi	法起
Faren	法忍
Fashun	法順
faxi	法系
faxiang	法相
Faxiang Daxue	法相大學
Faxiangzong	法相宗
faxing	法性
Faxingzong	法性宗
fei zongjiao	非宗教
Foguang	佛光

LIST OF CHINESE CHARACTERS

Foguangshan	佛光山
Fohua xin qingnian	佛化新青年
Fojiao chuxue keben	佛教初學課本
Fojiao gezong dayi	佛教各宗大意
Fojiao zhi sheng	佛教之聲
fotu	佛土
Foxue congbao	佛學叢報
Foxue Shuju	佛學書局
Foxue xiao congshu	佛學小叢書
"Foxue zhi zongpai"	佛學之宗派
Fozu tongji	佛祖統紀
Fu Jinqiu	傅近秋
gang	綱
gangyao	綱要
Gaomin	高旻
guan	觀
Guanfu	觀復
Guanghui	廣慧
Guangxiao Foxueyuan	光孝佛學院
guangxia zizai wuai	廣狹自在無礙
Guangxu	光緒
Guanyin Tang	觀音堂
Guanzong	觀宗
Guanzong Yanjiu She	觀宗研學社
Gui Bohua	桂伯華
Guoqin (Guo Cheen)	果琴
guoxue	國學
Gu	鼓
Gushan Foxueyuan	鼓山佛學
Gyōnen	凝然
Haichao	海潮
Haichao yin	海潮音
haiyin sanmei	海印三昧
Haiyun	海雲
Han Qingjing	韓清淨

LIST OF CHINESE CHARACTERS

Hanshan Deqing	憨山德清
Hasshū kōyō	八宗綱要
He Dong Lianjue	何東蓮覺
Hiei	比叡
hoa nghiêm	華嚴
Hongyi	弘一
huaixiang	壞相
Huang Chanhua	黃懺華
Huayan	華嚴
Huayan'an	華嚴庵
Huayan Dache Tang	華嚴大徹堂
Huayan Daxue	華嚴大學
Huayan Daxue Yuke	華嚴大學預科
Huayan foqi	華嚴佛七
Huayanhui	華嚴會
Huayan jiaoyi	華嚴教義
Huayanjing helun	華嚴經合論
Huayanjing jin shizi zhang zhu	華嚴經金師子章註
Huayanjing kongmu zhang	華嚴經孔目章
Huayan Jingshe	華嚴精舍
Huayanjingxue	華嚴經學
Huayanjing yihai baimen	華嚴經義海百門
Huayanjing yu Huayanzong	華嚴經與華嚴宗
Huayanjing zhuanji	華嚴經傳記
Huayan Lianshe	華嚴蓮社
Huayan nianfo sanmei lun	華嚴念佛三昧論
Huayan Shifan Xueyuan	華嚴師範學院
Huayan shuchao	華嚴疏鈔
Huayan Shuchao Bianyin Hui	華嚴疏鈔編印會
Huayan shuchao xuantan	華嚴疏鈔懸談
Huayan Xueyuan	華嚴學院
Huayan Yanjiushe	華嚴研究社
Huayan yuanren lun	華嚴原人論
Huayan Zhuanzong Xueyuan	華嚴專宗學院
Huayanzong	華嚴宗

LIST OF CHINESE CHARACTERS

Huayanzong jianlun	華嚴宗簡論
"Huayanzong jiaoyi lüeshuo"	華嚴宗教義略說
Huayanzongxue	華嚴宗學
Huiguang	慧光
Huijiang	慧江
Huiting	蕙庭
Huiyin Si	慧因
Huiyuan	慧苑
Huizong	惠宗
Huxin	湖心
Jiangdu Fojiao Zhuanxisuo	江都佛教傳習所
Jiangnan	江南
Jiangsu Seng Shifan Xuetang	江蘇僧師範學堂
Jiang Weiqiao	蔣維喬
Jiang Yiyuan	江易園
jianzhang	簡章
Jiao	焦
Jiaoguan gangzong	教觀綱宗
jiaomen	教門
Jiaoshan Foxue Tushuguan	焦山佛學圖書館
Jiaoshan Foxueyuan	焦山佛學院
jiazu	甲組
Jichan	寄禪
Jiechen	戒塵
Jiede	戒德
Ji Juemi	姬覺彌
Jimeng	繼夢
jin	晉
Ji'nan	濟南
Jingbo	靜波
Jingchan	淨禪
Jinghai	淨海
Jingjie	淨戒
Jingkong	淨空
Jinglian	淨蓮

LIST OF CHINESE CHARACTERS

jingwang	經王
"Jingxing pin"	淨行品
Jingyan	靜嚴
Jingying Huiyuan	淨影慧遠
jingzhong zhi wang	經中之王
Jinling Kejingchu	金陵刻經處
Jinshan	金山
Jinshui Jingyuan	晉水淨源
Jiqing	際清
Jiulianan	九蓮庵
jiu shixuan	舊十玄
Jiyang	暨陽
Jizu	雞足
Juemin	覺民
Jueshe congshu	覺社叢書
Jueshi Shuju Wenju She	覺世書局文具社
kaiti	楷體
Kang Youwei	康有為
Keduan	可端
Kefa	可法
kegon kanpō	華嚴觀法
Kegon kyōgaku	華嚴教學
Kegonshū yogi	華嚴宗要義
kong	空
Kuanrong	寬融
Kuiji	窺基
Lengding	楞定
Lengyan Foxueyuan	楞嚴佛學院
Li'an	栗庵
Liang Qichao	梁啟超
Lianxi	蓮溪
Liaochen	了塵
Liaozhong	了中
li fajie	理法界
Lingyuan	靈源

LIST OF CHINESE CHARACTERS

Linji	臨濟
lishi wuai guan	理事無礙觀
Li Tongxuan	李通玄
Liu Shipei	劉師培
liuxiang	六相
Liu Xianliang	劉顯亮
liuzong	六宗
Li Yinchen	李隱塵
Li Yuanjing	李圓淨
Li Zikuan	李子寬
Longhua Fojiaoshe	龍華佛教社
Long zangjing	龍藏經
Lu	廬
lüe	略
Luo Jialing	羅迦陵
Lüzong	律宗
Mei Guangxi	梅光羲
Meiguo Huayan Lianshe	美國華嚴蓮社
men	門
Miaofa	妙法
Mii-dera	御井寺
mimi yinxian jucheng	秘密隱顯俱成
Mingyuan	明源
Minnan Foxueyuan	閩南佛學院
mixin	迷信
Mo'an	默庵
Muxi	幕西
Myōe	明惠
Nanjing Fojiao Jingyeshe	南京佛教淨業社
Nanjing Huayanhui	南京華嚴會
Nanjō Bunyū	南條文雄
Nanting	南亭
nianfo	念佛
Oda Tokunō	識田德能
Ouyang Jingwu	歐陽竟無

panjiao	叛教
Peng Shaosheng	彭紹升
pianzuo	偏座
pianzuo fashi	偏座法師
Pilushe'na	毘盧舍那
Puji	普濟
Pushou	普壽
Puti	普提
Putuoshan	普陀山
"Puxian xingyuan pin"	普賢行願品
Qingliang	清涼
Qingliang Xueyuan	清涼學院
renkongguan	人空觀
Renshan	仁山
rentianjiao	人天教
ri	日
rumen	入門
Sakaino Kōyō	境野黃洋
sangoku	三國
Sangoku Bukkyō ryakushi	三國佛教略史
sanguan	三觀
sansheng	三乘
Sansheng yuanrong guanmen	三聖圓融觀門
sanshi	三時
Sanshi Xuehui	三時學會
sanxing	三性
se	色
Shandao	善導
Shanghai Lianshe	上海蓮社
Shaodian	少顛
sheli	舍利
Shengyan (Sheng Yen)	聖嚴
Shengyi	聖譯
shi	史
"Shidi pin"	十地品

LIST OF CHINESE CHARACTERS

shi fajie	事法界
shifang conglin	十方叢林
Shijie Fojiao Jushilin	世界佛教居士林
Shijie Fojiao Lianhehui	世界佛教聯合會
Shijie Foxueyuan Tushuguan	世界佛學苑圖書館
Shilin	士林
Shimaji Mokurai	島地磨雷
Shina Bukkyō shikō	支那佛教史綱
Shipu	十普
Shiqing	實清
shishi wuai	事事無礙
shishi wuai fajie	事事無礙法界
"Shishi xuetang neiban kecheng"	釋氏學堂內班課程
shixuanmen	十玄門
shiyi	十儀
Shi Yiru	史一如
shizong	十宗
"Shizong lüeshuo"	十宗略說
Shoupa Hutong	手帕胡同
Shouye	壽冶
shu	疏 (commentary)
shū	宗 (school or sect)
shūhai	宗派
sifajie	四法界
Sihong Xueyuan	四弘學院
Sui	隨
Su Manshu	蘇曼殊
Sun Liren	孫立人
Sun Yuyun	孫毓筠
Su Zhouchen	蘇宙忱
Tai	泰
Taixu	太虛
Tang Dayuan	唐大圓
Tang dynasty	唐代
Tang Yongtong	湯用彤

LIST OF CHINESE CHARACTERS

Tanxu	倓虛
tian	田
Tianjin Fojiao Gongdelin	天津佛教功德林
Tianning	天寧
Tiantai	天台
Tiantai sijiao yi	天台四教儀
Tiantong	天童
Tikong	體空
tongjiao yisheng	同教一乘
tongshi	通史
tongxiang	同相
Tung Lin Kok Yuen	東蓮覺苑
Ui Hakuju	宇井伯壽
Wanfo Shengcheng	萬佛聖城
Wang Guowei	王國維
Wang Senfu	王森甫
Weicheng	葦乘
Weifang	葦舫
weishi	唯識
Wenxi	文希
wuai	無礙
Wuchang Foxueyuan	武昌佛學院
wujiao	五教
Wujiao zhang	五教章
wuxiang	無相
Wuyunguan	五蘊觀
Wu Zetian	武則天
Xiandai sengqie	現代僧伽
Xiandu	賢度
Xiangrui	祥瑞
Xianshou chuandeng lu	賢首傳燈錄
Xianshou Fazang	賢首法藏
Xianshou wujiao yi	賢首五教儀
Xianshou wujiaoyi *kaimeng*	賢首五教儀開蒙
Xianshouzong Xueyuan	賢首宗學院

LIST OF CHINESE CHARACTERS

Xianyin	顯蔭
Xianyue	現月
xiaosheng	小乘
xiaoshengjiao	小乘教
Xiao Weisheng	蕭唯昇
Xiaozaogou	小棗溝
Xiding	習定
Xilai	西來
Xin Fohua Qingniantuan	新佛化青年團
xingbu	行布
Xingche	性徹
Xingfu	興福
xingju	性具
Xinglian	性蓮
xingqi	性起
xingqi guan	性起觀
Xingyun (Hsing Yun)	星雲
Xinhai	辛亥
Xinmin Zhongxuexiao	新民中學校
Xinsheng	新生
xin shixuan	新十玄
Xinyan	心巖
xiucai	秀才
Xiu huayan aozhi wanjing huanyuan guan	修華嚴奧旨妄盡還源觀
Xuanhua (Hsuan Hua)	宣化
xuanlun	玄論
xuanshu	玄疏
xuantan	懸談 or 玄談
xuanyi	玄義
Xuanzang	玄奘
Xuefan	雪煩
xueseng	學僧
xueyuan	學苑 or 學院
Xufa	續法
Xu Weiru	徐蔚如

LIST OF CHINESE CHARACTERS

Xuyun	虛雲
Yancheng	鹽城
Yang Wenhui	楊文會
Yangzhou Huayan Daxue	揚州華嚴大學
Yekai	冶開
Yihe	義和
Yijiaojing	遺教經
Yincun	印存
Yingci	應慈
Yinguang	印光
yinguo	因果
yiqie ji yi, yi ji yiqie	一切即一, 一即一切
yisheng yuanjiao	一乘圓教
yixiang	異相
yi xiang ru duo	一相入多
yi zhong yi, yiqie zhong yi, yi zhong yiqie, yiqie zhong yiqie	一中一, 一切中一, 一中一切, 一切中一切
yizu	乙組
Yongqing	永慶
Yongquan	湧泉
youjiao wuguan	有教無觀
youyi	遊意
Youzheng	有正
Youzheng Shuju	有正書局
Yu	虞
yuan	圓
Yuanjue Jing	圓覺經
yuanqi	緣起
yuanqi guan	緣起觀
yuanrong	圓融
Yuan Shikai	袁世凱
Yuexia	月霞
Yufo	玉佛
yuke	預科
Yunüfeng	玉女峰

LIST OF CHINESE CHARACTERS

Yuzhu	玉柱
zaowanke	早晚課
zhangcheng	章程
Zhang Qingyang	張清揚
Zhang Taiyan	章太炎
Zhanshansi Foxueyuan	湛山寺佛學院
Zhenchan	真禪
Zhengdao	正道
zhengke	正科
Zhengyan (Cheng Yen)	證嚴
Zhenhua	振華 or 震華
Zhenhua (Chen-hua)	真華
zhenkong guan	眞空觀
zhi	止
zhiguan	止觀
Zhiguang	智光
Zhihuan Jingshe	祇洹精舍
Zhina Neixueyuan	支那内學院
Zhiyan	智儼
Zhiyi	智顗
Zhongguo Fojiaohui	中國佛教會
Zhongguo Fojiao Xiehui	中國佛教協會
Zhongguo Foxueyuan	中國佛學院
Zhongnan	終南
zhoubian hanrong guan	周遍含容觀
Zhou Guoren	周果仁
Zhou Shujia	周叔迦
Zhou Xuande	周宣德
zhuanke	專科
zhuban yuanming jude	主伴圓明具德
Zhuji	諸暨
zhujiang	主講
zhuke	主課
Zhulin	竹林
Zhulin Foxueyuan	竹林佛學院

LIST OF CHINESE CHARACTERS

zili lita	自利利他
zisun miao	子孫廟
Zixuan	子璿
zong	宗
Zongjiao Shiwu Ju	宗教事務局
Zongliang	宗量
zongmen	宗門
zongxiang	總相
Zongyang	宗仰
zongyao	宗要
zongzhi	宗旨

Notes

Preface

1. Ōtake Susumu, "On the Origin and Early Development of the Buddhāvataṃsaka-sutra," in *Reflecting Mirrors: Perspectives on Huayan Buddhism*, ed. Imre Hamar (Wisebaden: Harrassowitz, 2007), 87–107.
2. George J. Tanabe, *Myoe the Dreamkeeper: Fantasy and Knowledge in Early Kamakura Buddhism* (Cambridge, MA: Harvard University Press, 1992), 216–217 n. 23.

Introduction

1. Stefania Travagnin, "Buddhist Education Between Tradition, Modernity, and Alternative Networks: Reconsidering the 'Revival' of Education for the Sangha," *Studies in Chinese Religion* 3, no. 3 (November 2017): 220–241.
2. For the case of Korea, see Richard McBride, *Domesticating the Dharma: Buddhist Cults and the Hwaom Synthesis in Silla Korea* (Honolulu: University of Hawai'i Press, 2007); and for China, see Chen Jinhua, *Philosopher, Practitioner, Politician: The Many Lives of Fazang (643-712)* (Leiden: Brill, 2007).
3. Jason Ananda Josephson, *The Invention of Religion in Japan* (Chicago: University of Chicago Press, 2012).
4. Chan Sin-wai, *Buddhism in Late Ch'ing Political Thought* (Hong Kong: Chinese University Press, 1985), 77–92, 148–149; Mori Noriko, "Liang

Qichao, Late-Qing Buddhism, and Modern Japan," in *The Role of Japan in Liang Qichao's Introduction of Modern Western Civilization to China*, ed. Joshua A. Fogel (Berkeley: University of California Press, 2004), 222–246. Yao Binbin says that the noted Chinese scholar Du Jiwen 杜繼文 also made the same argument (Yao Binbin 姚彬彬, *Xiandai wenhua sichao yu zhongguo foxue de zhuanxing* 現代文化思潮與中國佛學的轉型 [Modern cultural thought and the transformation of Chinese Buddhist studies] [Beijing: Zongjiao Wenhua, 2015], 172–174).

5. For example, scholars of the history of Huayan regularly argue both that there was very little creativity in Huayan during the Qing dynasty *and* that monks such as Xufa, who wrote new works on Huayan thought, misunderstood the tradition. For example, see Chen Bing 陳兵 and Deng Zimei 鄧子美, *Ershi shiji zhongguo fojiao* 二十世紀中國佛教 (Twentieth-century Chinese Buddhism) (Beijing: Renmin, 2000), 76. Even Yang Wenhui displayed this attitude. See Yang Wenhui 楊文會, "*Xianshou faji* xu 賢首法集敘" (Preface to the *Xianshou Dharma Collection*), in *Yang Renshan quanji* 楊仁山全集 (Complete works of Yang Renshan) (Anhui: Huangshan, 2000), 378–379.

6. For example, Bo Jing 鈤淨, "Ershi shiji de huyanxue yanjiu 20世紀的華嚴學研究" (Twentieth-century Huayan research), *Foxue yanjiu* 佛學研究 1, no. 1 (2005): 363–381. Like other scholars, Bo discusses the roles played by Yang Wenhui and Yuexia, but he also examines the connections that were drawn between Huayan thought and Marxism in mainland China and between Huayan and Western philosophy in Taiwan. Even he cannot avoid concluding by stating that the study of Huayan among Chinese thinkers continues to lag behind study of it in Japan.

7. Holmes Welch, *The Buddhist Revival in China* (Cambridge, MA: Harvard University Press, 1968), 99, 115.

8. Shi Dongchu 釋東初, *Zhongguo fojiao jindai shi* 中國佛教近代史 (A history of early contemporary Chinese Buddhism), vols. 1 and 2 of *Dongchu laoren quanji* 東初老人全集 (Collected works of Venerable Dongchu) (Taipei: Dongchu, 1974).

9. Chen and Deng, *Ershi shiji zhongguo fojiao*, 394–399, 406–407.

10. Yao, *Xiandai wenhua sichao yu zhongguo foxue de zhuanxing*, 193.

11. Erik Hammerstrom, "Avataṃsaka 華嚴 Transnationalism in Modern Sinitic Buddhism," *Journal of Global Buddhism* 17 (2016): 65–84.

12. King Pong Chiu, *Thomé H. Fang, Tang Junyi, and Huayan Thought: A Confucian Appropriation of Buddhist Ideas in Response to Scientism in the Twentieth Century* (Leiden: Brill, 2016).

13. Welch, *The Buddhist Revival in China*, 199–200.

14. Gregory Adam Scott, "The Publishing of Buddhist Books for Beginners in Modern China from Yang Wenhui to Master Sheng Yen," *Shengyan yanjiu* 聖嚴研究 5 (2014): 53.
15. Jan Kiely, "Spreading the Dharma with the Mechanized Press: New Buddhist Print Culture in the Modern Chinese Print Revolution, 1866–1949," in *From Woodblocks to the Internet: Chinese Publishing and Print Culture in Transition, Circa 1800 to 2008*, ed. Cynthia Brokaw and Christopher Bell (Leiden: Brill, 2010), 197.
16. Changxing 常惺, "Xianshou gailun 賢首概論" (Introduction to the Xianshou [School]) (1929), reprinted in *Huayan wenhui* 華嚴文匯 (Collected writings on Huayan), 2 vols., ed. Fan Guanlan 范觀瀾 (Beijing: Zongjiao Wenhua, 2007), 1:33–58; Nanting 南亭, "Huayanzong shilüe 華嚴宗史略" (Brief history of the Huayan School)" (1959), reprinted in *Huayan wenhui*, ed. Fan, 1:242–270.
17. Gong Jun 龔雋, "Minguo shiqi foxue tongshi de shuxie 民國時期佛學通史的書寫" (The writing of comprehensive Buddhist histories in the Republican period), *Shijie zongjiao yanjiu* 世界宗教研究 6 (2013): 1–8.
18. The works of Sakaino Kōyō 境野黃洋 (1871–1933) had a particularly large impact, especially *Shina Bukkyō shikō* 支那佛教史綱 (Outline of Chinese Buddhist history) (Tokyo: Morie Shoten, 1907), which was widely disseminated in China after Jiang Weiqiao translated and published it in 1929, with a few updates and under his own name, as *Zhongguo fojiao shi* 中國佛教史 (A history of Chinese Buddhism) (1929; reprint, Shanghai: Guji, 2004). Other works by Sakaino include *Indo Shina Bukkyō shikō* 印度支那佛教史綱 (Outline of Indian and Chinese Buddhist history) (Tokyo: Komeisha, 1907) and *Shina no Bukkyō* 支那の佛教 (Chinese Buddhism) (Tokyo: Heigo Shuppansha, 1918). Jiang's book went through several printings, as did two general histories derived from Japanese works by Huang Chanhua, *Fojiao gezong dayi* 佛教各宗大意 (Major ideas of the Buddhist sects) (n.p.: n.p., 1930) and *Zhongguo fojiao shi* 中國佛教史 (A history of Chinese Buddhism) (1940; reprint, Shanghai: Commercial Press, 1947).
19. For example, the essay "Brief Discussion of the Teachings of the Huayan School" (1936) by the lay Buddhist scholar Mei Guangxi is little more than a summary of the Huayan section of Huang Chanhua's *Fojiao gezong dayi*. See Mei Guangxi 梅光羲, "Huayanzong jiaoyi lüeshuo 華嚴宗教義略說" (Brief discussion of the teachings of the Huayan School), *HCY* 17, no. 5 (May 15, 1936): 22–31, MFQ 193:358–367.
20. The full name of this text is *Huayan yisheng jiaoyi fenqi zhang* 華嚴一乘教義分齊章 (Treatise Distinguishing the Teachings of the One Vehicle of the Huayan), CBETA, T 1866.

1. Huayan as a School of Chinese Buddhism

1. As is standard practice, I use modern Mandarin pronunciations throughout this book. The term *Huayan* is pronounced differently in the other standardized modern languages of East Asia: Japanese *kegon*, Korean *hwaŏm*, Vietnamese *hoa nghiêm*.
2. "Flower Adornment 華嚴," in *Digital Dictionary of Buddhism*, ed. A. Charles Muller, entry updated May 2, 2008, http://www.buddhism-dict.net/cgi-bin/xpr-ddb.pl?q=%E8%8F%AF%E5%9A%B4.
3. Kimura Kiyotaka 木村清孝, *Chūgoku kegon shisōshi* 中國華嚴思想史 (A history of Chinese Huayan thought) (Kyoto: Heirakuji, 1992), 11–14; Wei Daoru 魏道儒, *Zhongguo huayanzong tongshi* 中國華嚴宗通史 (Comprehensive history of the Chinese Huayan School) (Nanjing: Jiangsu guji, 2001), 1–23.
4. Wei, *Zhongguo huayanzong tongshi*, 27–37.
5. Du Jiwen 杜繼文, "Huayanzong xingcheng de sixiang yuanyuan yu shehui beijing 華嚴宗形成的思想淵源與社會背景" (The intellectual origins and social background for the formation of the Huayan School), in *Kegongaku ronshū* 華嚴學論集 (Collected writings in Kegon studies), ed. Kamata Shigeo 鎌田茂雄 (Tokyo: Daizō Shuppan, 1997), 1265–1278. Both Kimura Kiyotaka 木村清孝 and Wei Daoru 魏道儒 refer to the study and exegesis of the Huayan Sutra as "Huayan Sutra studies [Huayanjingxue 華嚴經學]." Kimura calls the teachers and teachings of the Huayan School "Huayan doctrine studies [*Kegon kyōgaku* 華嚴教學]" (Kimura, *Chūgoku kegon shisōshi*), and Wei calls them "Huayan School studies [Huayanzongxue 華嚴宗學]" (Wei, *Zhongguo huayanzong tongshi*).
6. Yang Wenhui, "*Xianshou faji* xu 賢首法集敘" (Preface to the *Xianshou Dharma Collection*), in *Yang Renshan quanji* 楊仁山全集 (Complete works of Yang Renshan) (Anhui: Huangshan, 2000), 378–379.
7. Wang Song 王頌, "Cong Riben Huayanzong de liang da paibie fanguan Zhongguo Huayan sixiangshi 從日本華嚴宗的兩大派別反觀中國華嚴思想史" (The intellectual history of Chinese Huayan as viewed from the perspective of the two major sects of Japanese Kegon), *Shijie zongjiao yanjiu* 世界宗教研究 4 (2005): 11–12.
8. Yang Wenhui used both names for the school in "Shizong lüeshuo 十宗略說" ([Brief explanation of the ten schools], in *Yang Renshan quanji*, 149–156) but used only the name "Xianshou School" in *Fojiao chuxue keben* 佛教初學課本 ([A primer on Buddhism], in *Yang Renshan quanji*, 101–145) and in his preface to the reprint collection of Fazang's writings. See also *Hasshū kōyō* 八宗綱要 (Essentials of the Eight Sects), written by Gyōnen 凝然 in 1268, and *Fozu tongji* 佛祖通記 (Chronicle of the Buddhist Patriarchs). Written by Zhipan 志磐 in 1269, CBETA, T 2035.

1. HUAYAN AS A SCHOOL OF CHINESE BUDDHISM

9. These exceptions are Jiang Weiqiao's *Zhongguo fojiao shi* 中國佛教史 (A history of Chinese Buddhism) (1929; reprint, Shanghai: Guji, 2004), which does not mention the patriarchs, and Sakaino Kōyō's *Shina Bukkyō shikō* 支那佛教史綱 (Outline of Chinese Buddhist history) (Tokyo: Morie Shoten, 1907), which mentions only the first three (242–255).
10. For both Dushun and Zhiyan, the best English study remains Robert Gimello, "Chih-Yen (602–668) and the Foundations of Hua-yen Buddhism," Ph.D. diss., Columbia University, 1976. For Fazang, one should consult Francis Cook, "Fa-Tsang's *Treatise on the Five Doctrines*: An Annotated Translation," Ph.D. diss., University of Wisconsin, 1970, and Chen Jinhua, *Philosopher, Practitioner, Politician: The Many Lives of Fazang (643–712)* (Leiden: Brill, 2007). For a complete critical biography of Chengguan, see Imre Hamar, *A Religious Leader in the Tang: Chengguan's Biography* (Tokyo: International Institute for Buddhist Studies, International College for Advanced Buddhist Studies, 2002). Finally, the life and thought of Zongmi are treated in detail in Peter Gregory, *Tsung-mi and the Sinification of Buddhism* (1991; reprint, Honolulu: University of Hawai'i Press, 2002).
11. Wang Song 王頌, *Songdai huayan sixiang yanjiu* 宋代華嚴思想研究 (Research on Song dynasty Huayan thought) (Beijing: Zongjiao Wenhua, 2008), 34–40.
12. *Fozu tongji*, CBETA, T 2035.294a23–28.
13. Gimello, "Chih-Yen," 64–67; Wang, *Songdai huayan sixiang yanjiu*, 112. Reflecting an alternate perspective, Kimura Kiyotaka leaves open the possibility that Dushun did contribute to the origins of Huayan as Jingyuan argued (*Chūgoku kegon shisōshi*, 81).
14. Shimaji Mokurai 島地磨雷 and Oda Tokunō 識田德能, *Sangoku Bukkyō ryakushi* 三國佛教略史 (A brief history of Buddhism of the Three Nations), 2 vols. (Tokyo: Kōmeisha, 1890). This text is discussed in greater detail in chapter 5.
15. Guo Cheen, *Translating Totality in Parts: Chengguan's Commentaries and Subcommentaries to the Avataṃsaka Sutra* (Lanham, MD: University Press of America, 2014), 1–2.
16. Imre Hamar, "Creating Huayan Lineage: Miraculous Stories About the Avataṃsaka-sūtra," *Oriens Extremus* 50 (2011): 181–192.
17. *Huayanjing zhuanji* 華嚴經傳記 (Record of the Transmission of the Huayan Sutra), written by Fazang 法藏, CBETA, T 2073.
18. Hamar, "Creating Huayan Lineage," 183–185.
19. Fan Gunong 范古農, "Shanghai Lianshe Huayan fahui yuanqi 上海蓮社華嚴法會緣起" (On the origin of the Shanghai Lotus Society's Huayan Assembly), *HCY* 11, no.1 (January 1930): n.p., *MFQ* 174:439.
20. "Nanjing Fojiao Jingyeshe lisong Huayanjing quanbu 南京佛教淨業社禮誦華嚴經全部" (The Nanjing Buddhist Pure Karma Society to bow to

1. HUAYAN AS A SCHOOL OF CHINESE BUDDHISM

and recite the entire Huayan Sutra), *Foxue banyuekan* 佛學半月刊 134 (September 1, 1936): 18, *MFQ* 53:20.
21. John Kieschnick, *The Impact of Buddhism on Chinese Material Culture* (Princeton, NJ: Princeton University Press, 2003), 176.
22. Holmes Welch, *The Practice of Chinese Buddhism, 1900–1950* (Cambridge, MA: Harvard University Press, 1967), 321–322.
23. Changguan started his period of retreat at the town's Guanyin Hall (Guanyin Tang 觀音堂), but after soldiers and workmen temporarily commandeered the hall, he used a room in the New People's Middle School (Xinmin Zhongxuexiao 新民中學校), where he had worked prior to his ordination ("Changguan fashi fenbai Huayanjing 常觀師焚拜華嚴經" [Venerable Changguan burns incense and bows to the Huayan Sutra], *Shanxi fojiao zazhi* 山西佛教雜志 1, no. 11 [November 15, 1934]: 69, *MFQ* 140:319).
24. Lin Yuanfan 林遠凡, "Xiding heshang biguan bai Huayanjing wei ge yi song 習定和尚閉關拜華嚴經爲偈以送" (Verse of praise sent to Monk Xiding, who is bowing to the Huayan Sutra in confinement), *Fojiao jushilin tekan* 佛教居士林特刊 42–43 (April 15, 1937): 9, *MFQ* 65:501.
25. Wang, *Songdai huayan sixiang yanjiu*, 8.
26. Raoul Birnbaum, "Master Hongyi Looks Back: A Modern Man Becomes a Monk in Twentieth-Century China," in *Buddhism in the Modern World: Adaptations of an Ancient Tradition*, ed. Steven Heine and Charles Prebish (Oxford: Oxford University Press, 2003), 110–111.
27. Mo'an 默庵, "Shaodian shangren shu Huayanjing xu 少顛上人書華嚴經敘" (Preface to the Huayan Sutra copied by Elder Shaodian), *HCY* 4, no. 2 (April 5, 1923): 1, *MFQ* 155:431.
28. Wang Xiaoxu 王小徐, "Su Zhouchen jushi xie Huayanjing ba 蘇宙忱居士寫華嚴經跋" (Postscript to Huayan Sutra copied by layman Su Zhouchen), *Foxue banyuekan* 佛學半月刊 130 (July 1, 1937): 11, *MFQ* 52:385. For more information on Wang Xiaoxu, see Erik Hammerstrom, "Science and Buddhist Modernism in Early 20th Century China: The Life and Works of Wang Xiaoxu 王小徐," *Journal of Chinese Religion* 39 ([2011] 2012): 1–32.
29. Cao Songqiao 曹崧喬, "Jingshu Dafang Guangfo Huayanjing zhengqiu baqi 敬書大方廣佛華嚴經徵求跋啓" (Announcement humbly requesting postscripts for a respectfully copied Huayan Sutra), *Honghua yuekan* 弘化月刊 25 (1934): 112–114, *MFQ* 24:130–132.
30. "Huayanjing quanbu xiecheng zhengqiu bawen 華嚴經全部寫成徵求跋文" (Humbly requesting postscripts for completion of a copy of the entire Huayan Sutra), *Fojiao jushilin tekan* 佛教居士林特刊 42–43 (May 15, 1937): 20–21, *MFQ* 65:512–513.
31. Jimmy Yu, *Sanctity and Self-Inflicted Violence in Chinese Religions, 1500–1700* (Oxford: Oxford University Press, 2012), 43, 47.

32. Shouye was born in Wuxi in Jiangnan, but his parents sent him to Shanghai to study and work when he was young. Running away from a marriage his mother had arranged for him when he was eighteen, he was tonsured in 1928 and received full ordination in 1930. Throughout his monastic career, he had a strong affiliation with Huayan, and in 1932, less than two years after his ordination, he traveled to Mt. Wutai's southern peak to recite and bow to the Huayan Sutra. He visited Wutai many times throughout his life. On August 15, 1936, he began to copy the Huayan Sutra in his own blood in a hut he built on Wutai. He pierced his tongue or finger to draw blood, which he mixed with sandalwood (to prevent coagulation) and ink. He wrote one character and then prostrated to it before moving on to the next character (Xiao Yu 肖雨, "Mangxie tabian Ya Meizhou de Wutaishan huayan xingzhe—Shouye fashi 芒鞋踏遍亞美洲的五台山華嚴行者—壽冶法師" [The Huayan practitioner of Mt. Wutai whose grass shoes wandered from Asia to America—Master Shouye], *Wutaishan yanjiu* 五臺山研究 2, no. 2 [1996]: 13–23). Shouye finished copying the entire sutra on June 19, 1940, but he had not been able to work on it continuously. In 1938, he had to return to Shanghai to become abbot of Puji 普濟 Temple. Less than two years later, Guanghui 廣慧 (n.d.), from whom Shouye had received dharma transmission in 1934, came to Shanghai to find someone to replace him as abbot of Bishan 碧山 Temple on Mt. Wutai. Shouye agreed and returned to Wutai. He completed his blood copy of the Huayan Sutra the year after he became abbot (Zhou Zhuying 周祝英, "Wutaishan Huayanzong xianzhuang 五台山華嚴宗現狀" [Current condition of the Huayan School on Mt. Wutai], *Wutaishan yanjiu* 五臺山研究 3 [2012]: 52–53).
33. Renshan 仁山, "Zongliang shangren shu Huayanjing yuanman ba 宗量上人書華嚴經圓滿跋" (Postscript to the complete Huayan Sutra copied by Venerable Zongliang), *Foxue banyuekan* 佛學半月刊 198 (February 1, 1940): 9, MFQ 55:209.
34. Welch, *The Practice of Chinese Buddhism*, 352.
35. Mo'an, "Shaodian shangren shu Huayanjing xu."
36. Fan was from Zhejiang and received a classical education but came to favor Buddhism. In his late twenties, he studied abroad in Japan, where he met Zhang Taiyan. Like Zhang, he studied Consciousness-Only thought, but he developed broad interests in Buddhism. He was a refuge disciple of the Tiantai master Dixian but also followed the work of many of the famous masters of the day. He was best known in the Buddhist world for his work in publishing. He took over as editor at Buddhist Books in Shanghai in 1929, and the following year he became the first editor of the company's newspaper *Buddhism*

Semimonthly (*Foxue Banyuekan* 佛學半月刊), which ran until 1944 (*XFRC*, 1:786c–789c).
37. Fan, "Shanghai Lianshe Huayanhui yuanqi."
38. Stanley Weinstein, "Schools of Buddhism," in *Encyclopedia of Religion*, 16 vols., ed. Mircea Eliade et al. (New York: Macmillan, 1987), 2:482, cited in T. Griffith Foulk, "The Ch'an Tsung in Medieval China: School, Lineage, or What?" *The Pacific World*, new series, 8 (1992): 18.
39. Robert Sharf, *Coming to Terms with Chinese Buddhism* (Honolulu: University of Hawai'i Press, 2002), 8–9.
40. Foulk, "The Ch'an Tsung in Medieval China"; Morten Schlütter, *How Zen Became Zen: The Dispute Over Enlightenment and Formation of Chan Buddhism in Song-Dynasty China* (Honolulu: University of Hawai'i Press, 2008); Jimmy Yu, "Revisiting the Notion of Zong: Contextualizing the Dharma Drum Lineage of Modern Chan Buddhism," *Chung-Hwa Buddhist Journal* 26 (2013): 113–151.
41. Erik Schicketanz, "Narratives of Buddhist Decline and the Concept of the Sect (*Zong*) in Modern Chinese Buddhist Thought," *Studies in Chinese Religions* 3, no. 3 (November 2017): 281–300.
42. Neil Donner and Daniel B. Stevenson, *The Great Calming and Contemplation: A Study and Annotated Translation of the First Chapter of Chih-i's Mo-ho-chih-kuan* (Honolulu: University of Hawai'i Press, 1999), 51.
43. T. Griffith Foulk, "Myth, Ritual, and Monastic Practice in Sung Ch'an Buddhism," in *Religion and Society in T'ang and Sung China*, ed. Peter Gregory and Patricia Ebrey (Honolulu: University of Hawai'i Press, 1993), 147–208.
44. Wang, *Songdai huayan sixiang yanjiu*, 34.
45. Wang, *Songdai huayan sixiang yanjiu*.
46. *Kaiyuan shijiao lu* 開元釋教錄 (Catalog of Buddhist Works Compiled During the Kaiyuan Period), written by Zhisheng 智昇 in 730, CBETA, T 2154; Wu Jiang, "The Chinese Buddhist Canon Through the Ages: Essential Categories and Critical Issues in the Study of a Textual Tradition," in *Spreading the Buddha's Word in East Asia: The Formation and Transformation of the Chinese Buddhist Canon*, ed. Wu Jiang and Lucille Chia (New York: Columbia University Press, 2016), 15–45.
47. James Ketelaar, *Of Heretics and Martyrs in Meiji Japan: Buddhism and Its Persecution* (Princeton, NJ: Princeton University Press, 1990), 178–183; *Sangoku buppō denzū engi* 三國佛法傳通緣起 (Record of the transmission of the Buddhadharma through the Three Nations), written by Gyōnen 凝然 in 1311, and *Hasshū kōyō*.
48. Despite the title *Essentials of the Eight Sects*, Gyōnen discussed ten sects in the text in that he included addenda on both Zen and Pure Land. Buddhist histories of the Meiji period usually expanded on Gyōnen's

model to include ten, twelve, or thirteen texts, depending on the sectarian affiliation of the scholar who wrote the text.
49. Erik Schicketanz, *Daraku to fukkō no kindai Chūgoku bukkyō: Nihon bukkyō to no kaikō to sono rekishizō no kōchiku* 堕落と復興の近代中國佛教：日本佛教との邂逅とその歴史像の構築 (Between decline and revival: Historical discourse and modern Chinese Buddhism's encounter with Japan) (Kyoto: Hōzōkan, 2016), 201.
50. Zhang Hua 張華, *Yang Wenhui yu Zhongguo jindai fojiao sixiang zhuanxing* 楊文會與中國近代佛教思想轉型 (Yang Wenhui and the formation of early-modern Chinese Buddhist thought) (Beijing: Zongjiao Wenhua, 2004), 157–158.
51. Chen Jidong 陳繼東, *Shinmatsu Bukkyō no kenkyū: Yō Bun'e o chūshin toshite* 清末仏教の研究：楊文会を中心として (Late-Qing Buddhist research: Centered on Yang Wenhui) (Tokyo: Sankibō Busshorin, 2003), 311–336.
52. Yang, "Shizong lüeshuo," 149.
53. "Brief Explanation of the Ten Schools" was an expanded and edited version of a Ming-era text with a Qing-era commentary that Yang Wenhui published in 1906 in collaboration with the monk Yinguang. For a full history of the publication of this text, see Gregory Adam Scott, "The Publishing of Buddhist Books for Beginners in Modern China from Yang Wenhui to Master Sheng Yen," *Shengyan yanjiu* 聖嚴研究 5 (2014): 51–107.
54. *Fojiao chuxue keben* and "Shizong lüeshuo" are reproduced in Yang, *Yang Renshan quanji*, 101–145, 149–156.
55. The complete curriculum for the Jetavana Hermitage is described in Lei Kuan Rongdao Lai, "Praying for the Republic: Buddhist Education, Student-Monks, and Citizenship in Modern China (1911–1949)," Ph.D. diss., McGill University, 2013, 113–117.
56. Scott, "The Publishing of Buddhist Books for Beginners," 66.
57. Schicketanz, *Daraku to fukkō no kindai Chūgoku bukkyō*, 201–211.
58. Foulk, "The Ch'an Tsung in Medieval China," 18.
59. Holmes Welch, *The Buddhist Revival in China* (Cambridge, MA: Harvard University Press, 1968), 199.
60. *Dasheng qixinlun* 大乘起信論 (Awakening of Faith in the Mahāyāna), probably written by Paramārtha 真諦, CBETA, T 1666.
61. Yang, *Fojiao chuxue keben*, 127.
62. Yang, "Xianshou faji xu," 378–379.
63. Taixu 太虛, "Lüeshuo Xianshou yi 略說賢首義" (Brief discussion of the meaning of the Xianshou [School]), *HCY* 4, no. 3 (1924): 3–9, *MFQ* 158:389.
64. Gong Jun 龔雋, *Dasheng qixinlun yu foxue zhongguohua* 大乘起信論與佛學中國化 (The *Awakening of Faith in Mahāyāna* and the Sinification of Buddhism) (Taipei: Wenjin, 1995), 150–158.

1. HUAYAN AS A SCHOOL OF CHINESE BUDDHISM

65. Eyal Aviv, "Differentiating the Pearl from the Fish Eye: Ouyang Jingwu (1871–1943) and the Revival of Scholastic Buddhism," Ph.D. diss., Harvard University, 2008, 134.
66. Ouyang Jingwu 歐陽境無, "Weishi jueze tan 唯識抉擇談" (Discussions on selected aspects of Consciousness-Only) (1922), reprinted in *Weishi wenti yanjiu* 唯識問題研究 (Research on questions related to Consciousness-Only), ed. Zhang Mantao 張曼濤 (Taipei: Dasheng Wenhua, 1980), 10.
67. Eyal Aviv, "Ouyang Jingwu: From Yogācāra Scholasticism to Soteriology," in *Transforming Consciousness: Yogācāra Thought in Modern China*, ed. John Makeham (Oxford: Oxford University Press, 2014), 294.
68. Liang Qichao 梁啓超, "*Dasheng qixinlun* kaozheng 大乘起信論考證" (Evidential analysis of the *Awakening of Faith*) (1922), reprinted in *Dasheng qixinlun yu Lengyanjing kaobian* 大乘起信論與楞嚴經考辨 (Critical analyses of the *Awakening of Faith in the Mahāyāna* and the *Śūraṅgama Sutra*), ed. Zhang Mantao 張曼濤 (Taipei: Dasheng Wenhua, 1978), 58.
69. Changxing 常惺, " '*Dasheng qixinlun* liaojian' boyi 大乘起信論料簡駁議" (A refutation of "Basic data related to the *Awakening of Faith in the Mahāyāna*") (1922), reprinted in *Dasheng qixinlun yu Lengyanjing kaobian*, ed. Zhang, 174. For a brief explanation of the issues involved in this doctrinal dispute, see Brook Ziporyn, "Anti-Chan Polemics in Post Tang Tiantai," *Journal of the International Association of Buddhist Studies* 17, no. 1 (Summer 1994): 26–65.
70. Taixu, "Lüeshuo Xianshou yi," 389.
71. Taixu 太虛, "Fofa zong jueze lun 佛法總抉擇論" (General selections and discussion of the Buddhdharma), *HCY* 3, nos. 11–12 (1922): 1–8, *MFQ* 155:163–170.
72. Zhang Taiyan 章太炎, "Shen Weishizong yi: Po Yuanrenlun 申唯識宗義: 駁原人論" (Expanding on the meaning of the Consciousness-Only School: A refutation of the *Inquiry Into the Origin of Humanity*), *Jueshe congshu* 覺社叢書 2 (February 1919): 14–21, *MFQ* 7:44–51; *Huayan yuanren lun* 華嚴原人論 (Huayan Inquiry Into the Origin of Humanity), written by Zongmi 宗密, CBETA, T 1886. For a full study and translation of the latter text, see Peter Gregory, *Inquiry Into the Origin of Humanity: An Annotated Translation of Tsung-Mi's Yuan Jen Lun with a Modern Commentary* (Honolulu: University of Hawai'i Press, 1995).
73. Taixu 太虛, " 'Shen Weishizong yi: Po *Yuanrenlun*': Fushi 申唯識宗義: 駁原人論: 附識" (Afterward to "Expanding on the Meaning of the Consciousness-Only School: A Refutation of the *Inquiry Into the Origin of Humanity*"), *Jueshe congshu* 覺社叢書 2 (February 1919): 20–21, *MFQ* 7:50–51.

74. Taixu 太虛, "Lun Xianshou yu Huiyuan zhi panjiao 論賢首與慧苑之判教" (Discussing Xianshou and Huiyuan's doctrinal classification), *HCY* 7, no. 12 (January 23, 1927): 7–10, *MFQ* 166:443–446.
75. Shi Dongchu 釋東初, *Zhongguo fojiao jindai shi* 中國佛教近代史 (A history of early contemporary Chinese Buddhism), vols. 1 and 2 of *Dongchu laoren quanji* 東初老人全集 (Collected works of Venerable Dongchu) (Taipei: Dongchu, 1974), 1:256–264.
76. *Shidi jinglun* 十地經論 (*Daśabhūmika-bhāṣya*, Commentary on the Sutra of the Ten Stages), written by Vasubandhu, CBETA, T 1522.
77. Taixu 太虛, "Xianshouxue yu Tiantaixue bijiao yanjiu 賢首學與天台學比較研究" (A comparative inquiry into Xianshou studies and Tiantai studies), *HCY* 13, no. 11 (November 15, 1932): 55–72, *MFQ* 182:229–230.
78. *XFRC*, 1:144a–147c.
79. Shen Quji 沈去疾, *Yingci fashi nianpu* 應慈法師年譜 (Chronicle of the life of Master Yingci) (Shanghai: Huadong Normal University, 1990).
80. *XFRC*, 1:954b–957b.
81. Keduan 可端, "Yangzhou Changshengsi Huayan Daxueyuan yuanqi 揚州長生寺華嚴大學院緣起" (On the origin of the Huayan University at Yangzhou's Changsheng Temple), *Foguang* 佛光 1 (March 2, 1923): 28–29, *MFQ* 12:76–77.

2. The Huayan Universities

1. James Ketelaar, *Of Heretics and Martyrs in Meiji Japan: Buddhism and Its Persecution* (Princeton, NJ: Princeton University Press, 1990), 179.
2. Makoto Hayashi, "General Education and the Modernization of Japanese Buddhism," *The Eastern Buddhist* 43, nos. 1–2 (2012): 133–152.
3. On these attitudes, see Holmes Welch, *The Buddhist Revival in China* (Cambridge, MA: Harvard University Press, 1968), 222–253.
4. Lei Kuan Rongdao Lai, "Praying for the Republic: Buddhist Education, Student-Monks, and Citizenship in Modern China (1911–1949)," Ph.D. diss., McGill University, 2013, 83–92.
5. Shi Dongchu 釋東初, *Zhongguo fojiao jindai shi* 中國佛教近代史 (A history of early contemporary Chinese Buddhism), vols. 1 and 2 of *Dongchu laoren quanji* 東初老人全集 (Collected works of Venerable Dongchu) (Taipei: Dongchu, 1974), 1:80.
6. See, for example, Ding Gang 丁鋼, *Zhongguo fojiao jiaoyu: Ru Fo Dao jiaoyu bijiao yanjiu* 中國佛教教育: 儒佛道教育比較研究 (Chinese Buddhist education: A comparative study of Confucian, Buddhist, and Daoist education) (Chengdu: Sichuan Publishing, 2010); Li Silong, "The Practice of Buddhist Education in Modern China," *Chinese Studies in History*

46, no. 3 (Spring 2013): 59–78; and Stefania Travagnin, "Concepts and Institutions for a New Buddhist Education: Reforming the Saṃgha Between and Within State Agencies," *East Asian History* 39 (December 2014): 89–102.

7. This is the opinion put forward in Chen Bing 陳兵 and Deng Zimei 鄧子美, *Ershi shiji zhongguo fojiao* 二十世紀中國佛教 (Twentieth-century Chinese Buddhism) (Beijing: Renmin, 2000); Ding, *Zhongguo fojiao jiaoyu*; and Li, "The Practice of Buddhist Education in Modern China." However, as Stefania Travagnin points out, the monk and historian Shi Dongchu included the earlier schools within his model ("Concepts and Institutions for a New Buddhist Education," 96).

8. On Ouyang and the Inner Studies Institute, see Eyal Aviv, "Differentiating the Pearl from the Fish Eye: Ouyang Jingwu (1871–1943) and the Revival of Scholastic Buddhism," Ph.D. diss., Harvard University, 2008; Chen and Deng, *Ershi shiji zhongguo fojiao*, 99–107; Shi, *Zhongguo fojiao jindai shi*, 1:205–206; and Welch, *The Buddhist Revival in China*, 117–120.

9. On the Wuchang Buddhist Institute, see Chen and Deng, *Ershi shiji zhongguo fojiao*, 84–93; Shi, *Zhongguo fojiao jindai shi*, 1:206–207, and Lai, "Praying for the Republic," 140–181.

10. There are several sources of information on the life of Yuexia. Here I have relied on the biographies in Shi, *Zhongguo fojiao jindai shi*, 2:755–757; *XFRC*, 1:144a–147c; and Zhiguang 智光, "Yuexia fashi lüezhuan 月霞法師略傳" (Brief biography of Master Yuexia), *HCY* 11, no. 3 (1931): 3–5, *MFQ* 175:83–85.

11. *XFRC*, 1:679a.

12. Yuzhu's interest in Huayan and his influence on Yuexia are discussed later in this chapter. Puchang focused on teaching Huayan in the late 1920s and early 1930s. For Puchang's biography, see *XFRC*, 2:1322a–1323b. Puchang gave a series of lectures on a text by Gyōnen in a program he ran from 1928 to 1931. These lectures were collected and published as *Brief Commentary on an Outline of Huayan Essentials* (*Huayan gangyao qianshuo* 華嚴綱要淺說). This text has unfortunately been lost.

13. The definitive biography of Yingci is Shen Quji 沈去疾, *Yingci fashi nianpu* 應慈法師年譜 (Chronicle of the life of Master Yingci) (Shanghai: Huadong Normal University, 1990). Two shorter accounts, which do not depart significantly from the one found in Shen, are Shi, *Zhongguo fojiao jindai shi*, 2:765–768, and *XFRC*, 2:1656b–1659c.

14. This general transmission practice as well as the dharma transmission in which Yuexia and Yingci participated in 1906 are discussed in some detail in Holmes Welch, *The Practice of Chinese Buddhism, 1900–1950* (Cambridge, MA: Harvard University Press, 1967), 450–453.

2. THE HUAYAN UNIVERSITIES

15. Shen, *Yingci fashi nianpu*, 14–15.
16. Xiao Ping 肖平, *Jindai zhongguo fojiao de fuxing yu Riben fojiaojie jiaowang lu* 近代中國佛教的復興與日本佛教界交往錄 (The early-modern Chinese Buddhist revival and the Japanese Buddhist world, a record) (Guangdong: Renmin, 2003).
17. Yang reports that he was particularly struck by Gui's diligent study of the *Awakening of Faith*, Yogācāra, Buddhist logic, and Huayan (Yang Wenhui 楊文會, "Yu Mei Xieyun shu 與梅擷芸書" [Letter to Mei Xieyun], in *Yang Renshan quanji* 楊仁山全集 [Complete works of Yang Renshan] [Anhui: Huangshan, 2000], 463).
18. Yingci 應慈, "Jinling Fu Jinqiu Huijiang jushi faxin shuxie sanyin Huayanjing xu 金陵傅近秋慧江居士發心書寫三譯華嚴經序" (Nanjing's Fu Jinqiu, Layman Huijiang has decided to copy out the three translations of the Huayan Sutra), *HCY* 28, no. 2 (February 1, 1947): 27, *MFQ* 203:283.
19. Fu was known in his neighborhood for his charitable Buddhist work, and he focused his study of Buddhism on Huayan because of Yuzhu's influence. See Huo Rui 霍銳, "Shu Fu Huijiang jushi xie Huayanjing hou 書傅慧江居士寫華嚴經後" (Letter to Layman Fu Hujiang after he copied the Huayan Sutra), *HCY* 28, no. 2 (February 1, 1947): 27–28, *MFQ* 203:283.
20. *XFRC*, 2:1657a–b.
21. I suspect the monk Tikong, another student at the original Huayan University, should be included in this list, but I have been unable to confirm that he was from Hubei.
22. Zhiguang, "Yuexia fashi lüezhuan," *MFQ* 175:84a.
23. Shi, *Zhongguo fojiao jindai shi*, 2:647, 736–738.
24. This canon was called the Pinjia Dazangjing 頻伽大藏經 (Kalaviṅka Canon). On its printing, see Gregory Adam Scott, "Conversion by the Book: Buddhist Print Culture in Early Republican China," Ph.D. diss., Columbia University, 2013, chap. 2.
25. "Huayan Daxue yuanqi yubai daixiaoshe wangong zai wei deng bao zhaokao 華嚴大學緣起預白待校舍完工再為登報招考" (Announcing commencement of activity and registration for entrance exams on the establishment of Huayan University), *Foxue congbao* 佛學叢報 10 (March 15, 1914): 1–6, *MFQ* 4:129–134.
26. Shi, *Zhongguo fojiao jindai shi*, 1:204.
27. Chen and Deng, *Ershi shiji zhongguo fojiao*, 395.
28. Zhiguang, "Yuexia fashi lüezhuan," *MFQ* 175:84a.
29. Juexing 覺醒, "Yuexia fashi changdao sengqie jiaoyu 月霞法師倡導僧伽教育" (Yuexia-initiated monastic education), *Xianggang fojiao* 佛教文化, no. 471 (1999): n.p.

30. Xia Boming 夏伯銘, *Shanghai jiushi zhi Hatong fufu* 上海舊事之哈同夫婦 (Tales of Mrs. Hardoon in Shanghai) (Shanghai: Shanghai Yuandong, 2008), 131–132, 218–220.
31. Shen, *Yingci fashi nianpu*.
32. Shaozu 紹祖, "Fajie Xueyuan zhuangkuang 法界學院狀況" (Circumstances at the Dharmadhātu Institute), *Jiangnan Jiuhua Foxueyuan yuankan* 江南九華佛學院院刊, September 1931, 13–16, *MFQB* 41:441–444.
33. Frank Dikötter, *Things Modern: Material Culture and Everyday Life in China* (London: Hurst, 2007), 135.
34. Stephen MacKinnon, "Wuhan's Search for Identity in the Republican Period," in *Remaking the Chinese City: Modernity and National Identity, 1900–1950*, ed. Joseph Esherick (Honolulu: University of Hawai'i Press, 1999), 163.
35. There is very little biographical information available about Liaochen. He should not be confused with the nineteenth-century Chan master of the same name, who was one of Yuexia's teachers.
36. "Hankou tongxun: Sengjie jiangbian Huayan Daxue yuke 漢口通訊: 僧界將辦華嚴大學預科" (News from Hankou: The monastic sector is organizing a Huayan University preparatory class), *HCY* 2, no. 6 (June 20, 1921): 4, *MFQ* 151:114.
37. Liaochen 了塵, "Zhonghua fojiao: Huayan Daxue yueke jianzhang 中華佛教: 華嚴大學預科簡章" (Chinese Buddhism: School charter for the Huayan University preparatory class), *HCY* 2, no. 7 (July 20, 1921): 2–4, *MFQ* 151:178–80.
38. The received biographical account gives Xuyun's date of birth as 1840, but most scholars do not accept this date. See, for example, Daniela Campo, *La construction de la sainteté dans la Chine moderne: La vie du maître bouddhiste Xuyun* (Paris: Les belles lettres, 2013).
39. *XFRC*, 1:481–482. The material in editor Yu Lingbo's entry mostly repeats the material in Shi, *Zhongguo fojiao jindai shi*, 1:360–361. Shi reports that Jiechen also served as a lecturer at Dixian's Guanzong Research Society in 1919, along with Changxing and Keduan (who is discussed in greater detail later in this chapter) (*Zhongguo fojiao jindai shi*, 2:516, 759). I have not seen this information anywhere else.
40. *XFRC*, 2:1544–1546.
41. "Hankou Huayan Daxue biye 漢口華嚴大學畢業" (Graduation at the Hankou Huayan University), *HCY* 5, no. 7 (August 20, 1924): 6, *MFQ* 159:384.
42. Liaochen, "Zhonghua fojiao," *MFQ* 151:180.
43. Lai, "Praying for the Republic," 111, 146.
44. Shi, *Zhongguo fojiao jindai shi*, 1:282. For more on this event, see Shi, *Zhongguo fojiao jindai shi*, 1:277–295, and Welch, *The Buddhist Revival in China*, 55–56.

2. THE HUAYAN UNIVERSITIES

45. Shi, *Zhongguo fojiao jindai shi*, 1:308–309. For more on this movement, see Lai, "Praying for the Republic," 162.
46. Lai, "Praying for the Republic," 157.
47. Shi, *Zhongguo fojiao jindai shi*, 1:206.
48. Lai, "Praying for the Republic," 152.
49. Nanting 南亭, "Zhenjiang Xiashan Zhulinsi Foxueyuan sannian zhi shilüe 鎮江夾山竹林寺佛學院三年之史略" (A brief history of the three years of the Zhulin Temple Buddhist Institute at Mt. Xia in Zhenjiang), *HCY* 12, no. 8 (August 15, 1931): 67–73, *MFQ* 178:451–457.
50. Lai, "Praying for the Republic," 155–156.
51. *XFRC*, 1:754c–757b.
52. Zhuren 竺人, "Hankou fojiaohui huanying Chisong Tikong liang fashi zhi shengkuang 漢口佛教會歡迎持松體空兩法師之盛況" (On the grand occasion of the Hankou Buddhist Association welcoming the two masters Chisong and Tikong), *HCY* 5, no. 4 (May 23, 1924): 5–6, *MFQ* 159:29–30.
53. There is almost no recorded information about Tikong beyond what is discussed here other than that he was heavily involved in the provincial Buddhist associations in the 1920s.
54. Liu Xianliang 劉顯亮, "Fu Wuchang Lianxisi Huayan Daxue Tikong fashi shu 覆武昌蓮溪寺華嚴大學體空法師書" (In reply to a letter from Master Tikong of Huayan University at Lianxi Temple in Wuchang), *Fobao xunkan* 佛寶旬刊 40 (June 2, 1928): 4, *MFQB* 33:20.
55. "Wuchang Lianxisi Huayan Daxue jiesan 武昌蓮溪寺華嚴大學解散" (Huayan University at Lianxi Temple in Wuchang is disbanding), *Xiandai senqie* 現代僧伽 2, nos. 43–44 (June 1930): 8, *MFQB* 39:271.
56. Lai, "Praying for the Republic," 158.
57. Welch, *The Practice of Chinese Buddhism*, 281.
58. Welch, *The Practice of Chinese Buddhism*, 398.
59. Xingzong Zuwang 興宗祖旺 and Jinglin Xinlu 景林心露, *Xianshou chuandeng lu* 賢首傳燈錄 (Record of the transmission of the Xianshou lineage), vols. 1–2 (Beijing: Guanyin Hermitage, 1805; reprint, Taipei: Dasheng Jingshe, 1996). Both Xingzong and Jinglin lived in the eighteenth century.
60. Lei Kuan Rongda Lai, "Lineage Networks and the Transnational Transmission of Modern Chinese Buddhism," paper presented at the American Academy of Religions annual meeting, November 19–22, 2016, San Antonio, TX.
61. Lai, "Praying for the Republic," 23.
62. Lai, "Praying for the Republic," 158–159.
63. It is unfortunate that we know too little about the students at the unaffiliated programs to be able to identify other connections of this type.

64. Vincent Goossaert, "Mapping Charisma Among Chinese Religious Specialists," *Novo Religio* 12, no. 2 (November 2008): 12–24.

3. Second- and Third-Generation Programs

1. Vincent Goossaert and David Palmer, *The Religious Question in Modern China* (Chicago: University of Chicago Press, 2011), 50–61.
2. Stephen MacKinnon, *Wuhan, 1938: War, Refugees, and the Making of Modern China* (Berkeley: University of California Press, 2008), 12–13.
3. Adam Chau, "The 'Religion Sphere' (*zongjiao jie* 宗教界) in the Construction of Modern China," in *Critical Concepts and Methods for the Study of Chinese Religions II: Intellectual History of Key Concepts*, ed. Stefania Travagnin and Gregory Adam Scott (Berlin: De Gruyter, 2020), 155–180.
4. Rebecca Nedostup, *Superstitious Regimes: Religion and the Politics of Chinese Modernity* (Cambridge, MA: Harvard University Press, 2009).
5. Goosaert and Palmer, *The Religious Question in Modern China*, 50–53.
6. Shen Quji 沈去疾, *Yingci fashi nianpu* 應慈法師年譜 (Chronicle of the life of Master Yingci) (Shanghai: Huadong Normal University, 1990), 26–27.
7. "Changzhou Qingliang Xueyuan yuanqi 常州清涼學院緣起" (On the origin of the Qingliang Institute in Changzhou), *HCY* 7, no. 3 (May 1926): 6–7, *MFQ* 164:538–539.
8. Qinghai 清海, "Guanyu Changzhou Qingliang Xueyuan zhi gongwen 關於常州清涼學院之公文" (Documents pertaining to the Qingliang Institute of Changzhou), *HCY* 7, no. 3 (May 1926): 12–13, *MFQ* 164:544–545.
9. "Changzhou Qingliang Xueyuan yuanqi."
10. Jiang Weiqiao 蔣維喬, "Changzhou Qingliang Xueyuan zhangcheng xu 常州清涼學院章程序" (Preface to the bylaws for the Qingliang Institute in Changzhou), *HCY* 7, no. 3 (May 1926): 6, *MFQ* 164:538.
11. Yingci 應慈, "Changzhou Qingliang Xueyuan zhangcheng 常州清涼學院章程" (Bylaws of the Qingliang Institute in Changzhou), *HCY* 7, no. 3 (May 1926): 7–11, *MFQ* 164:539–543.
12. Qinghai 清海 (recorded by Nanting 南亭), "Jiangsu Qingliang Xueyuan yuanzhang Qinghai lao heshang huanying Riben lai Hua fojiao tuan yanshuoci 江蘇清涼學院院長清海老和尚歡迎日本來華佛教團演說詞" (Formal words of welcome for the Japanese delegation visiting Chinese Buddhism, given by the Venerable Qinghai, principal of the Qingliang Institute in Jiangsu), *Fohua cejinhui huikan* 佛化策進會刊 2 (February 25, 1927): 80–81, *MFQ* 26:486–487.
13. "Changzhou Qingliang Xueyuan qianyi Shanghai 常州清涼學院遷移上海" (The Qingliang Institute of Changzhou is moving to Shanghai), *Xiandai sengqie* 現代僧伽, no. 5 (April 16, 1928): 25, *MFQ* 139:455.

3. SECOND- AND THIRD-GENERATION PROGRAMS

14. Jingming 淨名, "Tantan Qingliang Xueyuan zhi qianyin, houguo 談談清涼學院之前因後果" (Discussion of the fortunes of the Qingliang Institute), *Xiandai sengqie* 現代僧伽 2, nos. 29–30 (1929): 27–30, *MFQ* 66:131–134.
15. Shen, *Yingci fashi nianpu*, 29.
16. Shen, *Yingci fashi nianpu*, 29. *Introductory Discourse* is the introductory section of the *Commentary and Subcommentary on the Huayan Sutra* (*Huayan shuchao*) by Chengguan and is sometimes treated as an independent text; however, it does not have a separate entry or number in the standard catalog (CBETA, T).
17. Jingming, "Tantan Qingliang Xueyuan zhi qianyin, houguo."
18. Surprisingly, in October 1929 Abbot Qinghai announced that Qingliang Temple, located in the English Concession in Shanghai, would begin hosting daily lectures on the Huayan Sutra, which were to last three years ("Shanghai Qingliang Chansi kai jiang Huayanjing qi tonggao 上海清涼禪寺開講華嚴經期通告" [Shanghai's Qingliang Chan Temple to begin a lecture period on the Huayan Sutra], *HCY* 10, no. 9 [October 22, 1929]: 12, *MFQ* 173:456). This may have been a lecture series begun by Yingci before he departed, and he may have left Shanghai later than Shen Quji says he did, but that is unlikely, and Qinghai was probably able to hire a different monk to give the lecture. Unfortunately, the typeset for the announcement of this series in *HCY* is poor, and the lecturing master's name is not entirely clear. The second character is 西, but the first character is indistinct. It could be 慧 as there was a monk named Huixi 慧西 active at the time.
19. Shen, *Yingci fashi nianpu*, 29.
20. Nanting 南亭, "Zhenjiang Xiashan Zhulinsi Foxueyuan sannian zhi shilüe 鎮江夾山竹林寺佛學院三年之史略" (A brief history of the three years of the Zhulin Temple Buddhist Institute at Mt. Xia in Zhenjiang), *HCY* 12, no. 8 (August 15, 1931): 67–73, *MFQ* 178:453b.
21. In the traditional Chinese procedure for sutra lectures, the assistant lecturer is one of the primary lecturer's learned students, and each day he gives a supplemental explanatory talk (*pianzuo* 偏座) on the same section covered earlier that day by the primary lecturer during the main talk (*dazuo* 大座) (Holmes Welch, *The Practice of Chinese Buddhism, 1900-1950* [Cambridge, MA: Harvard University Press, 1967], 312). This procedure is discussed in greater detail in chapter 6.
22. As noted in the introduction, the forty-volume Huayan Sutra is the Gaṇḍhavyūha, which is the last section of the sixty- and eighty-volume versions of the sutra.
23. Shen, *Yingci fashi nianpu*, 44–46.
24. Shen, *Yingci fashi nianpu*, 59.

25. Guo Cheen, *Translating Totality in Parts: Chengguan's Commentaries and Subcommentaries to the Avatamsaka Sutra* (Lanham, MD: University Press of America, 2014).
26. This text is discussed in greater detail in chapter 6; it does not have a CBETA number.
27. *Huayanjing tanxuanji* 華嚴經探玄記 (Exploration of the Profundities of the Huayan Sutra), written by Fazang 法藏, CBETA, T 1733; *Sansheng yuanrong guanmen* 三聖圓融觀門 (Method of Contemplation on the Complete Interfusion of the Three Sages), written by Chengguan 澄觀, CBETA, T 1882.
28. "*Huayan shuchao* Bianyin Hui yuanqi 華嚴疏鈔編印會緣起" (Origins of the *Huayan Subcommentary* Publishing Committee), *Foxue banyuekan* 佛學半月刊 183 (June 16, 1939): 7–8, *MFQ* 55:7–8.
29. Shen, *Yingci fashi nianpu*, 48–49.
30. Shen, *Yingci fashi nianpu*, 56.
31. *XFRC*, 1:883–886.
32. Dading 大定, "Poshan Fajie Xueyuan kuochong xue'e ji qi xianzhuang 破山法界學院擴充學額及其現狀" (Expanding the class size at Poshan's Dharmadhātu Institute and its current situation), *HCY* 16, no. 5 (May 15, 1935): 73–77, *MFQ* 190:357b.
33. Shaozu 紹祖, "Fajie Xueyuan zhuangkuang 法界學院狀況" (Circumstances at the Dharmadhātu Institute), *Jiangnan Jiuhua Foxueyuan yuankan* 江南九華佛學院院刊, September 1931, 13–16, *MFQB* 41:441.
34. *XFRC*, 2:1130–1131.
35. *XFRC*, 1:482a.
36. Nanting, "Zhenjiang Xiashan Zhulinsi Foxueyuan sannian zhi shilüe," *MFQ* 178:453a.
37. "Fajie Xueyuan xuesheng shang Taixu fashi shu 法界學苑學生上太虛法師書" (Letter sent to Master Taixu by the students of the Dharmadhātu Institute), *HCY* 7, no. 1 (March 1926): 3–4, *MFQ* 164:267–268.
38. "Yushan Fajie Xueyuan tongxue pini cejinhui yuanqi bing jianzhang 虞山法界學院同學毗尼策進會緣起并簡章" (Origin and bylaws of the Yushan Dharmadhātu Institute Students' Association for the observance of the monastic rule), *Shijie fojiao jushilin linkan* 世界佛教居士林林刊 16 (January 1927): 8–9, *MFQ* 142:142–143.
39. Cizhou 慈舟, "Zhonghua minguo shiliunian Fajie Xueyuan shouzhi yinqian juesan biao: Fulu 中華民國十六年法界學院收支銀錢決算表: 附錄" (Statement of income and expenditures for the Dharmadhātu Institute in year 16 of the Republic of China: Appendix), *Chenzhong tekan* 晨鐘特刊 3 (April 1928): 5–6, *MFQB* 32:493–494.
40. "Changshu Xingfusi Fajie Xueyuan jianzhang 常熟興福寺法界學院簡章" (Bylaws of the Dharmadhātu Institute at Changshu's Xingfu Temple), *Chenzhong tekan* 晨鐘特刊 1 (September 9, 1927): 2–4, *MFQB* 32:210–212.

3. SECOND- AND THIRD-GENERATION PROGRAMS

41. Chisong 持松 (lecture recorded by Nengxin 能信), "Duiyu Fajie Xueyuan xuesheng zhi xiwang 對於法界學院學生之希望" (My hopes for the students of the Dharmadhātu Institute), *Chenzhong tekan* 晨鐘特刊 1 (September 9, 1927): 1–2, MFQB 32:181–182.
42. *XFRC*, 2:1616–1617.
43. Shaozu, "Fajie Xueyuan zhuangkuang."
44. *XFRC*, 2:1617.
45. Shaozu, "Fajie Xueyuan zhuangkuang."
46. Dading, "Poshan Fajie Xueyuan kuochong xue'e ji qi xianzhuang," *MFQ* 190:358–360.
47. "Changshu Xingfusi Fajie Xueyuan xianzhu xueseng yilanbiao 常熟興福寺法界學院現住學僧一覽表" (List of student monks currently residing at the Dharmadhātu Institute at Changshu's Xingfu Temple), *HCY* 16, no. 4 (April 15, 1935): 111–113, *MFQ* 190:249–251.
48. "Changshu Fajie Xueyuan juxing disijie biye 常熟法界學院舉行第四屆畢業" (Dharmadhātu Institute at Changshu held its fourth graduation), *HCY* 17, no. 8 (August 15, 1936): 89, *MFQ* 194:365.
49. "Changshu Fajie Xueyuan zhongzhen 常熟法界學院重振" (Revival of the Dharmadhātu Institute of Changshu), *Foxue yuekan* 佛學月刊 2, no. 2 (July 1942): 30, *MFQ* 95:468.
50. Shen, *Yingci fashi nianpu*, 35–36.
51. "Gushan Foxueyuan gaibian Fajie Xueyuan 鼓山佛學院改辦法界學院" (The Gushan Buddhist Institute has been transformed into a Dharmadhātu Institute), *Foxue banyuekan* 佛學半月刊 62 (September 1933): 14, *MFQ* 48:408.
52. "Fujian Gushan kuobian Fajie Xueyuan 福建鼓山擴辦法界學苑" (Gushan in Fujian will carry on the Dharmadhātu Institute), *Xianghai fohua* 香海佛化刊 5 (September 1933): 51–52, MFQB 47:339–340.
53. Zhou Zhuying 周祝英, "Wutaishan Huayanzong xianzhuang 五台山華嚴宗現狀" (Current condition of the Huayan School on Mt. Wutai), *Wutaishan yanjiu* 五臺山研究 3 (2012): 53; *XFRC*, 2:1425c–1427b.
54. "Fuzhou Luoshan Fajie Xueyuan juankuan jijin 福州羅山法界學苑募捐基金" (Raising funds for a Dharmadhātu Institute at Fuzhou's Mt. Luo), *Foxue banyuekan* 佛學半月刊 124 (April 1, 1936): 26, *MFQ* 52:210b.
55. "Fuzhou Luoshan Fajie Xueyuan jianzheng 福州羅山法界學苑簡章" (Bylaws of the Dharmadhātu Institute at Fuzhou's Mt. Luo), *Foxue banyuekan* 佛學半月刊 127 (May 16, 1936): 26, *MFQ* 52:308.
56. For a full biography of Tanxu, see James Carter, *Heart of Buddha, Heart of China: The Life of Tanxu, a Twentieth-Century Monk* (Oxford: Oxford University Press, 2010).
57. *XFRC*, 2:1278b.
58. Yu Lingbo states that the Dharmadhātu Institute at Fahai Temple did open under the direction of Daoyuan 道源 (1900–1988), a graduate of

the Dharmadhātu Institute at Changshu (*XFRC*, 2:1389b–c), but I have not found another source to confirm this information.

59. "Fuzhou Fajie Xueyuan qianwang Beiping 福州法界學苑遷往北平" (The Dahrmadhātu Institute of Fuzhou is moving to Beiping), *Wei miaosheng* 微妙聲 2 (November 15, 1936): 91, *MFQ* 84:203.
60. "Cizhou Fashi jiang Huayanjing 慈舟法師講華嚴經" (Master Cizhou is lecturing on the Huayan Sutra), *Foxue yuekan* 佛學月刊, no. 1 (June 1, 1941): 24b, *MFQ* 95:26b.
61. Dayin 達因, "Beijing Fajie Xueyuan chongxing yuanqi 北京法界學苑重興緣啟" (On the revival of the Beijing Dharmadhātu Institute), *Honghua Yuekan* 弘化月刊 49 (July 1945): 7, *MFQB* 69:453.
62. *XFRC*, 2:1279b.
63. *XFRC*, 2:1801a–1803b.
64. *Xianshou wujiaoyi* 賢首五教儀 (Outline of Xianshou's Five Teachings), written by Xufa 續法 in 1675, CBETA, X 1024.
65. Nanting, "Zhenjiang Xiashan Zhulinsi Foxueyuan sannian zhi shilüe," *MFQ* 178:455b.
66. Lei Kuan Rongdao Lai, "Praying for the Republic: Buddhist Education, Student-Monks, and Citizenship in Modern China (1911–1949)," Ph.D. diss., McGill University, 2013, 161–163, 168.
67. "Zhulin Xueyuan jiesan yu Qingliang Xueyuan tingbian 竹林學院解散與清涼學院停辦" (The Zhulin Institute is disbanding, and the Qingliang Institute is ceasing operations), *Xiandai sengqie* 現代僧伽 2, nos. 29–30 (1929): 1–2, *MFQ* 66:105–106.
68. Jingming, "Tantan Qingliang Xueyuan zhi qianyin, houguo," *MFQ* 66:132–133.
69. Yincun 印存, "Zhulinsi Foxueyuan jiesan 竹林寺佛學院解散" (Disbanding of the Zhulin Temple Buddhist Institute), *Xiandai senqie* 現代僧伽 2, nos. 29–30 (1929): 21–27, *MFQ* 66:125–131.
70. Nanting, "Zhenjiang Xiashan Zhulinsi Foxueyuan sannian zhi shilüe," *MFQ* 178:454a–b.
71. Chen-hua, *In Search of the Dharma: Memoirs of a Modern Chinese Buddhist Pilgrim* (Albany: State University of New York Press, 1992).
72. "Jiaoshan Dinghuisi Foxue Yanjiushe chengli 焦山定慧寺佛學研究社成立" (A Buddhist Studies Research Society is established at Jiaoshan's Dinghui Temple), *Renhai deng* 人海燈 1, no. 22 (October 15, 1934): 25, *MFQ* 69:387b.
73. *XFRC*, 1:642b–645a.
74. After his graduation from the Zhulin Buddhist Institute in 1931, Xuefan traveled with Weifang to Beijing to enroll in the Bailin Teaching Institute (Bailin Jiaoliyuan 柏林教理院), where they sought to further their studies of Buddhism as well as of the Chinese and Japanese languages, but the institute closed soon after their arrival. Xuefan then

briefly studied Consciousness-Only at the Three Times Study Association (Sanshi Xuehui 三時學會), run by the layman Han Qingjing 韓清淨 (1884–1949), before returning to Zhenjiang (XFRC, 1:1109c–1112a).

75. Haodong 皓東, "Jiaoshan Foxueyuan chengli jingguo ji qi jinkuang 焦山佛學苑成立經過及其近況" (On the establishment of the Jiaoshan Buddhist Institute and recent developments), HCY 15, no. 12 (December 15, 1934): 77–79, MFQ 189:85–87.

76. "Jiaoshan Foxueyuan xianzhu xueseng yilan 焦山佛學苑現住學僧一覽" (List of student monks currently residing at the Jiaoshan Buddhist Institute), HCY 15, no. 12 (December 15, 1934): 80–84, MFQ 189:88–92.

77. The history, holdings, and staff of the Jiaoshan Buddhist Studies Library are described in detail in Shi Dongchu 釋東初, Zhongguo fojiao jindai shi 中國佛教近代史 (A history of early contemporary Chinese Buddhism), vols. 1 and 2 of Dongchu laoren quanji 東初老人全集 (Collected works of Venerable Dongchu) (Taipei: Dongchu, 1974), 1:256–264.

78. Haodong, "Jiaoshan Foxueyuan chengli jingguo ji qi jinkuang," MFQ 189:87b.

79. "Zhenjiang Jiaoshan Foxueyuan jinkuang 鎮江焦山佛學苑近況" (Recent developments at the Jiaoshan Buddhist Institute), Zhengxin 正信 7, nos. 1–2 (October 15, 1935): 12–13, MFQ 62:266–267.

80. Like Zhiguang, Jingyan was from Jiangsu and had ordained at Zhenjiang's Baohuashan 寶華山 Temple in the mid-1920s, after which he moved to the nearby Dinghui Temple to study under its then abbot Dejun 德竣 (n.d.) (XFRC, 2:1635c).

81. Junling 峻嶺, "Jiaoshan Dingui Huayanqi zhi shengkuang 焦山定慧寺華嚴期之盛況" (On the grand occasion of the Huayan period of Jiaoshan's Dinghui Temple), Foxue banyuekan 佛學半月刊 128 (June 1, 1936): 21, MFQ 52:331c.

82. Shi, Zhongguo fojiao jindai shi, 1:213.

83. Shi Dongchu says that classes resumed in 1939 (Zhongguo fojiao jindai shi, 1:213), but a press release stated that the institute did not reopen until 1940 ("Dinghui Foxueyuan kaixue 定慧佛學院開學" [Opening of the Dinghui Buddhist Institute], Foxue banyuekan 佛學半月刊 201 [March 16, 1940]: 11, MFQ 55:271).

84. Shi, Zhongguo fojiao jindai shi, 1:213.

85. Liao Yanbo 廖彥博, Chengyi fashi fangtan lu 成一法師訪談錄 (Record of interviews with Master Chengyi) (Taipei: Sanmin Shuju, 2007), 29–39. The full title of the Treatise on the Five Teachings is Huayan yisheng jiaoyi fenqi zhang 華嚴一乘教義分齊章 (Treatise Distinguishing the Teachings of the One Vehicle of the Huayan), written by Fazang 法藏, CBETA, T 1866.

86. Liao, Chengyi fashi fangtan lu, 45.

3. SECOND- AND THIRD-GENERATION PROGRAMS

87. Yuehui 月慧, "Youxue Sanjiang canli Jiangdu Fojiao Zhuanxisuo jianwen jiangxi ji 遊學三江參禮江都佛教傳習所見聞講習記" (A record of the lectures and practice I experienced while visiting the Jiangdu Buddhist Teaching Center during my study around the Three Rivers region), *Da foxuebao* 大佛學報 2 (May 1, 1930): 66–68, *MFQ* 45:210–212.
88. Shi, *Zhongguo fojiao jindai shi*, 1:204, 2:759.
89. *Huayan yisheng shixuanmen* 華嚴一乘十玄門 (Ten Profound Gates of the Huayan One Vehicle), written by Zhiyan 智儼, CBETA, T 1868.
90. Keduan 可端, "Huayan Daxueyuan shang Jiangsu jiaoyuting chengwen 華嚴大學院上江蘇教育廳呈文" (Official petition to the Jiangsu Board of Education for the Huayan University), *Foguang* 佛光 1 (March 2, 1923): 29–30, *MFQ* 12:78. These concepts are explained in detail in chapter 5.
91. Keduan 可端, "Yangzhou Changshengsi Huayan Daxueyuan yuanqi 揚州長生寺華嚴大學院緣起" (On the origin of the Huayan University at Yangzhou's Changsheng Temple), *Foguang* 佛光 1 (March 2, 1923): 28–29, *MFQ* 12:76–77.
92. Xingjing 行靜, "Yangzhou Changshengsi Huayan Daxueyuan chengli ji 揚州長生寺華嚴大學院成立記" (Record of the establishment of the Huayan University at Yangzhou's Changsheng Temple), *Foguang* 佛光 1 (March 2, 1923): n.p., *MFQ* 12:48.
93. "Fen faxing bu 分發行部" (Subsidiary distribution sites), *Foguang* 佛光 1 (March 2, 1923): n.p., *MFQ* 12:123.
94. *XFRC*, 2:1797a–1799c.
95. See J. Brooks Jessup, "The Householder Elite: Buddhist Activism in Shanghai, 1920–1956," Ph.D. diss., University of California, Berkeley, 2010.
96. "Ben xueyuan tebie qishi 本學院特別啟事" (Special notice from this institute), *Foguang* 佛光 4 (September 2, 1923): n.p., *MFQ* 12:386.
97. Keduan 可端 and Xiao Weisheng 蕭唯昇, "Yangzhou Changshengsi jiangjing tonggao 揚州長生寺講經通告" (Announcement of sutra lectures at Yangzhou's Changsheng Temple), *HCY* 6, no. 4 (April 13, 1925): 34–36, *MFQ* 162:69a–b. For the original story of the founding of the Huayan University of Yangzhou, see Keduan, "Yangzhou Changshengsi Huayan Daxueyuan yuanqi."
98. Keduan and Xiao, "Yangzhou Changshengsi jiangjing tonggao."
99. Keduan 可端, "Yangzhou Changshengsi Huayan Daxueyuan zhengshi kaibian zuzhi fahui, zhaoji xueseng, yuanqi, bing tonggao 揚州長生寺華嚴大學院正式開辦組織法會招集學僧緣起並通告" (Statement of the origins and announcement of the organization of the rituals, formal opening, and call for students for the Huayan University at Yangzhou's Changsheng Temple), *HCY* 7, no. 8 (September 26, 1926): 5–7, *MFQ* 166:87–89.

100. Keduan and Xiao, "Yangzhou Changshengsi jiangjing tonggao," *MFQ* 162:70a.
101. Keduan, "Yangzhou Changshengsi Huayan Daxueyuan yuanqi," *MFQ* 12:76.
102. Keduan 可端, "Huayan Daxue gao zhushan zhanglao zhuchi shu 華嚴大學告諸山長老住持書" (Letter addressed to the venerable abbots of all temples sent from Huayan University), *HCY* 9, no. 1 (February 11, 1928): 2–6, *MFQ* 169:354–358.
103. Keduan 可端, "Jiangdu Fojiao Zhuanxisuo: Lingwen, chengpi, jianzhang, tongqi 江都佛教傳習所「令文」「呈批」「簡章」「通啟」" (Formal documents, bylaws, and announcement of the Jiangdu Buddhist Teaching Center), *Da foxuebao* 大佛學報 1 (March 1, 1930): 51–66, *MFQ* 45:109–124.
104. This center published two issues of its own periodical, *Great Journal of Buddhism* (*Da foxuebao* 大佛學報), both in 1930 (*MFQ* 45:54–127, 128–216).
105. Xiangrui 祥瑞 (recorded by Renhang 仁航), "*Xianshou wujiao* lüshuo 賢首五教略説" (Brief discussion of *Xianshou's Five Teachings*), *Fohua xin qingnian* 佛化新青年 2, no. 4 (August 1, 1924): 1, *MFQB* 3:439–441.
106. Xiangrui 祥瑞, "Jiangsu Yancheng Xianshouzong Xueyuan tonggao 江蘇鹽城賢首宗學院通告" (General announcement of the Institute of the Xianshou School in Yangcheng, Jinagsu), *HCY* 7, no. 9 (October 26, 1926): 2–3, *MFQ* 166:172–173.
107. *XFRC*, 1:74b–78a.
108. Xiangrui, "Jiangsu Yancheng Xianshouzong Xueyuan tonggao."
109. "Xianshouzong Xueyuan zhangcheng 賢首宗學院章程" (Bylaws of the Institute of the Xianshou School), *Shijie fojiao jushilin linkan* 世界佛教居士林林刊 14 (October 1926): 1–4, *MFQB* 9:309–312.
110. Xiangrui 祥瑞, "Xianshouzong Xueyuan zhangcheng 賢首宗學院章程" (Bylaws of the Institute of the Xianshou School), *Shijie fojiao jushilin linkan* 世界佛教居士林林刊 17 (April 1927): 9–11, *MFQ* 142:404–406.
111. Xiangrui 祥瑞, "Huaian Lengyan Foxueyuan xuanyan 淮安楞嚴佛學院宣言" (Announcement of the Śūraṅgama Buddhist Institute in Huaian), *HCY* 10, no. 12 (January 20, 1930): 21–24, *MFQ* 174:305–308.
112. "Huaian Lengyan Foxueyuan quanshuke yingshe 淮安楞嚴佛學院拳術科攝影" (Photograph of the martial arts class at the Śūraṅgama Buddhist Institute of Huaian), *HCY* 12, no. 8 (August 15, 1931): n.p., *MFQ* 178:384.

4. The Huayan University Network After 1949

1. Holmes Welch, *Buddhism Under Mao* (Cambridge, MA: Harvard University Press, 1971), 81.

4. THE HUAYAN UNIVERSITY NETWORK AFTER 1949

2. *XFRC*, 1:1427a.
3. *XFRC*, 1:885b–c.
4. Ma Mingbo 馬明博, "Wutai shenchu changming deng: Ji Mengcan zhanglao 五台深處長明燈: 記夢參長老" (An enduring lamp deep within Wutai: Remembering Venerable Mengcan), *Zhongguo zongjiao* 中國宗教 7 (2013): 32–35.
5. Aiting 靄亭, *Huayan yisheng jiaoyi zhang ji jie* 華嚴一乘教義章集解 (Collected explanations of the *Treatise on the Teachings of the Huayan One Vehicle*) (n.d.; reprint, Taipei: Xinwenfeng, 1991).
6. *XFRC*, 2:1802–1803.
7. Charles Jones, *Buddhism in Taiwan: Religion and the State, 1660–1990* (Honolulu: University of Hawai'i Press, 1999), 105–109.
8. Jones, *Buddhism in Taiwan*, 139–158, 175–183.
9. Chün-fang Yü, *Passing the Light: The Incense Light Community and Buddhist Nuns in Contemporary Taiwan* (Honolulu: University of Hawai'i Press, 2013), 76–80.
10. Stuart Chandler, "Spreading the Buddha's Light: The Internationalization of Foguang Shan," in *Buddhist Missionaries in the Era of Globalization*, ed. Linda Learman (Honolulu: University of Hawai'i Press, 2005), 162–184.
11. Julia Huang, "The Compassion Relief Diaspora," in *Buddhist Missionaries in the Era of Globalization*, ed. Learman, 185–209.
12. Shi Tianen 釋天恩, "Huayanzong de liuzhuan yu zai Taiwan de fazhan 華嚴宗的流傳與在臺灣的發展" (Transmission of the Huayan School and its development in Taiwan), M.A. thesis, Hua-yen Buddhist College, 2004, 47–49.
13. Liao Yanbo 廖彥博, *Chengyi fashi fangtan lu* 成一法師訪談錄 (Record of interviews with Master Chengyi) (Taipei: Sanmin Shuju, 2007), 112–113.
14. Liao, *Chengyi fashi fangtan lu*, 95–96, 100–101.
15. Nanting 南亭, "Zhongguo Huayanzong gaikuang 中國華嚴宗概況" (General survey of the Chinese Huayan School) (1988), reprinted in *Huayan wenhui* 華嚴文匯 (Collected writings on Huayan), 2 vols., ed. Fan Guanlan 范觀瀾 (Beijing: Zongjiao Wenhua, 2007), 277.
16. Liao, *Chengyi fashi fangtan lu*, 76–80, 98–99.
17. Liao, *Chengyi fashi fangtan lu*, 115–117.
18. Shi, "Huayanzong de liuzhuan yu zai Taiwan de fazhan," 53–59.
19. Rather than provide my own translation of the school's name, I use the English name that the institution uses for itself.
20. Liao, *Chengyi fashi fangtan lu*, 120–126.
21. See especially Nanting 南亭, "Huayanzong shilüe 華嚴宗史略" (Brief history of the Huayan School) (1959), reprinted in *Huayan wenhui*, ed. Fan, 1:242–270, and Chengyi 成一, "Huayanzong jianjie 華嚴宗簡介"

4. THE HUAYAN UNIVERSITY NETWORK AFTER 1949

(Brief introduction to the Huayan School), in *Huayan wenhui*, ed. Fan, 2:494–497.
22. Chengyi, "Huayanzong jianjie," 494; Chengyi 成一, "Huayanzong gangyao 華嚴宗綱要" (Essentials of the Huayan School), in *Huayan wenhui*, ed. Fan Guanlan, 2:517.
23. Chengyi, "Huayanzong jianjie," 495.
24. Nanting, "Zhongguo Huayanzong gaikuang," 271–274; Chengyi, "Huayanzong gangyao," 520–521.
25. Chengyi, "Huayanzong gangyao," 521–522.
26. Chengyi, "Huayanzong jianjie," 495.
27. Shi, "Huayanzong de liuzhuan yu zai Taiwan de fazhan," 63–65.
28. Liao, *Chengyi fashi fangtan lu*, 136–141.
29. Liao, *Chengyi fashi fangtan lu*, 125–126.
30. Jones, *Buddhism in Taiwan*, 152.
31. Yü, *Passing the Light*, 13.
32. Liao, *Chengyi fashi fangtan lu*, 127–131.
33. Liao, *Chengyi fashi fangtan lu*, 249–254.
34. "Xingshili 行事曆," Avatamsaka Lotus Society, n.d., http://www.huayenusa.org/%E8%A1%8C%E4%BA%8B%E8%A1%A8.
35. *XFRC*, 1:885b–886a.
36. Juexing 覺醒, "Jicheng yizhi, kaichuang Yufosi de jiaoyu hongfa xin jumian--jinian Zhenchan zhanglao shishi shizhounian 繼承遺志, 開創玉佛寺的教育弘法新局面--記念真禪長老逝世十週年" (Inheriting the goals left behind, creating a new situation for education and the propagation of the dharma at Yufo Temple--Commemorating the tenth anniversary of the death of Venerable Zhenchan), *Fojiao wenhua* 佛教文化 5 (October 1, 2005): 16–18.
37. *XFRC*, 1:886a–b.
38. Xia Jinhua 夏金華, "Chanzong yu Huayan de zonghe changdaozhe--cong Yingci laofashi dao Zhenchan fashi 禪宗與華嚴的綜合倡導者--從應慈老法師到真禪法師" (Advocates for unified Chan and Huayan—from the Venerable Yingci to Master Zhenchan), *Fojiao wenhua* 佛教文化 6 (December 1, 2005): 7–10.
39. Ma, "Wutai shenchu changming deng," 34.
40. Zhou Zhuying 周祝英, "Wutaishan Huayanzong xianzhuang 五台山華嚴宗現狀" (Current condition of the Huayan School on Mt. Wutai), *Wutaishan yanjiu* 五臺山研究 3 (2012): 53.
41. *XFRC*, 2:1427b.
42. Zhou, "Wutaishan Huayanzong xianzhuang," 53.
43. Liao, *Chengyi fashi fangtan lu*, 210–232.
44. Shi, "Huayanzong de liuzhuan yu zai Taiwan de fazhan," 48–49.
45. According to his organization's website, Jimeng holds several different Dharma lineages, including one as a forty-second-generation

holder of the Xianshou lineage. See "Daoshi shilüe 導師事略," *Huayen World*, January 1, 2018, https://www.huayenworld.org/HuayenNews.aspx?NewsID=1018.

5. Huayan Doctrine in Republican China

1. Yang Wenhui cited *Essentials of the Eight Sects* as the basis for his essay "Brief Explanation of the Ten Schools" ("Shizong lüeshuo 十宗略說," 1896) (in *Yang Renshan quanji* 楊仁山全集 [Complete works of Yang Renshan] [Anhui: Huangshan, 2000], 149). Unlike the *Essential Meaning of the Huayan School* (*Kegon shū yōgi* 華嚴宗要義, written by Gyōnen 凝然, CBETA, T 2335), the *Essentials of the Eight Sects* (*Hasshū kōyō* 八宗綱要, written by Gyōnen 凝然 in 1268) was printed as a stand-alone text in China multiple times in the modern period. As far as I have been able to determine, the *Essential Meaning of the Huayan School* was printed independently only once in Republican China, in 1934 by Shanghai's Buddhist Books as part of its Buddhists Texts Collection (Foxue xiao congshu 佛學小叢書) series. For this reason, it seems likely that *Essentials of the Eight Sects* had the greater impact on modern Chinese views of Huayan.
2. Shimaji Mokurai 島地磨雷 and Oda Tokunō 識田德能, *Sangoku Bukkyō ryakushi* 三國佛教略史 (A brief history of Buddhism of the Three Nations), 2 vols. (Tokyo: Kōmeisha, 1890), 2:31a.
3. *Fozu tongji* 佛祖通記 (Chronicle of the Buddhist Patriarchs), written by Zhipan 志磐 in 1269, CBETA, T 2035.292c8–16.
4. *Xianshou wujiaoyi kaimeng* 賢首五教儀開蒙 (Clarification of the *Outline of Xianshou's Five Teachings*), written by Xufa 續法 in 1682, CBETA, X 1025; *Xianshou wujiaoyi* 賢首五教儀 (Outline of Xianshou's Five Teachings), written by Xufa 續法 in 1675, CBETA, X 1024.
5. Wei Daoru 魏道儒, *Zhongguo huayanzong tongshi* 中國華嚴宗通史 (Comprehensive history of the Chinese Huayan School) (Nanjing: Jiangsu Guji, 2001), 295–297.
6. *Xianshou wujiaoyi*, CBETA, X 1024.58.631b09; *Xianshou wujiaoyi kaimeng*, CEBTA, X 1025.58689a9–10.
7. See, for example, Shengyi 聖譯, "Foxue zhi zongpai: Xianshouzong 佛學之宗派：賢首宗" (The sects of Buddhism: The Xianshou School), *Foxue xunkan* 佛學旬刊 17 (October 8, 1922): 4, *MFQ* 7:456; Taixu 太虛, "Lüeshuo Xianshou yi 略說賢首義" (Brief discussion of the meaning of the Xianshou [School]), *HCY* 4, no. 3 (1924): 3–9, *MFQ* 158:385–391.
8. Liu Ming-Wood, "The 'P'an'chiao' System of the Hua-yen School in Chinese Buddhism," *T'oung Pa*, second series, 67, nos. 1–2 (1981): 12.

5. HUAYAN DOCTRINE IN REPUBLICAN CHINA

9. Liu, "The 'P'an'chiao' System," 14 n. 12.
10. Robert Gimello, "Chih-Yen (602–668) and the Foundations of Hua-yen Buddhism," Ph.D. diss., Columbia University, 1976, 370–374.
11. Peter Gregory, *Tsung-mi and the Sinification of Buddhism* (1991; reprint, Honolulu: University of Hawai'i Press, 2002), 118; Wei, *Zhongguo huayanzong tongshi*, 156.
12. Liu, "The 'P'an'chiao' System," 16; Wei, *Zhongguo huayanzong tongshi*, 157–159; *Huayanjing kongmu zhang* 華嚴經孔目章 (Treatise on Topics in the Huayan Sutra), written by Zhiyan 智儼 between 661 and 668, CBETA, T 1870.
13. Kimura Kiyotaka 木村清孝, *Chūgoku kegon shisōshi* 中國華嚴思想史 (A history of Chinese Huayan thought) (Kyoto: Heirakuji, 1992), 127–128.
14. Wei, *Zhongguo huayanzong tongshi*, 158; *Huayanjing tanxuanji* 華嚴經探玄記 (Exploration of the Profundities of the Huayan Sutra), written by Fazang 法藏, CBETA, T 1733. *Treatise on the Golden Lion* can be found in the Song dynasty commentary by Chengqian 承遷 (fl. 997–1022) titled *Commentary on the Huayan Treatise on the Golden Lion* (*Huayanjing jin shizi zhang zhu* 華嚴經金師子章註), CBETA, T 1881.
15. For a full study and English translation of the *Treatise on the Golden Lion*, see Francis Cook, "Fa-Tsang's *Treatise on the Five Doctrines*: An Annotated Translation," Ph.D. diss., University of Wisconsin, 1970.
16. Gregory, *Tsung-mi and the Sinification of Buddhism*, 14.
17. *Huayan yuanren lun* 華嚴原人論 (Huayan Inquiry Into the Origin of Humanity), written by Zongmi 宗密, CBETA, T 1886.
18. Wang Song 王頌, *Songdai huayan sixiang yanjiu* 宋代華嚴思想研究 (Research on Song dynasty Huayan thought) (Beijing: Zongjiao Wenhua, 2008), 73.
19. Kimura, *Chūgoku kegon shisōshi*, 128.
20. Sakaino Kōyō 境野黃洋, *Shina Bukkyō shikō* 印度支那佛教史綱 (Outline of Chinese Buddhist history) (Tokyo: Morie Shoten, 1907), 246–248; Jiang Weiqiao 蔣維喬, *Zhongguo fojiao shi* 中國佛教史 (A history of Chinese Buddhism) (1929; reprint, Shanghai: Guji, 2004), 151–152; Huang Chanhua 黃懺華, *Fojiao gezong dayi* 佛教各宗大意 (Major ideas of the Buddhist schools) (N.p.: n.p., 1930), 235–240.
21. Imre Hamar, "A Huayan Paradigm for the Classification of Mahāyāna Teachings: The Origin and Meaning of *Faxingzong* and *Faxiangzong*," in *Reflecting Mirrors: Perspectives on Huayan Buddhism*, ed. Imre Hamar (Wiesbaden: Harrassowitz, 2007), 195–220.
22. Since the Tokugawa Period (1600–1868) in Japan, the basic Buddhist curriculum common for all sects was organized according to the twofold classification of Dharma Nature and Dharma Characteristic studies. See John Jorgensen, "Indra's Network: Zhang Taiyan's

5. HUAYAN DOCTRINE IN REPUBLICAN CHINA

Sino-Japanese Personal Networks and the Rise of Yogācāra in Modern China," in *Transforming Consciousness: Yogācāra Thought in Modern China*, ed. John Makeham (Oxford: Oxford University Press, 2014), 94.
23. See, for example, Wei, *Zhongguo huayanzong tongshi*, 6.
24. Wei, *Zhongguo huayanzong tongshi*, 186.
25. Kimura, *Chūgoku kegon shisōshi*, 92–93.
26. Gregory, *Tsung-mi and the Sinification of Buddhism*, 155–156.
27. Itō Zuiei 伊藤瑞叡, "Kegon kyōgaku ni okeru rokushōsetsu no denbo to uwa 華嚴教學における六相説の伝播と融和" (The source and development of the Six Characteristics theory of the Huayan sect), *Ōsaki gakuhō* 大崎學報 162 (March 2006): 63–70.
28. Wei, *Zhongguo huayanzong tongshi*, 77. The full title of *Record of Investigation* is *Huayanjing souxuan fenqi tongzhi fanggui* 華嚴經搜玄分齊通智方軌 (Outline for the Analysis, Comprehensive Understanding, and Investigation Into the Profundity of the Huayan Sutra), written by Zhiyan 智儼, CBETA, T 1732.
29. Gimello, "Chih-Yen," 169.
30. For English translations of these sections of Fazang's work, see Cook, "Fa-tsang's *Treatise on the Five Doctrines*," chap. 10, secs. 2 and 4.
31. Wei, *Zhongguo huayanzong tongshi*, 150.
32. For an examination of the Six Characteristics within the context of Huayan thought, see Francis Cook, *Hua-Yen Buddhism: The Jewel Net of Indra* (College Park: Pennsylvania State University Press, 1977), chap. 1. For an extended philosophical analysis, see Nicholaos J. Jones, "Mereological Heuristics for Huayan Buddhism," *Philosophy East and West* 60, no. 3 (2010): 355–368.
33. Wei, *Zhongguo huayanzong tongshi*, 4–5.
34. *Huayan yisheng shixuanmen* 華嚴一乘十玄門 (Ten Profound Gates of the Huayan One Vehicle), written by Zhiyan 智儼, CBETA, T 1868.
35. Ishii Kōsei 石井公成, "*Ichigyō jūgenmon* no sho mondai 『一乘十玄門』の諸問題" (Some problems concerning the *Ten Profound Gates of the One Vehicle*), *Bukkyōgaku* 佛教學 12 (October 1981): 85–112.
36. Kimura, *Chūgoku kegon shisōshi*, 93–96.
37. Chen Jinhua, *Philosopher, Practitioner, Politician: The Many Lives of Fazang (643–712)* (Leiden: Brill, 2007), 181–183.
38. Peter Gregory, "What Happened to the 'Perfect Teaching'? Another Look at Hua-yen Buddhist Hermeneutics," in *Buddhist Hermeneutics*, ed. Donald Lopez Jr. (Honolulu: University of Hawai'i Press, 1992), 213.
39. The Ten Profound Gates are: (1) "simultaneous complete correspondence" (*tongshi juzu xiangying* 同時具足相應); (2) "freedom and [nonobstruction] of extension and restriction or breadth and narrowness" (*guangxia zizai wuai* 廣狹自在無礙); (3) "the one and the many

containing each other without being the same" (*yiduo xiangrong butong* 一多相容不同); (4) "the mutual identification of all things" (*zhufa xiangji zizai* 諸法相即自在); (5) both concealment and revelation are completely attained (*mimi yinxian jucheng* 秘密隱顯俱成); (6) the tiniest particles contain one another, yet each stays in its own place (*weixi xiangrong anli* 微細相容安立); (7) "the realm of Indra's net" (*yinduoluo wang fajie* 因陀羅網法界); (8) "using a phenomenon to [explain the dharma] and produce understanding" (*tuoshi xianfa shengjie* 託事顯法生解); (9) various phenomena of the ten timeframes are different but united (*shishi gefa yicheng* 十世隔法異成); (10) each pair of subject ("lord") and object ("servant") completely illuminates the whole and contains all qualities (*zhuban yuanming jude* 主伴圓明具德). The quoted translations are taken from Thomas Cleary, *Entry Into the Inconceivable: An Introduction to Hua-yen Buddhism* (Honolulu: University of Hawai'i Press, 1983), 33–39; the remaining translations are my own.

40. Gyōnen included the concept of the Four Dharmadhātu in *Essentials of the Eight Sects* as a major element of Huayan doctrine (he writes about it directly after the Six Characteristics and the Ten Profound Gates), but because the concept is not mentioned in *Record of the Buddhist Patriarchs*, it does not appear in Shimaji and Oda's history *Sangoku Bukkyō ryakushi*. Sakaino Kōyō and those Chinese authors who copied him do not discuss it either. Yang Wenhui, however, mentioned it, even in his short "Brief Explanation of the Ten Schools," and Shengyi and Taixu, as they did on other topics, follow Yang in including it in their summaries of the Buddhist schools. It is also mentioned by the historians Zhou Shujia 周叔迦 (1899–1970), Huang Chanhua, and Mei Guangxi as well as by the monk Nanting. See Huang, *Fojiao gezong dayi*, 223–224; Mei Guangxi 梅光羲, "Huayanzong jiaoyi lüeshuo 華嚴宗教義略說" (Brief discussion of the teachings of the Huayan School), *HCY* 17, no. 5 (May 15, 1936): 22–31, *MFQ* 193:358–367; Nanting 南亭, "Huayanzong shilüe 華嚴宗史略" (Brief history of the Huayan School) (1959), reprinted in *Huayan wenhui* 華嚴文匯 (Collected writings on Huayan), 2 vols., ed. Fan Guanlan 范觀瀾 (Beijing: Zongjiao Wenhua, 2007), 1:265–267; Shengyi 聖譯, "Foxue zhi zongpai: Xianshouzong [xu qian] 佛學之宗派: 賢首宗 [續前]" (The sects of Buddhism: The Xianshou School [continued from previous]), *Foxue xunkan* 佛學旬刊 19 (October 29, 1922): 3–8, *MFQ* 8:5–10; Yang, "Shizong lüeshuo," 152; Zhou Shujia 周叔迦, *Zhongguo foxue shi* 中國佛學史 (A history of Chinese Buddhism) (N.p.: n.p., n.d.).

41. Jin Y. Park, *Buddhism and Postmodernity: Zen, Huayan, and the Possibility of Postmodern Buddhist Ethics* (Lanham, MD: Lexington Books, 2010), 161–162.

42. Wei, *Zhongguo huayanzong tongshi*, 197.

5. HUAYAN DOCTRINE IN REPUBLICAN CHINA

43. This history is described at length and in rather abstruse fashion in Brook Ziporyn, *Beyond Oneness and Difference: Li* 理 *and Coherence in Chinese Buddhist Thought and Its Antecedents* (Albany: State University of New York, Press, 2013).
44. Robert M. Gimello, "Apophatic and Kataphatic Discourse in Mahayana: A Chinese View," *Philosophy East and West* 26, no. 2 (1976): 125.
45. Jingyan 净嚴, "Shi hokkaikan no seiritsu to *Hokkai kanmon* 四法界観の成立と『法界観門』" (The formation of the doctrine of the Four Dharmadhātus and the *Contemplation of the Dharmadhātu*), *Indogaku Bukkyōgaku kenkyū* 印度佛教學研究 104, no. 52 (March 2004): 194–200.
46. Gimello, "Chih-Yen," 11–12.
47. Jingyan, "Shi hokkaikan no seiritsu to *Hokkai kanmon*."
48. Gimello, "Apophatic and Kataphatic Discourse in Mahayana."
49. For an extended explanation of Fazang's ideas about the Three Natures, see Cook, *Hua-yen Buddhism*, chap. 4.
50. Kimura, *Chūgoku kegon shisōshi*, 143–144.
51. Robert Gimello, "Li T'ung-hsüan and the Practical Dimensions of Hua-yen," in *Studies in Ch'an and Hua-Yen*, ed. Robert Gimello and Peter Gregory (Honolulu: University of Hawai'i Press, 1983), 321–389.
52. George J. Tanabe, *Myoe the Dreamkeeper: Fantasy and Knowledge in Early Kamakura Buddhism* (Cambridge, MA: Harvard University Press, 1992).
53. Gregory Adam Scott, "Conversion by the Book: Buddhist Print Culture in Early Republican China," Ph.D. diss., Columbia University, 2013, 86–90.
54. To search for titles across a range of Chinese canon collections, I used Chung-Hwa Institute of Buddhist Studies, *Fojiao zangjing mulu shuwei ziliaoku* 佛教藏經目錄數位資料庫 (Digital database of Buddhist Tripitaka catalogs), http://jinglu.cbeta.org/index.htm.
55. "Shanghai Youzheng Shuju fojing liutong shumu 上海有正書局佛經流通書目" (Catalog of Buddhist scriptures distributed by Shanghai Youzheng Press), *Foxue congbao* 佛學叢報 12 (June 15, 1914): 1–18, *MFQ* 4:551–568; *Foxue Shuju tushu mulu* 佛學書局圖書目錄 (Buddhist Books' catalog of works) 9 (May 1937), *MFQ* 54:29–140.
56. Gregory Adam Scott, *The Digital Catalogue of Chinese Buddhism, v. 3.0*, last modified October 3, 2013, http://bib.buddhiststudies.net/. The reliability of Scott's *Digital Catalogue* is, of course, limited by the quality of its original source data, but it is still a good way to get a general sense of what was available and when.
57. Chen Jidong 陳繼東, *Shinmatsu Bukkyō no kenkyū: Yō Bun'e o chūshin toshite* 清末佛教の研究: 楊文會を中心として (Late-Qing Buddhist research: Centered on Yang Wenhui) (Tokyo: Sankibō Busshorin, 2003), 311–336; Xiandu 賢度, *Huayanxue zhuanti yanjiu* 華嚴學專題研究 (Special topics in Huayan studies) (Taipei: Huayan Lianshe, 2008), 253, http://dev

.ddbc.edu.tw/hsiendu/interface.php?book=02; Zhang Hua 張華, *Yang Wenhui yu Zhongguo jindai fojiao sixiang zhuanxing* 楊文會與中國近代佛教思想轉型 (Yang Wenhui and the formation of early-modern Chinese Buddhist thought) (Beijing: Zongjiao Wenhua, 2004), 145–159.

58. *Foxue Shuju tushu mulu*, MFQ 54:65b–66a; Yang Wenhui 楊文會, ed., *Dafang guangfo huayanjing zhushu jiyao* 大方廣佛華嚴經著述集要 (Essential collected writings on the Huayan Sutra), 13 vols. (Nanjing: Jinling Kejingchu, 1876).

59. In counting the numbers of texts in these collections, I am treating as one work the seven brief essays by Fazang that are collectively referred to as *Huayanjing qike zhang* 華嚴經七科章 (Seven topical essays on the Huayan Sutra). In the Ming dynasty, these seven essays were combined into one *juan* text, which is present in the Taishō Canon under the title *Huayanjing mingfapin neili sanbao zhang* 華嚴經明法品內立三寶章 (The Treatise on the Three Treasures Found in the Huayan Sutra Chapter on Elucidating the Dharma), CEBTA, T 1874. Despite its inclusion in the title, "Sanbao zhang" is actually only the first of the seven essays. The others, in order, are "Liuzhuan zhang 流傳章" (Essay on transmigration), "Fajie yuanqi zhang 法界緣起章" (Essay on the origination of the Dharmadhātu), "Yuanyin zhang 圓音章" (Essay on the Perfect Voice [of the Buddha]), "Fashen zhang 法身章" (Essay on the Dharmakāya), "Shishi zhang 十世章" (Essay on the Ten Worlds), and "Xuanyi zhang 玄義章" (Essay on profound meaning).

60. *Fajiezong wuzu lüeji* 法界宗五祖略記 (Abbreviated Record of the Five Patriarchs of the Dharmadhātu School), written by Xufa 續法 in 1680, CBETA, X 1530.

61. Yang Wenhui 楊文會, "*Xianshou faji* xu 賢首法集敘" (Preface to the *Xianshou Dharma Collection*), in *Yang Renshan quanji*, 378; *Huayanjing yihai baimen* 華嚴經義海百門 (One Hundred Entrances Into the Ocean of Meanings in the Huayan Sutra), written by Fazang 法藏, CBETA, T 1875.

62. *Sansheng yuanrong guanmen* 三聖圓融觀門 (Method of Contemplation on the Complete Interfusion of the Three Sages), written by Chengguan 澄觀, CBETA, T 1882.

63. "Huayan Daxue yuanqi yubai daixiaoshe wangong zai wei chengbao zhaokao 華嚴大學緣起預白待校舍完工再為登報招考" (Announcing commencement of activity and registration for entrance exams on the establishment of Huayan University), *Foxue congbao* 佛學叢報 10 (March 15, 1914): 1–6, MFQ 4:131; *Foxue Shuju tushu mulu*, MFQ 54:65b–66a.

64. *Huayanjing zhuanji* 華嚴經傳記 (Record of the transmission of the Huayan Sutra), written by Fazang 法藏, CBETA, T 2073; Yang, "*Xianshou faji* xu," 380.

65. Scott, "Conversion by the Book," 86–90.

66. *Foxue Shuju tushu mulu*, MFQ 54:31-32.
67. *Foxue Shuju tushu mulu*, MFQ 54:64-66.
68. Xiandu, *Huayanxue zhuanti yanjiu*, 254-255.
69. These two texts were Fazang's *Record of the Transmission of the Huayan Sutra* and Zhiyan's *Record of Investigation into the Profound* (Outline for the Analysis, Comprehensive Understanding, and Investigation Into the Profundity of the Huayan Sutra).
70. *Huayan nianfo sanmei lun* 華嚴念佛三昧論 (Treatise on the Huayan Buddha Recollection Samādhi), written by Peng Shaosheng 彭紹升, CBETA, X 1030. For more information on Jiang Yiyuan, see Beverley Foulks McGuire, "Bringing Buddhism Into the Classroom: Jiang Qian's (1876-1942) Vision for Education in Republican China," *Journal of Chinese Religions* 39 (2011): 33-54. For an analysis of Peng's thought, see Liu Guijie 劉貴傑, "Qingchu Huayan nianfo sixiang shixi—yi Xufa yu Peng Shaosheng wei lie 清初華嚴念佛思想試析--以續法與彭紹升為例" (An examination of the Huayan Nianfo thought of the early Qing: Xufa and Peng Shaosheng as case studies), *Chung Hwa Buddhist Journal* 22 (2007): 227-250.
71. Taixu 太虛 (recorded by Liaocan 了參), "Tingjiang *Wujiaoyi* shiling 聽講五教儀拾零" (Listening to a brief lecture on *Outline of the Five Teachings*), *HCY* 24, no. 12 (December 1943): 15, *MFQ* 201:359; Taixu 太虛 (recorded by Liaocan 了參), "Tingjiang *Wujiaoyi* shiling 聽講五教儀拾零" (Listening to a brief lecture on *Outline of the Five Teachings*, final part), *HCY* 25, no. 3 (March 1943): 15, *MFQ* 201:416-418.
72. "Tianjin Fojiao Gongdelin yanjiu Huayanjing 天津佛教功德林研究華嚴經" (The Tianjin Buddhist Grove of Virtue is researching the Huayan Sutra), *Foxue banyuekan* 佛學半月刊 104 (June 1935): 23, *MFQ* 51:95c.
73. "Tianjin Fojiao Gongdelin yihai zhongqiu tongsong Huayanjing yuanman sheying 天津佛教功德林乙亥中秋同誦華嚴經圓滿攝影" (Photograph on the completion of the Tianjin Grove of Virtue's group recitation of the Huayan Sutra at the Midautumn Festival of 1935), *Beiping fojiaohui yuekan* 北平佛教會月刊 2, no. 3 (January 1936): n.p., MFQ 74:5.

6. A Common Curriculum

1. For example, in 1931 Nanting wrote an extensive reflection on the first three-year run of the Zhulin Buddhist Institute. It included a summary of the texts taught in each of the institute's six semesters as well as the name of the person responsible for teaching each of them (Nanting 南亭, "Zhenjiang Xiashan Zhulinsi Foxueyuan sannian zhi shilüe 鎮江夾山竹林寺佛學院三年之史略" [A brief history of

6. A COMMON CURRICULUM

the three years of the Zhulin Temple Buddhist Institute at Mt. Xia in Zhenjiang], *HCY* 12, no. 8 [August 15, 1931]: 67–73, *MFQ* 178:452–455). In this case, the curriculum that was taught only partially matched the curriculum proposed during the institute's founding in 1928. The most significant records of any institute's actual curriculum are the student articles and essay exams published for the Huayan University of Yangzhou, which I examine in greater detail later in this chapter.
2. Stefania Travagnin, "Concepts and Institutions for a New Buddhist Education: Reforming the Saṃgha Between and Within State Agencies," *East Asian History* 39 (December 2014): 96–98.
3. Shi Dongchu 釋東初, *Zhongguo fojiao jindai shi* 中國佛教近代史 (A history of early contemporary Chinese Buddhism), vols. 1 and 2 of *Dongchu laoren quanji* 東初老人全集 (Collected works of Venerable Dongchu) (Taipei: Dongchu, 1974), 1:203, cited in Travagnin, "Concepts and Institutions for a New Buddhist Education," 96.
4. Lei Kuan Rongdao Lai, "The Wuchang Ideal: Buddhist Education and Identity Production in Republican China," *Studies in Chinese Religion* 3, no. 1 (2017): 55–70.
5. Yang Wenhui 楊文會, "Shishi xuetang neiban kecheng 釋氏學堂内班課程" (Curriculum for inner classes at Buddhist schools), in *Yang Renshan quanji* 楊仁山全集 (Complete works of Yang Renshan) (Anhui: Huangshan, 2000), 334–335. For a complete list in English, see Lei Kuan Rongdao Lai, "Praying for the Republic: Buddhist Education, Student-Monks, and Citizenship in Modern China (1911–1949)," Ph.D. diss., McGill University, 2013, 113–114.
6. The full canonical title of this text is *Fochui niepan lüeshuo jiaojie jing* 佛垂般涅槃略説教誡經 (Sutra of Briefly Explained Admonishments Handed Down by the Buddha at the Time of His Entry Into Nirvana), translated by Kumārajīva, CBETA, T 389. This was a very popular text in East Asia. Although it is associated with the Chan School, it was studied by all types of Buddhists in China. See A. Charles Muller, "Sutra of the Deathbed Injunction 遺教經," in *Digital Dictionary of Buddhism*, ed. A. Charles Muller, entry updated July 22, 2014, http://www.buddhism-dict.net/cgi-bin/xpr-ddb.pl?q=%E9%81%BA%E6%95%99%E7%B6%93.
7. *Baifa mingmen lun* 百法明門論 (Clear Explanation of the One Hundred Dharmas), written by Vasubandhu, translated by Xuanzang, CBETA, T 1614. *Verses on the Structure of the Eight Consciousnesses* does not have a CBETA number because it no longer exists as an independent text, but it is still treated as one by scholars.
8. *Fajie wuchabie lunshu* 法界無差別論疏 (Commentary on the Treatise on the Nondistinction of the Dharmadhātu), written by Fazang 法藏, CBETA, T 1838.

9. *Dazong dixuan wenben lun* 大宗地玄文本論 (Foundational Treatise on the Mysteries of the Stages of the Great Lineage), CBETA, T 1669. On this text, see Michael Radich, "*Dazong dixuan wenben lun* 大宗地玄文本論," in *Digital Dictionary of Buddhism*, ed. Muller, entry updated July 10, 2013, http://www.buddhism-dict.net/cgi-bin/xpr-ddb.pl?q=%E5%A4%A7%E5%AE%97%E5%9C%B0%E7%8E%84%E6%96%87%E6%9C%AC%E8%AB%96. The English title I have provided here is only a tentative interpretation.
10. Holmes Welch, *The Practice of Chinese Buddhism, 1900–1950* (Cambridge, MA: Harvard University Press, 1967), 310–315.
11. Welch, *The Practice of Chinese Buddhism*, 311.
12. Welch, *The Practice of Chinese Buddhism*, 110–111.
13. "Huayan Daxue yuanqi yubai daixiaoshe wangong zai wei chengbao zhaokao 華嚴大學緣起預白待校舍完工再為登報招考" (Announcing commencement of activity and registration for entrance exams on the establishment of Huayan University), *Foxue congbao* 佛學叢報 10 (March 15, 1914): 1–6, *MFQ* 4:134.
14. Yingci 應慈, "Changzhou Qingliang Xueyuan zhangcheng 常州清涼學院章程" (Bylaws of the Qingliang Institute in Changzhou), *HCY* 7, no. 3 (May 1926): 7–11, *MFQ* 164:541.
15. Chengguan's *Introductory Discourse* is one example of an introductory essay (*xuantan* 懸談 or 玄談), a specific type of writing within Chinese Buddhist literature that appears at the beginning of a sutra commentary (*shu* 疏) and summarizes the main points it will discuss. These texts are also referred to as "profound meaning" (*xuanyi* 玄義), "profound commentary" (*xuanshu* 玄疏), "passing thoughts" (*youyi* 遊意), and "profound discourse" (*xuanlun* 玄論). Although they were initially created to serve as introductions to larger commentaries, since the time of the Tiantai master Zhiyi they have also circulated as independent texts. See Tao Jin, "The Formulation of Introductory Topics and the Writing of Exegesis in Chinese Buddhism," *Journal of the International Association of Buddhist Studies* 30, nos. 1–2 ([2007] 2009): 41–45.
16. Shen Quji 沈去疾, *Yingci fashi nianpu* 應慈法師年譜 (Chronicle of the life of Master Yingci) (Shanghai: Huadong Normal University, 1990), 29, 34, 41–42, 50, 53.
17. Keduan 可端, "Huayan Dasheng Foxueyuan zhangcheng 華嚴大乘佛學院章程" (Bylaws of the Huayan Mahāyāna Buddhist Institute), *Foguang* 佛光 3 (August 2, 1923): 53–55, *MFQ* 12:313–315.
18. Keduan 可端, "Huayan Dasheng Foxueyuan chunqi shijian kechengbiao 華嚴大乘佛學院春期時間課程表" (Spring term class schedule for the Huayan Mahāyāna Buddhist Institute), *Foguang* 佛光 2 (June 2, 1923): 62, *MFQ* 12:208.

19. Keduan 可端 and Xiao Weisheng 蕭唯昇, "Yangzhou Changshengsi jiangjing tonggao 揚州長生寺講經通告" (Announcement of sutra lectures at Yangzhou's Changsheng Temple), HCY 6, no. 4 (April 13, 1925): 34–36, MFQ 162:68–70; Huayanjing helun 華嚴經合論 (Combined Commentary on the Huayan Sutra), written by Li Tongxuan 李通玄, CBETA, X 223.
20. "Fujian Gushan kuobian Fajie Xueyuan 福建鼓山擴辦法界學苑" (Gushan in Fujian will carry on the Dharmadhātu Institute), Xianghai fohua 香海佛化刊 5 (September 1933): 51–52, MFQB 47:339–340.
21. Wuyunguan 五蘊觀 (Contemplation of the Five Skandha), written by Chengguan 澄觀, CBETA, X 1004.
22. Xiu huayan aozhi wangjin huanyuan guan 修華嚴奧旨妄盡還源觀 (Contemplation for Practicing the Huayan's Mysterious Teaching for Eliminating Delusions and Returning to the Origin), written by Fazang 法藏, CBETA, T 1876.
23. Of the programs mentioned in the current study, Treatise on the Five Teachings was assigned at all of them except the Anqing Monastic School, the Huayan University of Yangzhou, and Cizhou's Dharmadhātu Institutes.
24. Xianshou wujiaoyi 賢首五教儀 (Outline of Xianshou's Five Teachings), written by Xufa 續法 in 1675, CBETA, X 1024.
25. Francis Cook, "Fa-Tsang's Treatise on the Five Doctrines: An Annotated Translation," Ph.D. diss., University of Wisconsin, 1970.
26. Chen Bing 陳兵 and Deng Zimei 鄧子美, Ershi shiji zhongguo fojiao 二十世紀中國佛教 (Twentieth-century Chinese Buddhism) (Beijing: Renmin, 2000), 76.
27. Xianshou wujiaoyi, CBETA, X 1024.626b8–627a10.
28. Xianshou wujiaoyi kaimeng 賢首五教儀開蒙 (Clarification of the Outline of Xianshou's Five Teachings), written by Xufa 續法 in 1682, CBETA, X 1025.688c6–24.
29. Holmes Welch, The Buddhist Revival in China (Cambridge, MA: Harvard University Press, 1968), 203.
30. Welch, The Buddhist Revival in China, 196.
31. Chengguan's Profound Mirror of the Huayan Dharmadhātu (Huayan fajie xuanjing 華嚴法界玄鏡, CBETA, T 1883), was listed in the Qianlong Canon, and Yang Wenhui also included it in Essential Collected Writings on the Huayan Sutra (Dafang guangfo huayanjing zhushu jiyao 大方廣佛華嚴經著述集要, 13 vols. [Nanjing: Jinling Kejingchu, 1876]). An English translation of Chengguan's complete text can be found in Thomas Cleary, Entry Into the Inconceivable: An Introduction to Hua-yen Buddhism (Honolulu: University of Hawai'i Press, 1983), 69–124.
32. In China and Korea, Fazang's commentary on Method for Contemplation is commonly referred to as the Sanmei zhang 華嚴三昧章 (Treatise on

the Huayan Samādhi), which was probably its original title. In Japan, it is known as the *Huayan fa putixin zhang* 華嚴發菩提心章 (Treatise on Giving Rise to the Thought of Enlightenment in Huayan), which is the title used for it in the modern Taishō Canon (CBETA, T 1878). The relationship between these two texts is discussed in Robert Gimello, "Chih-Yen (602–668) and the Foundations of Hua-yen Buddhism," Ph.D. diss., Columbia University, 1976, 80–82.

33. Several of the most influential arguments about the provenance of *Method for Contemplation* are summarized in Wang Song 王頌, *Songdai huayan sixiang yanjiu* 宋代華嚴思想研究 (Research on Song dynasty Huayan thought) (Beijing: Zongjiao Wenhua, 2008), 114–117.
34. Wei Daoru 魏道儒, *Zhongguo huayanzong tongshi* 中國華嚴宗通史 (Comprehensive history of the Chinese Huayan School) (Nanjing: Jiangsu Guji, 2001), 112–113.
35. There are several different versions of the *sanguan* in the Sinitic Buddhist tradition, with the Tiantai and Consciousness-Only Schools having their own versions. Here the focus is on the Huayan version.
36. Gimello, "Chih-Yen," 14–28. This phrase can be found embedded in Fazang's *Treatise on Giving Rise to the Thought of Enlightenment in Huayan* (*Huayan fa putixin zhang*, CBETA, T 1878.45.653c29) and in Chengguan's *Profound Mirror of the Huayan Dharmadhātu* (*Huayan fajie xuanjing*, CBETA, T 1883.45.680c18).
37. Gimello, "Chih-Yen," 89–90.
38. Imre Hamar, "The Doctrines of Perfect Teaching in Ch'eng-kuan's Introduction to his Commentary on the Hua-yen ching," *Journal of the Center for Buddhist Studies* 3 (1998): 348.
39. Ishibashi Shinkai 石橋真誠, "Kegon kanpō no tenkai 華嚴觀法の展開" (The development of Huayan contemplation methods), *Indogaku Bukkyōgaku kenkyū* 印度佛教學研究 53, no. 27 (December 1978): 267–270.
40. Jin Yŏngyu 陳永裕, *Kegon kanpō no kisoteki kenkyū* 華嚴觀法の基礎研究 (Basic research into Huayan contemplation methods) (Seoul: Minjang Munhwasa, 1995), 16–19.
41. *Mohe zhiguan* 摩訶止觀 (Great Calming and Contemplation), written by Tiantai Zhiyi 天台智顗, CBETA, T 1911.
42. Neil Donner and Daniel B. Stevenson, *The Great Calming and Contemplation: A Study and Annotated Translation of the First Chapter of Chih-i's Mo-ho-chih-kuan* (Honolulu: University of Hawai'i Press, 1999).
43. Robert Sharf, "Experience," in *Critical Terms for Religious Studies*, ed. Marc Taylor (Chicago: University of Chicago Press, 1998), 94–116.
44. Halvor Eifring, "What Is Meditation?" in *Asian Traditions of Meditation*, ed. Halvor Eifring (Honolulu: University of Hawai'i Press, 2016), 1–26.
45. Halvor Eifring, "Types of Meditation," in *Asian Traditions of Meditation*, ed. Eifring, 27.

46. Eifring, "Types of Meditation."
47. For example, see the discussion in Livia Kohn, "Taoist Insight Meditation: The Tang Practice of *Neiguan*," in *Taoist Meditation and Longevity Techniques*, ed. Livia Kohn and Sakade Yoshinobu (Ann Arbor: Center for Chinese Studies, University of Michigan, 1989), 193–224.
48. A. Charles Muller, "Meditative Insight 觀," in *Digital Dictionary of Buddhism*, ed. Muller, entry updated December 27, 2013, http://www.buddhism-dict.net/cgi-bin/xRadicpr-ddb.pl?q=%E8%A7%80.
49. Donner and Stevenson, *The Great Calming and Contemplation*, 8.
50. Alan Sponberg, "Traditions of Meditation in Fa-hsiang Buddhism," in *Traditions of Meditation in Chinese Buddhism*, ed. Peter Gregory (Honolulu: University of Hawai'i Press, 1986), 21.
51. Sponberg, "Traditions of Meditation in Fa-hsiang Buddhism," 34–35.
52. Keduan 可端, "Keduan fashi shang Xian laofashi *Sanguan yixin lun* 可端法師上閑老法師三觀一心論" (Master Keduan lectures on Venerable Dixian's *Treatise on the Three Contemplations and One Mind*), *Foguang* 佛光 2 (June 2, 1923): 6–7, *MFQ* 12:152–153.
53. The two student essays are in *Foguang* 佛光 2 (June 2, 1923), *MFQ* 12:202–204.
54. Keduan 可端, "Huayan fajieguan 華嚴法界觀" (The Huayan contemplation of the Dharmadhātu), *Foguang* 佛光 3 (August 2, 1923): 1–3, *MFQ* 12:261–263.
55. The student essays are in *Foguang* 佛光 3 (August 2, 1923), *MFQ* 12:328–352.
56. The student exam essays are in *Foguang* 佛光 4 (September 2, 1923), *MFQ* 12:443–455.
57. Wang, *Songdai huayan sixiang yanjiu*, 120.

Bibliography

Abbreviations

CBETA, T	Chinese Buddhist Electronic Text Association. *Taishō Shinshū Daizōkyō* 大正新修大藏經 (Revised Tripiṭaka of the Taishō period). https://www.cbeta.org/.
CBETA, X	Chinese Buddhist Electronic Text Association. *Xuzangjing* 續藏經 (Supplemental Tripiṭaka). https://www.cbeta.org/.
HCY	*Haichao yin* 海潮音 (Sound of the sea tide).
MFQ	Huang Xianian 黃夏年, ed. *Minguo fojiao qikan wenxian jicheng* 民國佛教期刊文獻集成 (Collection of Republican-era Buddhist periodical literature). 209 vols. Beijing: Quanguo Tushuguan, 2006.
MFQB	Huang Xianian 黃夏年, ed. *Minguo fojiao qikan wenxian jicheng bubian* 民國佛教期刊文獻集成補編 (Supplement to the collection of Republican-era Buddhist periodical literature). 83 vols. Beijing: Zhongguo Shudian, 2008.
XFRC	Yu Lingbo 于凌波, ed. *Xiandai fojiao renwu cidian* 現代佛教人物辭典 (A dictionary of modern Buddhist persons). 2 vols. Taipei: Foguang, 2004.

Canonical Works

Baifa mingmen lun 百法明門論 (Clear Explanation of the One Hundred Dharmas). Written by Vasubandhu, translated by Xuanzang. CBETA, T 1614.

BIBLIOGRAPHY

Bashi guiju song 八識規矩頌 (Verses on the Structure of the Eight Consciousnesses). Written by Vasubhandu. No CBETA number because it no longer exists as an independent text.

Dasheng qixinlun 大乘起信論 (Awakening of Faith in the Mahāyāna). Probably written by Paramārtha 真諦. CBETA, T 1666.

Dazong dixuan wenben lun 大宗地玄文本論 (Foundational Treatise on the Mysteries of the Stages of the Great Lineage). CBETA, T 1669.

Fajie wuchabie lunshu 法界無差別論疏 (Commentary on the Treatise on the Nondistinction of the Dharmadhātu). Written by Fazang 法藏. CBETA, T 1838.

Fajiezong wuzu lüeji 法界宗五祖略記 (Abbreviated Record of the Five Patriarchs of the Dharmadhātu School). Written by Xufa 續法 in 1680. CBETA, X 1530.

Fochui niepan lüeshuo jiaojie jing 佛垂般涅槃略說教誡經 (Sutra of Briefly Explained Admonishments Handed Down by the Buddha at the Time of His Entry Into Nirvana). Translated by Kumārajīva. CBETA, T 389.

Fozu tongji 佛祖通記 (Chronicle of the Buddhist Patriarchs). Written by Zhipan 志磐 in 1269. CBETA, T 2035.

Hasshū kōyō 八宗綱要 (Essentials of the Eight Sects). Written by Gyōnen 凝然 in 1268.

Huayan fajie xuanjing 華嚴法界玄鏡 (Profound Mirror of the Huayan Dharmadhātu). Written by Chengguan 澄觀. CBETA, T 1883.

Huayan fa putixin zhang 華嚴發菩提心章 (Treatise on Giving Rise to the Thought of Enlightenment in Huayan). Written by Fazang 法藏. CEBTA, T 1878.

Huayanjing helun 華嚴經合論 (Combined Commentary on the Huayan Sutra). Written by Li Tongxuan 李通玄. CBETA, X 223.

Huayanjing jin shizi zhang zhu 華嚴經金師子章註 (Commentary on the Huayan Treatise on the Golden Lion). Written by Chengqian 承遷, early eleventh century. CBETA, T 1881.

Huayanjing kongmu zhang 華嚴經孔目章 (Treatise on Topics in the Huayan Sutra). Written by Zhiyan 智儼 between 661 and 668. CBETA, T 1870.

Huayanjing mingfapin neili sanbao zhang 華嚴經明法品內立三寶章 (The Treatise on the Three Treasures Found in the Huayan Sutra Chapter on Elucidating the Dharma). Written by Fazang 法藏. CEBTA, T 1874.

Huayanjing souxuan fenqi tongzhi fanggui 華嚴經搜玄分齊通智方軌 (Outline for the Analysis, Comprehensive Understanding, and Investigation Into the Profundity of the Huayan Sutra). Written by Zhiyan 智儼. CBETA, T 1732.

Huayanjing tanxuanji 華嚴經探玄記 (Exploration of the Profundities of the Huayan Sutra). Written by Fazang 法藏. CBETA, T 1733.

Huayanjing yihai baimen 華嚴經義海百門 (One Hundred Entrances Into the Ocean of Meanings in the Huayan Sutra). Written by Fazang 法藏. CBETA, T 1875.

Huayanjing zhuanji 華嚴經傳記 (Record of the Transmission of the Huayan Sutra). Written by Fazang 法藏. CBETA, T 2073.

Huayan nianfo sanmei lun 華嚴念佛三昧論 (Treatise on the Huayan Buddha Recollection Samādhi). Written by Peng Shaosheng 彭紹升. CBETA, X 1030.

Huayan yisheng jiaoyi fenqi zhang 華嚴一乘教義分齊章 (Treatise Distinguishing the Teachings of the Huayan One Vehicle). Written by Fazang 法藏. CBETA, T 1866.

Huayan yisheng shixuanmen 華嚴一乘十玄門 (Ten Profound Gates of the Huayan One Vehicle). Written by Zhiyan 智儼. CBETA, T 1868.

Huayan yuanren lun 華嚴原人論 (Huayan Inquiry Into the Origin of Humanity). Written by Zongmi 宗密. CBETA, T 1886.

Kaiyuan shijiao lu 開元釋教錄 (Catalog of Buddhist Works Compiled During the Kaiyuan Period). Written by Zhisheng 智昇 in 730. CBETA, T 2154.

Kegon shū yōgi 華嚴宗要義 (Essential Meaning of the Huayan School). Written by Gyōnen 凝然. CBETA, T 2335.

Mohe zhiguan 摩訶止觀 (Great Calming and Contemplation). Written by Zhiyi 智顗. CBETA, T 1911.

Sangoku buppō denzū engi 三國佛法傳通緣起 (Record of the transmission of the Buddhadharma through the Three Nations). Written by Gyōnen 凝然 in 1311.

Sansheng yuanrong guanmen 三聖圓融觀門 (Method of Contemplation on the Complete Interfusion of the Three Sages). Written by Chengguan 澄觀. CBETA, T 1882.

Shidi jinglun 十地經論 (*Daśabhūmika-bhāṣya*, Commentary on the Sutra of the Ten Stages). Written by Vasubhandu. CBETA, T 1522.

Wuyunguan 五蘊觀 (Contemplation of the Five Skandha). Written by Chengguan 澄觀. CBETA, X 1004.

Xianshou wujiaoyi 賢首五教儀 (Outline of Xianshou's Five Teachings). Written by Xufa 續法 in 1675. CBETA, X 1024.

Xianshou wujiaoyi kaimeng 賢首五教儀開蒙 (Clarification of the *Outline of Xianshou's Five Teachings*). Written by Xufa 續法 in 1682. CBETA, X 1025.

Xiu huayan aozhi wangjin huanyuan guan 修華嚴奧旨妄盡還源觀 (Contemplation for Practicing the Huayan's Mysterious Teaching for Eliminating Delusions and Returning to the Origin). Written by Fazang 法藏. CBETA, T 1876.

Other Primary Works

Aiting 靄亭. Huayan yisheng jiaoyi zhang ji jie 華嚴一乘教義章集解 (Collected explanations of the *Treatise on the Teachings of the Huayan One Vehicle*). N.d. Reprint. Taipei: Xinwenfeng, 1991.

"Ben xueyuan tebie qishi 本學院特別啟事" (Special notice from this institute). *Foguang* 佛光 4 (September 2, 1923): n.p.; *MFQ* 12:386.

Cao Songqiao 曹崧喬. "Jingshu Dafang Guangfo Huayanjing zhengqiu baqi 敬書大方廣佛華嚴經徵求跋啓" (Announcement humbly requesting postscripts for a respectfully copied Huayan Sutra). *Honghua yuekan* 弘化月刊 25 (1934): 112–114; *MFQ* 24:130–132.

"Changguan fashi fenbai Huayanjing 常觀師焚拜華嚴經" (Venerable Changguan burns incense and bows to the Huayan Sutra). *Shanxi fojiao zazhi* 山西佛教雜志 1, no. 11 (November 15, 1934): 69; *MFQ* 140:319.

"Changshu Fajie Xueyuan juxing disijie biye 常熟法界學院舉行第四屆畢業" (The Dharmadhātu Institute of Changshu held its fourth graduation). *HCY* 17, no. 8 (August 15, 1936): 89; *MFQ* 194:365.

"Changshu Fajie Xueyuan zhongzhen 常熟法界學院重振" (Revival of the Dharmadhātu Institute of Changshu). *Foxue yuekan* 佛學月刊 2, no. 2 (July 1942): 30; *MFQ* 95:468.

"Changshu Xingfusi Fajie Xueyuan jianzhang 常熟興福寺法界學院簡章" (Bylaws of the Dharmadhātu Institute at Changshu's Xingfu Temple). *Chenzhong tekan* 晨鐘特刊 1 (September 9, 1927): 2–4; *MFQB* 32:210–212.

"Changshu Xingfusi Fajie Xueyuan xianzhu xueseng yilanbiao 常熟興福寺法界學院現住學僧一覽表" (List of student monks currently residing at the Dharmadhātu Institute at Changshu's Xingfu Temple). *HCY* 16, no. 4 (April 15, 1935): 111–113; *MFQ* 190:249–251.

Changxing 常惺. "'Dasheng qixinlun liaojian' boyi 大乘起信論料簡駁議" (A refutation of "Basic Data Related to the *Awakening of Faith in the Mahāyāna*") (1922). Reprinted in *Dasheng qixinlun yu Lengyanjing kaobian* 大乘起信論與楞嚴經考辨 (Critical analyses of the *Awakening of Faith in the Mahāyāna* and the *Śūraṅgama Sutra*), ed. Zhang Mantao 張曼濤, 165–175. Taipei: Dasheng Wenhua, 1978.

———. "Xianshou gailun 賢首概論" (Introduction to the Xianshou [School]) (1929). Reprinted in *Huayan wenhui* 華嚴文匯 (Collected writings on Huayan), 2 vols., ed. Fan Guanlan 范觀瀾, 1:33–58. Beijing: Zongjiao Wenhua, 2007.

"Changzhou Qingliang Xueyuan qianyi Shanghai 常州清涼學院遷移上海" (The Qingliang Institute of Changzhou is moving to Shanghai). *Xiandai sengqie* 現代僧伽, no. 5 (April 16, 1928): 25; *MFQ* 139:455.

"Changzhou Qingliang Xueyuan yuanqi 常州清涼學院緣起" (On the origin of the Qingliang Institute in Changzhou). *HCY* 7, no. 3 (May 1926): 6–7; *MFQ* 164:538–539.

Chengyi 成一. "Huayanzong gangyao 華嚴宗綱要" (Essentials of the Huayan School). In *Huayan wenhui* 華嚴文匯 (Collected writings on Huayan), 2 vols., ed. Fan Guanlan 范觀瀾, 2:517–522. Beijing: Zongjiao Wenhua, 2007.

——. "Huayanzong jianjie 華嚴宗簡介" (Brief introduction to the Huayan School). In *Huayan wenhui* 華嚴文匯 (Collected writings on Huayan), 2 vols., ed. Fan Guanlan 范觀瀾, 2:494–497. Beijing: Zongjiao Wenhua, 2007.

Chen-hua. *In Search of the Dharma: Memoirs of a Modern Chinese Buddhist Pilgrim*. Albany: State University of New York Press, 1992.

Chisong 持松 (recorded by Nengxin 能信). "Duiyu Fajie Xueyuan xuesheng zhi xiwang 對於法界學院學生之希望" (My hopes for the students of the Dharmadhātu Institute). *Chenzhong tekan* 晨鐘特刊 1 (September 9, 1927): 1–2; *MFQB* 32:181–182.

Cizhou 慈舟. "Zhonghua minguo shiliunian Fajie Xueyuan shouzhi yinqian juesan biao: Fulu 中華民國十六年法界學院收支銀錢決算表: 附錄" (Statement of income and expenditures for the Dharmadhātu Institute in year 16 of the Republic of China: Appendix). *Chenzhong tekan* 晨鐘特刊 3 (April 1928): 5–6; *MFQB* 32:493–494.

"Cizhou Fashi jiang Huayanjing 慈舟法師講華嚴經" (Master Cizhou is lecturing on the Huayan Sutra). *Foxue yuekan* 佛學月刊, no. 1 (June 1, 1941): 24b; *MFQ* 95:26b.

Dading 大定. "Poshan Fajie Xueyuan kuochong xue'e ji qi xianzhuang 破山法界學院擴充學額及其現狀" (Expanding the class size at Poshan's Dharmadhātu Institute and its current situation). *HCY* 16, no. 5 (May 15, 1935): 73–77; *MFQ* 190:357–361.

Dayin 達因. "Beijing Fajie Xueyuan chongxing yuanqi 北京法界學苑重興緣啟" (On the revival of the Beijing Dharmadhātu Institute). *Honghua Yuekan* 弘化月刊 49 (July 1945): 7; *MFQB* 69:453.

"Dinghui Foxueyuan kaixue 定慧佛學院開學" (Opening of the Dinghui Buddhist Institute). *Foxue banyuekan* 佛學半月刊 201 (March 16, 1940): 11; *MFQ* 55:271.

"Fajie Xueyuan xuesheng shang Taixu fashi shu 法界學苑學生上太虛法師書" (Letter sent to Master Taixu by the students of the Dharmadhātu Institute). *HCY* 7, no. 1 (March 1926): 3–4; *MFQ* 164:267–268.

Fan Guanlan 范觀瀾, ed. *Huayan wenhui* 華嚴文匯 (Collected writings on Huayan). 2 vols. Beijing: Zongjiao Wenhua, 2007.

Fan Gunong 范古農. "Shanghai Lianshe Huayan fahui yuanqi 上海蓮社華嚴法會緣起" (On the origin of the Shanghai Lotus Society's Huayan Assembly). *HCY* 11, no. 1 (January 1930): n.p.; *MFQ* 174:439.

"Fen faxing bu 分發行部" (Subsidiary distribution sites). *Foguang* 佛光 1 (March 2, 1923): n.p.; *MFQ* 12:123.

Foxue Shuju tushu mulu 佛學書局圖書目錄 (Buddhist Books' catalog of works) 9 (May 1937); *MFQ* 54:29–140.

"Fujian Gushan kuobian Fajie Xueyuan 福建鼓山擴辦法界學苑" (Gushan in Fujian will carry on the Dharmadhātu Institute). *Xianghai fohua* 香海佛化刊 5 (September 1933): 51–52; *MFQB* 47:339–340.

"Fuzhou Fajie Xueyuan qianwang Beiping 福州法界學苑遷往北平" (The Dharmadhātu Institute of Fuzhou is moving to Beiping). *Wei miaosheng* 微妙聲 2 (November 15, 1936): 91; *MFQ* 84:203.

"Fuzhou Luoshan Fajie Xueyuan jianzheng 福州羅山法界學苑簡章" (Bylaws of the Dharmadhātu Institute at Fuzhou's Mt. Luo). *Foxue banyuekan* 佛學半月刊 127 (May 16, 1936): 26; *MFQ* 52:308.

"Fuzhou Luoshan Fajie Xueyuan juankuan jijin 福州羅山法界學苑募捐基金" (Raising funds for a Dharmadhātu Institute at Fuzhou's Mt. Luo). *Foxue banyuekan* 佛學半月刊 124 (April 1, 1936): 26; *MFQ* 52:210b.

"Gushan Foxueyuan gaibian Fajie Xueyuan 鼓山佛學院改辦法界學院" (The Gushan Buddhist Institute has been transformed into a Dharmadhātu Institute). *Foxue banyuekan* 佛學半月刊 62 (September 1933): 14; *MFQ* 48:408.

"Hankou Huayan Daxue biye 漢口華嚴大學畢業" (Graduation at the Hankou Huayan University). *HCY* 5, no. 7 (August 20, 1924): 6; *MFQ* 159:384.

"Hankou tongxun: Sengjie jiangbian Huayan Daxue yuke 漢口通訊: 僧界將辦華嚴大學預科" (News from Hankou: The monastic sector is organizing a Huayan University preparatory class). *HCY* 2, no. 6 (June 20, 1921): 4; *MFQ* 151:114.

Haodong 皓東. "Jiaoshan Foxueyuan chengli jingguo ji qi jinkuang 焦山佛學苑成立經過及其近況" (On the establishment of the Jiaoshan Buddhist Institute and recent developments). *HCY* 15, no. 12 (December 15, 1934): 77–79; *MFQ* 189:85–87.

"Huaian Lengyan Foxueyuan quanshuke yingshe 淮安楞嚴佛學院拳術科攝影" (Photograph of the martial arts class at the Śūraṅgama Buddhist Institute of Huaian). *HCY* 12, no. 8 (August 15, 1931): n.p.; *MFQ* 178:384.

Huang Chanhua 黃懺華. *Fojiao gezong dayi* 佛教各宗大意 (Major ideas of the Buddhist schools). N.p.: n.p., 1930.

———. *Zhongguo fojiao shi* 中國佛教史 (A history of Chinese Buddhism). 1940. Reprint. Shanghai: Commercial Press, 1947.

"Huayan Daxue yuanqi yubai daixiaoshe wangong zai wei deng bao zhaokao 華嚴大學緣起預白待校舍完工再為登報招考" (Announcing commencement of activity and registration for entrance exams on the establishment of Huayan University). *Foxue congbao* 佛學叢報 10 (March 15, 1914): 1–6; *MFQ* 4:129–134.

"Huayanjing quanbu xiecheng zhengqiu bawen 華嚴經全部寫成徵求跋文" (Humbly requesting postscripts for completion of a copy of the entire Huayan Sutra). *Fojiao jushilin tekan* 佛教居士林特刊 42–43 (May 15, 1937): 20–21; *MFQ* 65:512–513.

"*Huayan shuchao* Bianyin Hui yuanqi 華嚴疏鈔編印會緣起" (Origins of the Huayan Subcommentary Publishing Committee). *Foxue banyuekan* 佛學半月刊 183 (June 16, 1939): 7–8; *MFQ* 55:7–8.

Huo Rui 霍銳. "Shu Fu Huijiang jushi xie Huayanjing hou 書傅慧江居士寫華嚴經後" (Letter to Layman Fu Hujiang after he copied the Huayan Sutra). *HCY* 28, no. 2 (February 1, 1947): 27–28; *MFQ* 203:283.

Jiang Weiqiao 蔣維喬. "Changzhou Qingliang Xueyuan zhangcheng xu 常州清涼學院章程序" (Preface to the bylaws for the Qingliang Institute in Changzhou). *HCY* 7, no. 3 (May 1926): 6; *MFQ* 164:538.

———. *Zhongguo fojiao shi* 中國佛教史 (A history of Chinese Buddhism). 1929. Reprint. Shanghai: Guji, 2004.

"Jiaoshan Dinghuisi Foxue Yanjiushe chengli 焦山定慧寺佛學研究社成立" (A Buddhist Studies Research Society is established at Jiaoshan's Dinghui Temple). *Renhai deng* 人海燈 1, no. 22 (October 15, 1934): 25; *MFQ* 69:387b.

"Jiaoshan Foxueyuan xianzhu xueseng yilan 焦山佛學苑現住學僧一覽" (List of student monks currently residing at the Jiaoshan Buddhist Institute). *HCY* 15, no. 12 (December 15, 1934): 80–84; *MFQ* 189:88–92.

Jingming 淨名. "Tantan Qingliang Xueyuan zhi qianyin, houguo 談談清涼學院之前因後果" (Discussion of the fortunes of the Qingliang Institute). *Xiandai sengqie* 現代僧伽 2, nos. 29–30 (1929): 27–30; *MFQ* 66:131–134.

Junling 峻嶺. "Jiaoshan Dingui Huayanqi zhi shengkuang 焦山定慧寺華嚴期之盛況" (On the grand occasion of the Huayan period of Jiaoshan's Dinghui Temple). *Foxue banyuekan* 佛學半月刊 128 (June 1, 1936): 21; *MFQ* 52:331c.

Keduan 可端. "Huayan Dasheng Foxueyuan chunqi shijian kechengbiao 華嚴大乘佛學院春期時間課程表" (Spring term class schedule for the Huayan Mahāyāna Buddhist Institute). *Foguang* 佛光 2 (June 2, 1923): 62; *MFQ* 12:208.

———. "Huayan Dasheng Foxueyuan zhangcheng 華嚴大乘佛學院章程" (Bylaws of the Huayan Mahāyāna Buddhist Institute). *Foguang* 佛光 3 (August 2, 1923): 53–55; *MFQ* 12:313–315.

———. "Huayan Daxue gao zhushan zhanglao zhuchi shu 華嚴大學告諸山長老住持書" (Letter addressed to the venerable abbots of All Temples sent from Huayan University). *HCY* 9, no. 1 (February 11, 1928): 2–6; *MFQ* 169:354–358.

———. "Huayan Daxueyuan shang Jiangsu jiaoyuting chengwen 華嚴大學院上江蘇教育廳呈文" (Official petition to the Jiangsu Board of Education for the Huayan University). *Foguang* 佛光 1 (March 2, 1923): 29–30; *MFQ* 12:77–78.

———. "Huayan fajieguan 華嚴法界觀" (The Huayan contemplation of the Dharmadhātu). *Foguang* 佛光 3 (August 2, 1923): 1–3; *MFQ* 12:261–263.

——. "Jiangdu Fojiao Zhuanxisuo: Lingwen, chengpi, jianzhang, tongqi 江都佛教傳習所「令文」「呈批」「簡章」「通啟」" (Formal documents, bylaws, and announcement of the Jiangdu Buddhist Teaching Center). *Da foxuebao* 大佛學報 1 (March 1, 1930): 51–66; *MFQ* 45:109–124.

——. "Keduan fashi shang Xian laofashi *Sanguan yixin lun* 可端法師上閑老法師三觀一心論" (Master Keduan lectures on Venerable Dixian's *Treatise on the Three Contemplations and One Mind*). *Foguang* 佛光 2 (June 2, 1923): 6–7; *MFQ* 12:152–153.

——. "Yangzhou Changshengsi Huayan Daxueyuan yuanqi 揚州長生寺華嚴大學院緣起" (On the origin of the Huayan University at Yangzhou's Changsheng Temple). *Foguang* 佛光 1 (March 2, 1923): 28–29; *MFQ* 12:76–77.

——. "Yangzhou Changshengsi Huayan Daxueyuan zhengshi kaibian zuzhi fahui, zhaoji xueseng, yuanqi, bing tonggao 揚州長生寺華嚴大學院正式開辦組織法會招集學僧緣起並通告" (Statement of the origins and announcement of the organization of the rituals, formal opening, and call for students for the Huayan University at Yangzhou's Changsheng Temple). *HCY* 7, no. 8 (September 26, 1926): 5–7; *MFQ* 166:87–89.

Keduan 可端 and Xiao Weisheng 蕭唯昇. "Yangzhou Changshengsi jiangjing tonggao 揚州長生寺講經通告" (Announcement of sutra lectures at Yangzhou's Changsheng Temple). *HCY* 6, no. 4 (April 13, 1925): 34–36; *MFQ* 162:68–70.

Liang Qichao 梁啟超. "*Dasheng qixinlun* kaozheng 大乘起信論考證" (Evidential analysis of the *Awakening of Faith*) (1922). Reprinted *Dasheng qixinlun yu Lengyanjing kaobian* 大乘起信論與楞嚴經考辨 (Critical analyses of the *Awakening of Faith in the Mahāyāna* and the *Śūraṅgama Sutra*), ed. Zhang Mantao 張曼濤, 13–72. Taipei: Dasheng Wenhua, 1978.

Liaochen 了塵. "Zhonghua fojiao: Huayan Daxue yueke jianzhang 中華佛教: 華嚴大學預科簡章" (Chinese Buddhism: School charter for the Huayan University preparatory class). *HCY* 2, no. 7 (July 20, 1921): 2–4; *MFQ* 151:178–80.

Lin Yuanfan 林遠凡. "Xiding heshang biguan bai Huayanjing wei ge yi song 習定和尚閉關拜華嚴經爲偈以送" (Verse of praise sent to Monk Xiding, who is bowing to the Huayan Sutra in Confinement). *Fojiao jushilin tekan* 佛教居士林特刊 42–43 (April 15, 1937): 9; *MFQ* 65:501.

Liu Xianliang 劉顯亮. "Fu Wuchang Lianxisi Huayan Daxue Tikong fashi shu 覆武昌蓮溪寺華嚴大學體空法師書" (In reply to a letter from Master Tikong of Huayan University at Lianxi Temple in Wuchang). *Fobao xunkan* 佛寶旬刊 40 (June 2, 1928): 4; *MFQB* 33:20.

Mei Guangxi 梅光羲. "Huayanzong jiaoyi lüeshuo 華嚴宗教義略說" (Brief discussion of the teachings of the Huayan School). *HCY* 17, no. 5 (May 15, 1936): 22–31; *MFQ* 193:358–367.

Mo'an 默庵. "Shaodian shangren shu Huayanjing xu 少顛上人書華嚴經敘" (Preface to the Huayan Sutra copied by Elder Shaodian). *HCY* 4, no. 2 (April 5, 1923): 1; *MFQ* 155:431.

"Nanjing Fojiao Jingyeshe lisong Huayanjing quanbu 南京佛教淨業社禮誦華嚴經全部" (The Nanjing Buddhist Pure Karma Society to bow to and recite the entire Huayan Sutra). *Foxue banyuekan* 佛學半月刊 134 (September 1, 1936): 18; *MFQ* 53:20.

Nanting 南亭. "Huayanzong shilüe 華嚴宗史略" (Brief history of the Huayan School) (1959). Reprinted in *Huayan wenhui* 華嚴文匯 (Collected writings on Huayan), 2 vols., ed. Fan Guanlan 范觀瀾, 1:242–270. Beijing: Zongjiao Wenhua, 2007.

———. "Zhenjiang Xiashan Zhulinsi Foxueyuan sannian zhi shilüe 鎮江夾山竹林寺佛學院三年之史略" (A brief history of the three years of the Zhulin Temple Buddhist Institute at Mt. Xia in Zhenjiang). *HCY* 12, no. 8 (August 15, 1931): 67–73; *MFQ* 178:451–457.

———. "Zhongguo Huayanzong gaikuang 中國華嚴宗概況" (General survey of the Chinese Huayan School) (1988). Reprinted in *Huayan wenhui* 華嚴文匯 (Collected writings on Huayan), 2 vols., ed. Fan Guanlan 范觀瀾, 1:271–278. Beijing: Zongjiao Wenhua, 2007.

Ouyang Jingwu 歐陽境無. "Weishi jueze tan 唯識抉擇談" (Discussions on selected aspects of Consciousness-Only)" (1922). Reprinted in *Weishi wenti yanjiu* 唯識問題研究 (Research on questions related to Consciousness-Only), ed. Zhang Mantao 張曼濤, 1–50. Taipei: Dasheng Wenhua, 1980.

Qinghai 清海. "Guanyu Changzhou Qingliang Xueyuan zhi gongwen 關於常州清涼學院之公文" (Documents pertaining to the Qingliang Institute of Changzhou). *HCY* 7, no. 3 (May 1926): 12–13; *MFQ* 164:544–545.

Qinghai 清海 (recorded by Nanting 南亭). "Jiangsu Qingliang Xueyuan yuanzhang Qinghai lao heshang huanying Riben lai Hua fojiao tuan yanshuoci 江蘇清涼學院院長清海老和尚歡迎日本來華佛教團演說詞" (Formal words of welcome for the Japanese delegation visiting Chinese Buddhism, given by the Venerable Qinghai, principal of the Qingliang Institute in Jiangsu). *Fohua cejinhui huikan* 佛化策進會會刊 2 (February 25, 1927): 80–81; *MFQ* 26:486–487.

Renshan 仁山. "Zongliang shangren shu Huayanjing yuanman ba 宗量上人書華嚴經圓滿跋" (Postscript to the complete Huayan Sutra copied by Venerable Zongliang). *Foxue banyuekan* 佛學半月刊 198 (February 1, 1940): 9; *MFQ* 55:209.

Sakaino Kōyō 境野黃洋. *Indo Shina Bukkyō shikō* 印度支那佛教史綱 (Outline of Indian and Chinese Buddhist history). Tokyo: Komeisha, 1907.

———. *Shina Bukkyō shikō* 支那佛教史綱 (Outline of Chinese Buddhist history). Tokyo: Morie Shoten, 1907.

———. *Shina no Bukkyō* 支那の佛教 (Chinese Buddhism). Tokyo: Heigo Shuppansha, 1918.

"Shanghai Qingliang Chansi kai jiang Huayanjing qi tonggao 上海清涼禪寺開講華嚴經期通告" (Shanghai's Qingliang Chan Temple to begin a lecture period on the Huayan Sutra). *HCY* 10, no. 9 (October 22, 1929): 12; *MFQ* 173:456.

"Shanghai Youzheng Shuju fojing liutong shumu 上海有正書局佛經流通書目" (Catalog of Buddhist scriptures distributed by Shanghai Youzheng Press). *Foxue congbao* 佛學叢報 12 (June 15, 1914): 1–18; *MFQ* 4:551–568.

Shaozu 紹祖. "Fajie Xueyuan zhuangkuang 法界學院狀況" (Circumstances at the Dharmadhātu Institute). *Jiangnan Jiuhua Foxueyuan yuankan* 江南九華佛學院院刊, September 1931, 13–16; *MFQB* 41:441–444.

Shengyi 聖譯. "Foxue zhi zongpai: Xianshouzong 佛學之宗派: 賢首宗" (The sects of Buddhism: The Xianshou School). *Foxue xunkan* 佛學旬刊 17 (October 8, 1922): 2–9; *MFQ* 7:454–461.

———. "Foxue zhi zongpai: Xianshouzong [xu qian] 佛學之宗派: 賢首宗 [續前]" (The sects of Buddhism: The Xianshou School [continued from previous]). *Foxue xunkan* 佛學旬刊 19 (October 29, 1922): 3–8; *MFQ* 8:5–10.

Shimaji Mokurai 島地磨雷 and Oda Tokunō 識田德能. *Sangoku Bukkyō ryakushi* 三國佛教略史 (A brief history of Buddhism of the Three Nations). 2 vols. Tokyo: Kōmeisha, 1890.

Taixu 太虛. "Fofa zong jueze lun 佛法總抉擇論" (General selections and discussion of the Buddhdharma). *HCY* 3, nos. 11–12 (1922): 1–8; *MFQ* 155:163–170.

———. "Lüeshuo Xianshou yi 略說賢首義" (Brief discussion of the meaning of the Xianshou [School]). *HCY* 4, no. 3 (1924): 3–9; *MFQ* 158:385–391.

———. "Lun Xianshou yu Huiyuan zhi panjiao 論賢首與慧苑之判教" (Discussing Xianshou and Huiyuan's doctrinal classification). *HCY* 7, no. 12 (January 23, 1927): 7–10; *MFQ* 166:443–446.

———. "'Shen Weishizong yi: Po *Yuanrenlun*': Fushi 申唯識宗義: 駁原人論: 附識" (Afterward to "Expanding on the Meaning of the Consciousness-Only School: A Refutation of the *Inquiry Into the Origin of Humanity*"). *Jueshe congshu* 覺社叢書 2 (February 1919): 20–21; *MFQ* 7:50–51.

———. "Xianshouxue yu Tiantaixue bijiao yanjiu 賢首學與天台學比較研究" (A comparative inquiry into Xianshou studies and Tiantai studies). *HCY* 13, no. 11 (November 15, 1932): 55–72; *MFQ* 182:213–230.

Taixu 太虛 (recorded by Liaocan 了參). "Tingjiang *Wujiaoyi* shiling 聽講五教儀拾零" (Listening to a brief lecture on *Outline of the Five Teachings*). *HCY* 24, no. 12 (December 1943): 15; *MFQ* 201:359.

———. "Tingjiang *Wujiaoyi* shiling 聽講五教儀拾零" (Listening to a brief lecture on *Outline of the Five Teachings*, final part). *HCY* 25, no. 3 (March 1943): 15; *MFQ* 201:416–418.

"Tianjin Fojiao Gongdelin yanjiu Huayanjing 天津佛教功德林研究華嚴經" (The Tianjin Buddhist Grove of Virtue is researching the Huayan Sutra). *Foxue banyuekan* 佛學半月刊 104 (June 1935): 23; *MFQ* 51:95c.

"Tianjin Fojiao Gongdelin yihai zhongqiu tongsong Huayanjing yuanman sheying 天津佛教功德林乙亥中秋同誦華嚴經圓滿攝影" (Photograph on the completion of the Tianjing Grove of Virtue's group recitation of the Huayan Sutra at the Midautumn Festival of 1935). *Beiping fojiaohui yuekan* 北平佛教會月刊 2, no. 3 (January 1936): n.p.; *MFQ* 74:5.

Wang Xiaoxu 王小徐. "Su Zhouchen jushi xie Huayanjing ba 蘇宙忱居士寫華嚴經跋" (Postscript to Huayan Sutra copied by Layman Su Zhouchen). *Foxue banyuekan* 佛學半月刊 130 (July 1, 1937): 11; *MFQ* 52:385.

"Wuchang Lianxisi Huayan Daxue jiesan 武昌蓮溪寺華嚴大學解散" (Huayan University at Lianxi Temple in Wuchang is disbanding). *Xiandai senqie* 現代僧伽 2, nos. 43–44 (June 1930): 8; *MFQB* 39:271.

Xiangrui 祥瑞. "Huaian Lengyan Foxueyuan xuanyan 淮安楞嚴佛學院宣言" (Announcement of the Śūraṅgama Buddhist Institute in Huaian). *HCY* 10, no. 12 (January 20, 1930): 21–24; *MFQ* 174:305–308.

——. "Jiangsu Yancheng Xianshouzong Xueyuan tonggao 江蘇鹽城賢首宗學院通告" (General announcement of the Institute of the Xianshou School in Yangcheng, Jinagsu). *HCY* 7, no. 9 (October 26, 1926): 2–3; *MFQ* 166:172–173.

——. "Xianshouzong Xueyuan zhangcheng 賢首宗學院章程" (Bylaws of the Institute of the Xianshou School). *Shijie fojiao jushilin linkan* 世界佛教居士林林刊 17 (April 1927): 9–11; *MFQ* 142:404–406.

Xiangrui 祥瑞 (recorded by Renhang 仁航). "*Xianshou wujiao* lüshuo 賢首五教略說" (Brief discussion of *Xianshou's Five Teachings*). *Fohua xin qingnian* 佛化新青年 2, no. 4 (August 1, 1924): 1; *MFQB* 3:439–441.

"Xianshouzong Xueyuan zhangcheng 賢首宗學院章程" (Bylaws of the Institute of the Xianshou School). *Shijie fojiao jushilin linkan* 世界佛教居士林林刊 14 (October 1926): 1–4; *MFQB* 9:309–312.

Xingjing 行靜. "Yangzhou Changshengsi Huayan Daxueyuan chengli ji 揚州長生寺華嚴大學院成立記" (Record of the establishment of the Huayan University at Yangzhou's Changsheng Temple). *Foguang* 佛光 1 (March 2, 1923): n.p.; *MFQ* 12:48.

Xingzong Zuwang 興宗祖旺 and Jinglin Xinlu 景林心露. *Xianshou chuandeng lu* 賢首傳燈錄 (Record of the transmission of the Xianshou lineage). Vols. 1–2. 1805. Reprint. Taipei: Dasheng Jingshe, 1996.

Yang Wenhui 楊文會, ed. *Dafang guangfo huayanjing zhushu jiyao* 大方廣佛華嚴經著述集要 (Essential collected writings on the Huayan Sutra). 13 vols. Nanjing: Jinling Kejingchu, 1876.

——. *Fojiao chuxue keben* 佛教初學課本 (A primer on Buddhism). In *Yang Renshan quanji* 楊仁山全集 (Complete works of Yang Renshan), 101–145. Anhui: Huangshan, 2000.

———. "Shishi xuetang neiban kecheng 釋氏學堂內班課程" (Curriculum for inner classes at Buddhist Schools). In *Yang Renshan quanji* 楊仁山全集 (Complete works of Yang Renshan), 334–335. Anhui: Huangshan, 2000.

———. "Shizong lüeshuo 十宗略說" (Brief explanation of the ten schools). In *Yang Renshan quanji* 楊仁山全集 (Complete works of Yang Renshan), 149–156. Anhui: Huangshan, 2000.

———. "*Xianshou faji* xu 賢首法集敘" (Preface to the *Xianshou Dharma Collection*). In *Yang Renshan quanji* 楊仁山全集 (Complete works of Yang Renshan), 375–380. Anhui: Huangshan, 2000.

———. "Yu Mei Xieyun shu 與梅擷芸書" (Letter to Mei Xieyun). In *Yang Renshan quanji* 楊仁山全集 (Complete works of Yang Renshan), 462–463. Anhui: Huangshan, 2000.

Yincun 印存. "Zhulinsi Foxueyuan jiesan 竹林寺佛學院解散" (Disbanding of the Zhulin Temple Buddhist Institute). *Xiandai senqie* 現代僧伽 2, nos. 29–30 (1929): 21–27; *MFQ* 66:125–131.

Yingci 應慈. "Changzhou Qingliang Xueyuan zhangcheng 常州清涼學院章程" (Bylaws of the Qingliang Institute in Changzhou). *HCY* 7, no. 3 (May 1926): 7–11; *MFQ* 164:539–543.

———. "Jinling Fu Jinqiu Huijiang jushi faxin shuxie sanyin Huayanjing xu 金陵傅近秋慧江居士發心書寫三譯華嚴經序" (Nanjing's Fu Jinqiu, Layman Huijiang has decided to copy out the three translations of the Huayan Sutra). *HCY* 28, no. 2 (February 1, 1947): 27; *MFQ* 203:283.

Yuehui 月慧. "Youxue Sanjiang canli Jiangdu Fojiao Zhuanxisuo jianwen jiangxi ji 遊學三江參禮江都佛教傳習所見聞講習記" (A record of the lectures and practice I experienced while visiting the Jiangdu Buddhist Teaching Center during my study around the Three Rivers region). *Da foxuebao* 大佛學報 2 (May 1, 1930): 66–68; *MFQ* 45:210–212.

"Yushan Fajie Xueyuan tongxue pini cejinhui yuanqi bing jianzhang 虞山法界學院同學毗尼策進會緣起并簡章" (Origin and bylaws of the Yushan Dharmadhātu Institute Students' Association for the observance of the monastic rule). *Shijie fojiao jushilin linkan* 世界佛教居士林林刊 16 (January 1927): 8–9; *MFQ* 142:142–143.

Zhang Mantao 張曼濤, ed. *Dasheng qixinlun yu Lengyanjing kaobian* 大乘起信論與楞嚴經考辨 (Critical analyses of the *Awakening of Faith in the Mahāyāna* and the *Śūraṅgama Sutra*). 1922. Reprint. Taipei: Dasheng Wenhua, 1978.

Zhang Taiyan 章太炎. "Shen Weishizong yi: Po *Yuanrenlun* 申唯識宗義：駁原人論" (Expanding on the meaning of the Consciousness-Only School: A refutation of the *Inquiry into the Origin of Humanity*). *Jueshe congshu* 覺社叢書 2 (February 1919): 14–21; *MFQ* 7:44–51.

"Zhenjiang Jiaoshan Foxueyuan jinkuang 鎮江焦山佛學苑近況" (Recent developments at the Jiaoshan Buddhist Institute). *Zhengxin* 正信 7, nos. 1–2 (October 15, 1935): 12–13; *MFQ* 62:266–67.

Zhiguang 智光. "Yuexia fashi lüezhuan 月霞法師略傳" (Brief biography of Master Yuexia). *HCY* 11, no. 3 (1931): 3–5; *MFQ* 175:83–85.

Zhou Shujia 周叔迦. *Zhongguo foxue shi* 中國佛學史 (A history of Chinese Buddhism). N.p.: n.p., n.d.

"Zhulin Xueyuan jiesan yu Qingliang Xueyuan tingbian 竹林學院解散與清涼學院停辦" (The Zhulin Institute is disbanding, and the Qingliang Institute is ceasing operations). *Xiandai sengqie* 現代僧伽 2, nos. 29–30 (1929): 1–2; *MFQ* 66:105–106.

Zhuren 竺人. "Hankou Fojiaohui huanying Chisong Tikong liang fashi zhi shengkuang 漢口佛教會歡迎持松體空兩法師之盛況" (On the grand occasion of the Hankou Buddhist Association welcoming the two masters Chisong and Tikong). *HCY* 5, no. 4 (May 23, 1924): 5–6; *MFQ* 159:29–30.

Secondary Works

Aviv, Eyal. "Differentiating the Pearl from the Fish Eye: Ouyang Jingwu (1871–1943) and the Revival of Scholastic Buddhism." Ph.D. diss., Harvard University, 2008.

——. "Ouyang Jingwu: From Yogācāra Scholasticism to Soteriology." In *Transforming Consciousness: Yogācāra Thought in Modern China*, ed. John Makeham, 285–316. Oxford: Oxford University Press, 2014.

Birnbaum, Raoul. "Master Hongyi Looks Back: A Modern Man Becomes a Monk in Twentieth-Century China." In *Buddhism in the Modern World: Adaptations of an Ancient Tradition*, ed. Steven Heine and Charles Prebish, 74–124. Oxford: Oxford University Press, 2003.

Bo Jing 鉑淨. "Ershi shiji de huyanxue yanjiu 20世紀的華嚴學研究" (Twentieth-century Huayan research). *Foxue yanjiu* 佛學研究 1, no. 1 (2005): 363–381.

Campo, Daniela. *La construction de la sainteté dans la Chine moderne: La vie du maître bouddhiste Xuyun*. Paris: Les belles lettres, 2013.

Carter, James. *Heart of Buddha, Heart of China: The Life of Tanxu, a Twentieth-Century Monk*. Oxford: Oxford University Press, 2010.

Chan Sin-wai. *Buddhism in Late Ch'ing Political Thought*. Hong Kong: Chinese University Press, 1985.

Chandler, Stuart. "Spreading the Buddha's Light: The Internationalization of Foguang Shan." In *Buddhist Missionaries in the Era of Globalization*, ed. Linda Learman, 162–184. Honolulu: University of Hawai'i Press, 2005.

Chau, Adam. "The 'Religion Sphere' (*zongjiao jie* 宗教界) in the Construction of Modern China." In *Critical Concepts and Methods for the Study of Chinese Religions II: Intellectual History of Key Concepts*, ed. Stefania Travagnin and Gregory Adam Scott, 155–180. Berlin: De Gruyter, 2020.

BIBLIOGRAPHY

Chen Bing 陳兵 and Deng Zimei 鄧子美. *Ershi shiji zhongguo fojiao* 二十世紀中國佛教 (Twentieth-century Chinese Buddhism). Beijing: Renmin, 2000.

Chen Jidong 陳繼東. *Shinmatsu Bukkyō no kenkyū: Yō Bun'e o chūshin toshite* 清末佛教の研究: 楊文會を中心として (Late-Qing Buddhist research: Centered on Yang Wenhui). Tokyo: Sankibō Busshorin, 2003.

Chen Jinhua. *Philosopher, Practitioner, Politician: The Many Lives of Fazang (643–712)*. Leiden: Brill, 2007.

Chiu, King Pong. *Thomé H. Fang, Tang Junyi, and Huayan Thought: A Confucian Appropriation of Buddhist Ideas in Response to Scientism in the Twentieth Century*. Leiden: Brill, 2016.

Chung-Hwa Institute of Buddhist Studies. *Fojiao zangjing mulu shuwei ziliaoku* 佛教藏經目錄數位資料庫 (Digital database of Buddhist Tripiṭaka catalogs). http://jinglu.cbeta.org/index.htm.

Cleary, Thomas. *Entry Into the Inconceivable: An Introduction to Hua-yen Buddhism*. Honolulu: University of Hawai'i Press, 1983.

Cook, Francis. "Fa-Tsang's *Treatise on the Five Doctrines*: An Annotated Translation." Ph.D. diss., University of Wisconsin, 1970.

——. *Hua-yen Buddhism: The Jewel Net of Indra*. College Park: Pennsylvania State University Press, 1977.

"Daoshi shilüe 導師事略." *Huayen World*, January 1, 2018. https://www.huayenworld.org/HuayenNews.aspx?NewsID=1018.

Dikötter, Frank. *Things Modern: Material Culture and Everyday Life in China*. London: Hurst, 2007.

Ding Gang 丁鋼. *Zhongguo fojiao jiaoyu: Ru Fo Dao jiaoyu bijiao yanjiu* 中國佛教教育: 儒佛道教育比較研究 (Chinese Buddhist education: A comparative study of Confucian, Buddhist, and Daoist education). Chengdu: Sichuan Publishing, 2010.

Donner, Neil, and Daniel B. Stevenson. *The Great Calming and Contemplation: A Study and Annotated Translation of the First Chapter of Chih-i's Mo-ho-chih-kuan*. Honolulu: University of Hawai'i Press, 1999.

Du Jiwen 杜繼文. "Huayanzong xingcheng de sixiang yuanyuan yu shehui beijing 華嚴宗形成的思想淵源與社會背景" (The intellectual origins and social background for the formation of the Huayan School). In *Kegongaku ronshū* 華厳學論集 (Collected writings in Kegon studies), ed. Kamata Shigeo 鎌田茂雄, 1265–1278. Tokyo: Daizō Shuppan, 1997.

Eifring, Halvor. "Types of Meditation." In *Asian Traditions of Meditation*, ed. Halvor Eifring, 27–47. Honolulu: University of Hawai'i Press, 2016.

——. "What Is Meditation?" In *Asian Traditions of Meditation*, ed. Halvor Eifring, 1–26. Honolulu: University of Hawai'i Press, 2016.

Eliade, Mircea, et al., eds. *Encyclopedia of Religion*. 16 vols. New York: Macmillan, 1987.

Foulk, T. Griffith. "The Ch'an Tsung in Medieval China: School, Lineage, or What?" *The Pacific World*, new series, 8 (1992): 18–31.

——. "Myth, Ritual, and Monastic Practice in Sung Ch'an Buddhism." In *Religion and Society in T'ang and Sung China*, ed. Peter Gregory and Patricia Ebrey, 147–208. Honolulu: University of Hawai'i Press, 1993.
Gimello, Robert. "Apophatic and Kataphatic Discourse in Mahayana: A Chinese View." *Philosophy East and West* 26, no. 2 (1976): 117–136.
——. "Chih-Yen (602–668) and the Foundations of Hua-yen Buddhism." Ph.D. diss., Columbia University, 1976.
——. "Li T'ung-hsüan and the Practical Dimensions of Hua-yen." In *Studies in Ch'an and Hua-Yen*, ed. Robert Gimello and Peter Gregory, 321–389. Honolulu: University of Hawai'i Press, 1983.
Gong Jun 龔雋. Dasheng qixinlun yu foxue zhongguohua 大乘起信論與佛學中國化 (The *Awakening of Faith in Mahāyāna* and the Sinification of Buddhism). Taipei: Wenjin, 1995.
——. "Minguo shiqi foxue tongshi de shuxie 民國時期佛學通史的書寫" (The writing of comprehensive Buddhist histories in the Republican period). *Shijie zongjiao yanjiu* 世界宗教研究 6 (2013): 1–8.
Goossaert, Vincent. "Mapping Charisma Among Chinese Religious Specialists." *Novo Religio* 12, no. 2 (November 2008): 12–24.
Goossaert, Vincent and David Palmer. *The Religious Question in Modern China*. Chicago: University of Chicago Press, 2011.
Gregory, Peter, trans. Inquiry Into the Origin of Humanity: *An Annotated Translation of Tsung-Mi's Yuan Jen Lun with a Modern Commentary*. Honolulu: University of Hawai'i Press, 1995.
——. *Tsung-mi and the Sinification of Buddhism*. 1991. Reprint. Honolulu: University of Hawai'i Press, 2002.
——. "What Happened to the 'Perfect Teaching'? Another Look at Hua-yen Buddhist Hermeneutics." In *Buddhist Hermeneutics*, ed. Donald Lopez Jr., 207–230. Honolulu: University of Hawai'i Press, 1992.
Guo Cheen. *Translating Totality in Parts: Chengguan's Commentaries and Subcommentaries to the Avatamsaka Sutra*. Lanham, MD: University Press of America, 2014.
Hamar, Imre. "Creating Huayan Lineage: Miraculous Stories About the Avataṃsaka-sūtra." *Oriens Extremus* 50 (2011): 181–192.
——. "The Doctrines of Perfect Teaching in Ch'eng-kuan's Introduction to His Commentary on the Hua-yen ching," *Journal of the Center for Buddhist Studies* 3 (1998): 331–349.
——. "A Huayan Paradigm for the Classification of Mahāyāna Teachings: The Origin and Meaning of *Faxingzong* and *Faxiangzong*." In *Reflecting Mirrors: Perspectives on Huayan Buddhism*, ed. Imre Hamar, 195–220. Wiesbaden: Harrassowitz, 2007.
——. *A Religious Leader in the Tang: Chengguan's Biography*. Tokyo: International Institute for Buddhist Studies, International College for Advanced Buddhist Studies, 2002.

Hammerstrom, Erik. "Avataṃsaka 華嚴 Transnationalism in Modern Sinitic Buddhism." *Journal of Global Buddhism* 17 (2016): 65–84.

———. "Science and Buddhist Modernism in Early 20th Century China: The Life and Works of Wang Xiaoxu 王小徐." *Journal of Chinese Religion* 39 ([2011] 2012): 1–32.

Hayashi, Makoto. "General Education and the Modernization of Japanese Buddhism." *The Eastern Buddhist* 43, nos. 1–2 (2012): 133–152.

Huang, Julia. "The Compassion Relief Diaspora." In *Buddhist Missionaries in the Era of Globalization*, ed. Linda Learman, 185–209. Honolulu: University of Hawai'i Press, 2005.

Ishibashi Shinkai 石橋真誠. "Kegon kanpō no tenkai 華嚴觀法の展開" (The development of Huayan contemplation methods). *Indogaku Bukkyōgaku kenkyū* 印度佛教學研究 53, no. 27 (December 1978): 267–270.

Ishii Kōsei 石井公成. "*Ichigyō jūgenmon* no sho mondai 『一乘十玄門』の諸問題" (Some problems concerning the *Ten Profound Gates of the One Vehicle*). *Bukkyōgaku* 佛教學 12 (October 1981): 85–112.

Itō Zuiei 伊藤瑞叡. "Kegon kyōgaku ni okeru rokushōsetsu no denbo to uwa 華嚴教學における六相説の傳播と融和" (The source and development of the Six Characteristics theory of the Huayan sect). *Ōsaki gakuhō* 大崎學報 162 (March 2006): 63–70.

Jessup, J. Brooks. "The Householder Elite: Buddhist Activism in Shanghai, 1920–1956." Ph.D. diss., University of California, Berkeley, 2010.

Jin Yǒngyu 陳永裕. *Kegon kanpō no kisoteki kenkyū* 華嚴觀法の基礎研究 (Basic research into Huayan contemplation methods). Seoul: Minjang Munhwasa, 1995.

Jingyan 浄嚴. "Shi hokkaikan no seiritsu to *Hokkai kanmon* 四法界觀の成立と『法界観門』" (The formation of the doctrine of the Four Dharmadhātus and the *Contemplation of the Dharmadhātu*). *Indogaku Bukkyōgaku kenkyū* 印度佛教學研究 104, no. 52 (March 2004): 194–200.

Jones, Charles. *Buddhism in Taiwan: Religion and the State, 1660–1990*. Honolulu: University of Hawai'i Press, 1999.

Jones, Nicholaos J. "Mereological Heuristics for Huayan Buddhism." *Philosophy East and West* 60, no. 3 (2010): 355–368.

Jorgensen, John. "Indra's Network: Zhang Taiyan's Sino-Japanese Personal Networks and the Rise of Yogācāra in Modern China." In *Transforming Consciousness: Yogācāra Thought in Modern China*, ed. John Makeham, 64–99. Oxford: Oxford University Press, 2014.

Josephson, Jason Ananda. *The Invention of Religion in Japan*. Chicago: University of Chicago Press, 2012.

Juexing 覺醒. "Jicheng yizhi, kaichuang Yufosi de jiaoyu hongfa xin jumian--jinian Zhenchan zhanglao shishi shizhounian 繼承遺志, 開創玉佛寺的教育弘法新局面--記念真禪長老逝世十週年" (Inheriting the goals left behind, creating a new situation for education and the propagation of the dharma at Yufo Temple—Commemorating the tenth anniversary of the death of Venerable Zhenchan). *Fojiao wenhua* 佛教文化 5 (October 1, 2005): 16–18.

——. "Yuexia fashi changdao sengqie jiaoyu 月霞法師倡導僧伽教育" (Yuexia-initiated monastic education). *Xianggang fojiao* 香港佛教, no. 471 (1999): n.p.

Ketelaar, James. *Of Heretics and Martyrs in Meiji Japan: Buddhism and Its Persecution.* Princeton, NJ: Princeton University Press, 1990.

Kiely, Jan. "Spreading the Dharma with the Mechanized Press: New Buddhist Print Culture in the Modern Chinese Print Revolution, 1866–1949." In *From Woodblocks to the Internet: Chinese Publishing and Print Culture in Transition, Circa 1800 to 2008*, ed. Cynthia Brokaw and Christopher Bell, 185–210. Leiden: Brill, 2010.

Kieschnick, John. *The Impact of Buddhism on Chinese Material Culture.* Princeton, NJ: Princeton University Press, 2003.

Kimura Kiyotaka 木村清孝. *Chūgoku kegon shisōshi* 中國華嚴思想史 (A history of Chinese Huayan thought). Kyoto: Heirakuji, 1992.

Kohn, Livia. "Taoist Insight Meditation: The Tang Practice of *Neiguan*." In *Taoist Meditation and Longevity Techniques*, ed. Livia Kohn and Sakade Yoshinobu, 193–224. Ann Arbor: Center for Chinese Studies, University of Michigan, 1989.

Lai, Lei Kuan Rongdao. "Lineage Networks and the Transnational Transmission of Modern Chinese Buddhism." Paper presented at the American Academy of Religions annual meeting, November 19–22, 2016, San Antonio, TX.

——. "Praying for the Republic: Buddhist Education, Student-Monks, and Citizenship in Modern China (1911–1949)." Ph.D. diss., McGill University, 2013.

——. "The Wuchang Ideal: Buddhist Education and Identity Production in Republican China." *Studies in Chinese Religion* 3, no. 1 (2017): 55–70.

Li Silong. "The Practice of Buddhist Education in Modern China." *Chinese Studies in History* 46, no. 3 (Spring 2013): 59–78.

Liao Yanbo 廖彥博. *Chengyi fashi fangtan lu* 成一法師訪談錄 (Record of interviews with Master Chengyi). Taipei: Sanmin Shuju, 2007.

Liu Guijie 劉貴傑. "Qingchu Huayan nianfo sixiang shixi—yi Xufa yu Peng Shaosheng wei lie 清初華嚴念佛思想試析 ——以續法與彭紹升為例" (An examination of the Huayan Nianfo thought of the early Qing: Xufa and Peng Shaosheng as case studies). *Chung Hwa Buddhist Journal* 22 (2007): 227–250.

Liu Ming-Wood. "The 'P'an'chiao' System of the Hua-yen School in Chinese Buddhism." *T'oung Pao*, second series, 67, nos. 1–2 (1981): 10–47.

Ma Mingbo 馬明博. "Wutai shenchu changming deng: Ji Mengcan zhanglao 五台深處長明燈: 記夢參長老" (An enduring lamp deep within

Wutai: Remembering Venerable Mengcan). *Zhongguo zongjiao* 中國宗教 7 (2013): 32–35.

MacKinnon, Stephen. *Wuhan, 1938: War, Refugees, and the Making of Modern China.* Berkeley: University of California Press, 2008.

———. "Wuhan's Search for Identity in the Republican Period." In *Remaking the Chinese City: Modernity and National Identity, 1900-1950,* ed. Joseph Esherick, 161–173. Honolulu: University of Hawai'i Press, 1999.

McBride, Richard. *Domesticating the Dharma: Buddhist Cults and the Hwaom Synthesis in Silla Korea.* Honolulu: University of Hawai'i Press, 2007.

McGuire, Beverley Foulks. "Bringing Buddhism Into the Classroom: Jiang Qian's (1876–1942) Vision for Education in Republican China." *Journal of Chinese Religions* 39 (2011): 33–54.

Mori Noriko. "Liang Qichao, Late-Qing Buddhism, and Modern Japan." In *The Role of Japan in Liang Qichao's Introduction of Modern Western Civilization to China,* ed. Joshua A. Fogel, 222–246. Berkeley: University of California Press, 2004.

Muller, A. Charles, ed. *Digital Dictionary of Buddhism.* Last modified January 2, 2017. http://buddhism-dict.net/ddb.

Nedostup, Rebecca. *Superstitious Regimes: Religion and the Politics of Chinese Modernity.* Cambridge, MA: Harvard University Press, 2009.

Ōtake Susumu. "On the Origin and Early Development of the Buddhāvataṃsaka-sutra." In *Reflecting Mirrors: Perspectives on Huayan Buddhism,* ed. Imre Hamar, 87–107. Wisebaden: Harrassowitz, 2007.

Park, Jin Y. *Buddhism and Postmodernity: Zen, Huayan, and the Possibility of Postmodern Buddhist Ethics.* Lanham, MD: Lexington Books, 2010.

Schicketanz, Erik. *Daraku to fukkō no kindai Chūgoku bukkyō: Nihon bukkyō to no kaikō to sono rekishizō no kōchiku* 堕落と復興の近代中國佛教: 日本佛教との邂逅とその歴史像の構築 (Between decline and revival: Historical discourse and modern Chinese Buddhism's encounter with Japan). Kyoto: Hōzōkan, 2016.

———. "Narratives of Buddhist Decline and the Concept of the Sect (*Zong*) in Modern Chinese Buddhist Thought." *Studies in Chinese Religions* 3, no. 3 (November 2017): 281–300.

Schlütter, Morten. *How Zen Became Zen: The Dispute Over Enlightenment and Formation of Chan Buddhism in Song-Dynasty China.* Honolulu: University of Hawai'i Press, 2008.

Scott, Gregory Adam. "Conversion by the Book: Buddhist Print Culture in Early Republican China." Ph.D. diss., Columbia University, 2013.

———. *The Digital Catalogue of Chinese Buddhism, v. 3.0.* Last modified October 3, 2013. http://bib.buddhiststudies.net/.

———. "The Publishing of Buddhist Books for Beginners in Modern China from Yang Wenhui to Master Sheng Yen." *Shengyan yanjiu* 聖嚴研究 5 (2014): 51–107.

Sharf, Robert. *Coming to Terms with Chinese Buddhism*. Honolulu: University of Hawai'i Press, 2002.
———. "Experience." In *Critical Terms for Religious Studies*, ed. Marc Taylor, 94–116. Chicago: University of Chicago Press, 1998.
Shen Quji 沈去疾. *Yingci fashi nianpu* 應慈法師年譜 (Chronicle of the life of Master Yingci). Shanghai: Huadong Normal University, 1990.
Shi Dongchu 釋東初. *Zhongguo fojiao jindai shi* 中國佛教近代史 (A history of early contemporary Chinese Buddhism). Vols. 1 and 2 of *Dongchu laoren quanji* 東初老人全集 (Collected works of Venerable Dongchu). Taipei: Dongchu, 1974.
Shi Tianen 釋天恩. "Huayanzong de liuzhuan yu zai Taiwan de fazhan 華嚴宗的流傳與在臺灣的發展" (Transmission of the Huayan School and its development in Taiwan). M.A. thesis, Hua-yen Buddhist College, 2004.
Sponberg, Alan. "Traditions of Meditation in Fa-hsiang Buddhism." In *Traditions of Meditation in Chinese Buddhism*, ed. Peter Gregory, 15–43. Honolulu: University of Hawai'i Press, 1986.
Tanabe, George J. *Myoe the Dreamkeeper: Fantasy and Knowledge in Early Kamakura Buddhism*. Cambridge, MA: Harvard University Press, 1992.
Tao Jin. "The Formulation of Introductory Topics and the Writing of Exegesis in Chinese Buddhism." *Journal of the International Association of Buddhist Studies* 30, nos. 1–2 ([2007] 2009): 33–79.
Travagnin, Stefania. "Buddhist Education Between Tradition, Modernity, and Alternative Networks: Reconsidering the 'Revival' of Education for the Sangha." *Studies in Chinese Religions* 3, no. 3 (November 2017): 220–241.
———. "Concepts and Institutions for a New Buddhist Education: Reforming the Saṃgha Between and Within State Agencies." *East Asian History* 39 (December 2014): 89–102.
Wang Song 王頌. "Cong Riben Huayanzong de liang da paibie fanguan Zhongguo Huayan sixiangshi 從日本華嚴宗的兩大派別反觀中國華嚴思想史" (The intellectual history of Chinese Huayan as viewed from the perspective of the two major sects of Japanese Kegon). *Shijie zongjiao yanjiu* 世界宗教研究 4 (2005): 9–17.
———. *Songdai huayan sixiang yanjiu* 宋代華嚴思想研究 (Research on Song dynasty Huayan thought). Beijing: Zongjiao Wenhua, 2008.
Wei Daoru 魏道儒. *Zhongguo huayanzong tongshi* 中國華嚴宗通史 (Comprehensive history of the Chinese Huayan School). Nanjing: Jiangsu Guji, 2001.
Welch, Holmes. *Buddhism Under Mao*. Cambridge, MA: Harvard University Press, 1971.
———. *The Buddhist Revival in China*. Cambridge, MA: Harvard University Press, 1968.
———. *The Practice of Chinese Buddhism, 1900–1950*. Cambridge, MA: Harvard University Press, 1967.

Wu Jiang. "The Chinese Buddhist Canon Through the Ages: Essential Categories and Critical Issues in the Study of a Textual Tradition." In *Spreading the Buddha's Word in East Asia: The Formation and Transformation of the Chinese Buddhist Canon*, ed. Wu Jiang and Lucille Chia, 15–45. New York: Columbia University Press, 2016.

Xia Boming 夏伯銘. *Shanghai jiushi zhi Hatong fufu* 上海舊事之哈同夫婦 (Tales of Mrs. Hardoon in Shanghai). Shanghai: Shanghai Yuandong, 2008.

Xia Jinhua 夏金華. "Chanzong yu Huayan de zonghe changdaozhe--cong Yingci laofashi dao Zhenchan fashi 禪宗與華嚴的綜合倡導者--從應慈老法師到真禪法師" (Advocates for unified Chan and Huayan—from the Venerable Yingci to Master Zhenchan). *Fojiao wenhua* 佛教文化 6 (December 1, 2005): 7–10.

Xiandu 賢度. *Huayanxue zhuanti yanjiu* 華嚴學專題研究 (Special topics in Huayan studies). Taipei: Huayan lianshe, 2008. http://devol.ddbc.edu.tw/hsiendu/interface.php?book=02.

Xiao Ping 肖平. *Jindai zhongguo fojiao de fuxing yu Riben fojiaojie jiaowang lu* 近代中國佛教的復興與日本佛教界交往錄 (The early modern Chinese Buddhist revival and the Japanese Buddhist world, a record). Guangdong: Renmin, 2003.

Xiao Yu 肖雨. "Mangxie tabian Ya Meizhou de Wutaishan huayan xingzhe—Shouye fashi 芒鞋踏遍亞美洲的五台山華嚴行者—壽冶法師" (The Huayan practitioner of Mt. Wutai whose grass shoes wandered from Asia to America—Master Shouye). *Wutaishan yanjiu* 五臺山研究 2, no. 2 (1996): 13–23.

"Xingshili 行事曆." Avatamsaka Lotus Society, n.d. http://www.huayenusa.org/%E8%A1%8C%E4%BA%8B%E8%A1%A8.

Yao Binbin 姚彬彬. *Xiandai wenhua sichao yu zhongguo foxue de zhuanxing* 現代文化思潮與中國佛學的轉型 (Modern cultural thought and the transformation of Chinese Buddhist studies). Beijing: Zongjiao Wenhua, 2015.

Yü, Chün-fang. *Passing the Light: The Incense Light Community and Buddhist Nuns in Contemporary Taiwan*. Honolulu: University of Hawai'i Press, 2013.

Yu, Jimmy. "Revisiting the Notion of Zong: Contextualizing the Dharma Drum Lineage of Modern Chan Buddhism." *Chung-Hwa Buddhist Journal* 26 (2013): 113–151.

——. *Sanctity and Self-Inflicted Violence in Chinese Religions, 1500-1700*. Oxford: Oxford University Press, 2012.

Zhang Hua 張華. *Yang Wenhui yu Zhongguo jindai fojiao sixiang zhuanxing* 楊文會與中國近代佛教思想轉型 (Yang Wenhui and the formation of early-modern Chinese Buddhist thought). Beijing: Zongjiao Wenhua, 2004.

Zhou Zhuying 周祝英. "Wutaishan Huayanzong xianzhuang 五台山華嚴宗現狀" (Current condition of the Huayan School on Mt. Wutai). *Wutaishan yanjiu* 五臺山研究 3 (2012): 51–55.

Ziporyn, Brook. "Anti-Chan Polemics in Post Tang Tiantai." *Journal of the International Association of Buddhist Studies* 17, no. 1 (Summer 1994): 26–65.

———. *Beyond Oneness and Difference: Li* 理 *and Coherence in Chinese Buddhist Thought and Its Antecedents*. Albany: State University of New York Press, 2013.

Index

abbots: Chisong as, 85; Huizong as, 85; Qinghai as, 78, 217n18; Tikong as, 64; of Xingfu Temple, 84–85, 87; Yekai as, 52–53, 55, 66
Aiting, 69, 80, 92, 95; curriculum announcements by, 156; as disciple, 66–67; forced exile of, 108; as student, 58
Amitābha Buddha meditation, 168
Anhui Monastic School, 45, 69, 80, 85, 88, 158
antireligion movements, 75
antisectarian trend, 8–9, 38, 41–42
Anyang Hermitage, 91
Aśvaghoṣa, 23, 40
Awakening of Faith in the Mahāyāna, 39–40, 131; Changxing on, 41; Fazang's commentary on, 147; influence of, 171; lectures on, 44–45, 55, 114, 183; study of, 159, 164–165, 183

BAC. *See* Buddhist Association of China
Bailin Teaching Institute, 220n74
Baohuashan Temple, 221n80
biguan, 27, 29, 60

blood copying of sutras, 4, 28–29, 207n32
bodhisattva precepts, 19, 90; in Huayan Sutra, 136
Bo Jing, 202n6
"Brief Explanation of the Ten Schools" (Yang Wenhui), 37, 209n53, 226n1, 229n40
Brief History of Buddhism of the Three Nations, The (Shimaji and Oda), 127, 146
Buddha: Amitābha Buddha, 168; bathing rite, 118; Buddha lands, 126, 146; central, cosmic, 4, 18–19; enlightenment of, 3, 43, 129; Huayan Sutra taught by, 182; nature of, 126; preaching by, 151; Śākyamuni Buddha, 128; Sutra of Briefly Explained Admonishments, 233n6; teachings, 21, 40, 128, 182; Vairocana Buddha, 18, 19, 28, 29, 114
Buddhahood, 146
Buddha's Light, 45, 100, 101, 177–178
Buddhism, 37, 39, 127; Korean Buddhism, 146; Mahāyāna

[261]

Buddhism (*continued*)
    Buddhism, 41, 170, 182. *See also* Chinese Buddhism; Huayan Buddhism; Japanese Buddhism
Buddhism Semimonthly, 207n36
Buddhist Association of China (BAC), 110, 113, 116–117
Buddhist Books publishing house, 148, 207n36
Buddhist Journal, 55
Buddhist New Youth, 93
Buddhist Revival in China, The (Welch), 5–6

calligraphy, 27, 28, 96, 100, 180
Cangsheng Mingzhi University, 57
Cao Songqiao, 28
Caotangshan Great Huayan Temple, Taiwan, 121
Catalog of Buddhist Works Compiled During the Kaiyuan Period (Zhisheng), 34–35
CBA. *See* Chinese Buddhist Association
CCP. *See* Chinese Communist Party
Changguan, 27, 206n23
Changshu Dharmadhātu Institutes, 69, 75, 84–89
Changshui Zixuan, 23, 115
Changxing, 22, 44–45, 88; on *Awakening of Faith in the Mahāyāna*, 41; at Jetavana Hermitage, 157–158; on meditative practice, 146; as monastic exponent, 10; as student, 58
Chan meditation, 168–169, 177
Chan School, 20, 23, 33, 65, 131; Chan lineage, 65–66; meditation in, 174
charity, 136
Che'gwan, 127, 167
Chen Bing, 6, 166–167

Chengguan, 13, 20–23, 78; commentaries of, 24–25, 79, 81–83, 99, 101, 149–150, 152, 154, 156, 159, 162, 164–165, 167, 171, 178; essays, 234n15; Five Teachings and, 132; on Four Dharmadhātu, 142–143; on meditation, 171; mereology and, 135; as patriarch, 9, 22, 134, 142; on Ten Profound Gates, 138
Chengkong, 88
Chengyi, 98, 113; Guangxiao Temple and, 121; at Huayan Lotus Society, Taiwan, 114–116; U.S. visit, 117
Chen-hua, 94
Chen Yuanbai, 61, 86
Chiang Kai-shek, 76
Chinese Buddhism: Chisong on, 86–87; debates within, 4; education, 1–2, 48–51; Huayan thought and, 24; internationalization of, 181; introductory texts for study, 10; Japanese histories and, 11; monastic life, 1; periodicals, 11; PRC and, 104, 181; revival of, 48–51; role of monastic schools, 1, 12, 48–50, 73, 157; sects in, 38; student monks in, 67–68; study of, 181; in Taiwan, 109–112; temples, 65–66; *zong*-centric model of, 30–33, 35. *See also* Huayan Buddhism; Japanese Buddhism; Sinitic Buddhist tradition
Chinese Buddhist Association (CBA), 106–107
Chinese Civil War, 1949, 105
Chinese Communist Party (CCP): fear of, 109; reform by, 118; religion and, 106–107
Chinese diaspora, 67, 104, 111, 120, 181

INDEX

Chinul, 146
Chisong, 63–64, 66, 88; as abbot, 85; lecture attendance, 55; ordination of, 61; on state of Chinese Buddhism, 86–87; as student, 58
Ch'oe Ch'i-wŏn, 150
Chronicle of the Buddhist Patriarchs, 22–23, 36, 126–127, 146
Cizhou, 44, 60, 63, 85–86; as celebrated master, 7; death of, 107; Dharmadhātu Institutes of, 89–91; lectures of, 89–90; programs of, 160, 163; as student, 58; teaching by, 105
Clarification of the Outline of Xianshou's Five Teachings (Xufa), 127, 149, 167
Clear Explanation of the One Hundred Dharmas (Vasubandhu), 159
Combined Commentary on the Huayan Sutra (Li Tongxuan), 163
commentaries: of Chengguan, 24–25, 79, 81–83, 99, 101, 149–150, 152, 154, 156, 159, 162, 164–165, 167, 171, 178; of Fazang, 25, 82, 147, 149, 150, 152, 153, 154, 159, 164–165, 167, 171, 178–179; of Li Tongxuan, 78, 162, 163, 165, 167, 178; of Xufa, 10, 13, 39; of Yang Wenhui, 11; of Zongmi, 171. *See also specific commentaries*
Commentary and Subcommentary on the Huayan Sutra (Chengguan), 81, 83, 152, 154, 159, 162
Commentary on the Treatise on the Nondistinction of the Dharmadhātu (Fazang), 159
Communist government, 76, 83, 105. *See also* Chinese Communist Party
concealment, 140, 229n39

concentration, 173, 174
Conditioned Origination, 155
Confucianism, 132
conglin, 99, 109, 156
Consciousness-Only School, 6, 61, 175, 207n36, 236n35. *See also* Yogācāra
Contemplation of Origination, 171
Contemplation of the Dharmadhātu, 156–157, 169, 182; as foundation of Huayan thought, 179; at Huayan University, 176; at Institute of the Xianshou School, 176; Keduan on, 177; as meditative praxis, 172–176; at Qingliang Institute, 176; student essays on, 177–178; at Śūraṅgama Buddhist Institute, 176; three contemplations in, 170–171; Xufa on, 179
Contemplation of the Five Skandha (Chengguan), 164–165
Contemplation of the Nonobstruction of Phenomena, 170–171
Contemplation of the Universal Pervasion and Inclusion, 171
Contemplation of True Emptiness, 170
copying of Huayan Sutra, 26–27; blood copying, 4, 28–29, 207n32
cultivation of wisdom, 173
Cultural Revolution (1966–1976), 8, 104, 107–108, 111, 118, 181
curriculum. *See* Huayan curriculum
"Curriculum for Inner Classes at Buddhist Schools" (Yang Wenhui), 158

Daoism, 132, 159, 174
Daopei, 90
Daoyuan, 219n58

INDEX

Deng Zimei, 6, 166–167
Dharma Characteristics, 134, 227n22
Dharmadhātu Institutes, 59, 69, 75, 163; in Changshu, 69, 75, 84–89; of Cizhou, 89–91; at Fahai Temple, 91, 219n58; in Fujian, 107; for lecture series, 74; meditation at, 169; strategic location of, 72. *See also* Xingfu Temple
Dharma Nature, 134, 227n22
Dharma Realm, 19, 30, 41, 46, 85; as total of reality, 135
dharma transmission, 207n32, 212n14; in Huayan University network, 64–67; mass dharma transmission, 53; of Xuefan and Dongchu, 95; of Yingci, 66; of Zhiguang, 67
Diamond Sutra, 44, 99, 120
Di Chuqing, 55, 151
difference, 137
Digital Catalogue of Chinese Buddhism (Scott), 148
Dinghui Temple, 95–97, 220n72, 221n80
directive meditation, 174, 176
disintegration, 137
Dixian, 2, 68, 99, 207n36
Doctrinal Tiger of the Southeast, 167
doctrine. *See* Huayan doctrine
Dongchu. *See* Shi Dongchu
Dushun, 169–170, 205n10; as Mañjuśrī, 27; as patriarch, 22–23

education, 73; in Chinese Buddhism, 1–2, 48–51; desire for reform, 48; at Huayan Lotus Society, Taiwan, 114. *See also* Huayan curriculum

Eifring, Halvor, 173–176
Eight Schools model, 133
emptiness, 142, 143–144, 164, 170, 175, 182
Encyclopedia of Religion (Eliade et. al.), 31–32
enlightenment, 135–136; of Buddha, 3, 43, 129; goal of, 175; nature of, 19; path to, 136, 182; Sutra of Perfect Enlightenment, 40, 44, 54, 135, 151, 159, 165
Essential Collected Writings on the Huayan Sutra, 149, 152, 159
Essential Meaning of the Huayan School (Gyōnen), 126, 226n1
Essentials of the Eight Sects (Gyōnen), 22, 36–37, 114, 126, 146, 208n48; Four Dharmadhātu in, 229n40; impact of, 226n1
Exploration of the Profundities of the Huayan Sutra (Fazang), 82, 130, 138, 147, 150, 152, 154

Fahai Temple, 91, 219n58
faithfulness, 136
"Fajie yuanqi zhang" (Fazang), 231n59
Fang, Thomé H., 7
Fan Gunong, 30, 207n36
Faren, 52, 54
"Fashen zhang" (Fazang), 231n59
Faxiang University, 50–51, 75
Fazang, 39, 42–43, 164, 235n32; commentaries of, 25, 82, 147, 149, 150, 152, 153, 154, 159, 164–165, 167, 171, 178–179; doctrinal classification by, 13, 156, 166; essays, 231n59; on Five Teachings, 13, 115, 129–133, 135, 145; as Huayan patriarch, 21–23, 127, 132; influence of, 145; mereology and, 135; Origination of the Dharmadhātu and,

136; on Six Characteristics, 137, 145; teaching of, 128–129; on Ten Profound Gates, 138, 145
Final Mahāyāna Teachings, 131
Five Teachings, 34, 39, 42, 46, 99, 103; Chengguan and, 132; Fazang on, 13, 115, 129–133, 135, 145; as key doctrine, 99, 127–134, 166, 179, 182. *See also Treatise on the Five Teachings*
Fochui niepan lüeshuo jiaojie jing, 233n6
Foguangshan, 111, 119
Foulk, T. Griffith, 31, 38
Foundational Treatise on the Mysteries of the Stages of the Great Lineage (CBETA), 159
Four Dharmadhātu, 135; Chengguan on, 142–143; in *Essentials of the Eight Sects*, 22; Gyōnen on, 229n40; as key doctrine, 99, 125, 141–144; principle and phenomena in, 142–143; reality perspectives in, 143–144; Yang Wenhui on, 229n40
Four Noble Truths, 130
Four Teachings, 46, 99, 127, 131, 167
freedom, 140, 228n39
Fu Jinqiu, 54–55, 213n19
funeral rites, 79

Gimello, Robert, 142, 144, 170
Goossaert, Vincent, 70–71
Great Calming and Contemplation (Zhiyi), 172–173, 175
Great Cloud, 153
Great Leap Forward (1958–1962), 107
Great Vehicle, 40
guan, 174–175
Guanghui, 207n32
Guangxiao Buddhist Institute, 97–98, 167

Guangxiao Temple, 95, 97, 121
Guanzong Research Society, 2, 67, 68, 214n39
Gui Bohua, 53–54
Guo Cheen, 24
Gushan Buddhist Institute, 90
Gyōnen, 36–37, 114, 126, 133, 226n1; followers of, 22–23; on Four Dharmadhātu, 229n40; influence of, 146; on meditation, 172; sect-centric histories and, 145; on ten sects, 208n48

Hankou, Huayan University of, (1921–1924), 60–63, 69–70, 75, 85–86, 92, 158, 164–165
Hanshan Deqing, 28–29
Hardoon, Liza Roos, 1, 55–57, 79
Hardoon, Silas, 1, 55
HCY. *See Sound of the Sea Tide*
Heart Sutra, 44, 84, 107
Hongyi, 27–28
Huang Chanhua, 22, 229n40
huayan, meaning of, 17–18
Huayan Assemblies, 26, 30
Huayan Buddhism, 17, 20, 24, 32; devotion in, 37; during Republican China, 3–7; teaching of, 104–105
Huayan Buddhist College, 116–117
Huayan Commentary and Subcommentary Publishing Committee, 82–83
Huayan curriculum: ads for, 160; announcements of, 156; class schedule for, 161; common, for educational programs, 163–169; Conditioned Origination of, 155; *Contemplation of the Five Skandha* in, 164–165; elements of, 156–157; Huayan Sutra as central to, 160–163; at Huayan University, 163–164; meditation

INDEX

Huayan curriculum (*continued*)
and, 168–179; *Outline of Xianshou's Five Teachings* in, 165–167; overview, 155–157; in Qingliang Institute, 165; student lectures in, 161; *Treatise on the Five Teachings* in, 164–166; Yang Wenhui and, 157–160, 162, 164–165; Yingci and, 164; Yuexia and, 164

Huayan Dharma Assemblies, 104

Huayan doctrine: comparisons of, 128–134; elements downplayed during modern period, 144–147; Five Teachings as key, 99, 127–134, 166, 179, 182; Four Dharmadhātu as key, 99, 125, 141–144; Marxism and, 202n6; overview, 125–126; recovered texts of, 147–154, 181; Six Characteristics as key, 99, 125, 136–137, 179, 182; sources of, 126–128; Ten Profound Gates as key, 99, 125, 138–141, 165, 179, 182; Three Natures paradigm, 145, 166

Huayan Inquiry Into the Origin of Humanity (Zongmi), 42, 165

Huayan Institute, Shanghai, 73

Huayanjing qike zhang (Fazang), 231n59

Huayan Lotus Society, Taiwan: changes in, 115–116; Chengyi at, 114–116; educational activities, 114; growth of, 113–114; launch by Zhiguang, 112; Nanting as lecturer, 112–113; nuns at, 116–117; U.S. branch, 117

Huayan Normal Institute, 83

Huayan patriarchs. *See* patriarchs

Huayan Research Society, 95–96

Huayan School, 4; atrophy of, 8; doctrine of, 24, 126; Huayan Sutra and, 17–20; institutional presence of, 35; names and founders of, 19–23; references to, 18; weak institutional existence of, 47

Huayan sectarianism: absent in Republican China, 38–46; Japanese scholarship and, 30–38

Huayan Sutra, 1, 4; bodhisattva precepts in, 136; Buddha teaching, 182; as central to Huayan curriculum, 160–163; copying of, 4, 26–29, 207n32; as course work, 90; creation of, 18–19; full reality in, 3–4, 182; Huayan School and, 17–20; lectures on, 9, 56, 104; Mengcan and, 120; practices of, 13, 24–30; publication of, 4–5, 9; recitation of, 6, 25–26; references to, 18; study of, 163, 178; teaching of, 182; themes in, 19; widespread reverence for, 47; Yuexia and, 70–71

Huayan University: Contemplation of the Dharmadhātu at, 176; curriculum of, 163–164; founding of, 1, 47; graduates of, 7–8, 69, 77, 183; of Hankou (1921–1924), 60–63, 75, 85; influence and significance of, 7–10, 183; naming of, 160; original graduates of, 58; original university, 55–58; revival and, 5–6; second university (1920–1921), 58–59, 84; students at, 3; study in, 56–57; teaching in, 44; of Wuchang, 63–64; Wuhan universities, 59–64; of Yangzhou, 98–102, 162, 165, 167, 168–169, 177; Yuexia moving, 57

[266]

INDEX

Huayan University network: dharma transmission in, 64–67; in early PRC, 105–109; expansion of, 91–98; horizontal relationships in, 69; origins of, 64; Qingliang Institute, 78–80; revival of in mainland China, 118–121; second-and-third generation programs, 72–77; unaffiliated programs, 98–103; Yingci, as student and master in, 77–84. *See also* Dharmadhātu Institutes; *specific network institutes*; *specific topics*
Huiguang, 136
Huiting, 87
Huiyuan (disciple of Fazang), 42, 132, 143
Huiyuan, Jingying. *See* Jingying Huiyuan
Huizong, 66; as abbot, 85; as student, 58
Hundred Days Reform, 1898, 157

identification of all things, 229n39
identity, 137, 139–141
idioms of religious excellence, 71
inclusion, 143, 171; nature inclusion, 41; universal, 177–178
Indra's net, 8, 229n39
Initial Mahāyāna Teachings, 130
Inquiry Into the Origin of Humanity (Zongmi), 132, 151, 152–153
Institute of the Xianshou School, 102–103, 165; Contemplation of the Dharmadhātu at, 176; meditation in, 169
institutes, 74. *See also specific institutes*
integration, 137
Introductory Discourse to Commentary on the Huayan Sutra (Chengguan), 79, 81, 99, 162, 234n15

Japanese Buddhism, 9, 11, 109; Huayan sectarianism and Japanese scholarship, 30–38; for a modern Japanese nation, 48
Jetavana Hermitage, 2, 50; Changxing at, 157–158; closing of, 159; curriculum at, 157–159, 162, 163, 165, 209n53; Zhiguang at, 158
Jiangsu Monastic Normal School, 49, 54–55, 103
Jiang Weiqiao, 22, 45, 83
Jiang Yiyuan, 153, 232n70
Jiaoshan Buddhist Institute, 95–97
Jiaoshan Buddhist Studies Library, 96, 221n77
Jiechen, 63, 85–86, 214n39; lecture attendance, 55; meditation by, 60; as student, 58
Jiede, 112
Ji Juemi, 57
Jimeng, 121, 225n45
Jingbo, 77–79, 93
Jinghai, 116
Jinglian Temple, Beijing, 91
Jingyan, 96, 221n80
Jingying Huiyuan, 136
Jingyuan, 22–23
Jinling Scriptural Press, 39, 50, 149–150, 152
Jueshi Book and Stationery Company, 113

Kang Youwei, 57
Keduan, 45–46, 69; on Contemplation of the Dharmadhātu, 177; curriculum announcements by, 156, 162–163; lectures of, 98–99, 101, 162; programs of, 160; reform and, 102; study by, 99

INDEX

Kefa, 29
Kiely, Jan, 10
Korean Buddhism, 146
Kuanrong, 86, 88

Lai, Rongdao, 62, 64; on student monks, 67–68
language, 51, 96
Laṅkāvatāra Sutra, 131
lectures: on *Awakening of Faith*, 44–45, 55, 114, 183; Chisong attending, 55; of Cizhou, 89–90; Dharmadhātu Institutes, 74; and Huayan Sutra, 9, 56, 104; Jiechen attending, 55; of Keduan, 98–99, 101, 162; of Nanting, 112–113; procedure for, 217n21; at Qingliang Temple, 217n18; of students, in Huayan curriculum, 161; of Taixu, 42–44, 153; of Yingci, 44, 79, 81–83, 90, 107, 152, 161–162, 217n18; of Yuexia, 44, 45, 55, 56, 70, 160; of Zhenchan, 161
Lengding, 94
Lesser Vehicle, 129–130, 133
Li'an, 69, 85, 92
Liang Qichao, 37, 41
Liaochen, 60–61, 63, 214n35; as student, 58
Liaozhong, 116
libraries, 96, 221n77
Lingyuan, 112
Li Tongxuan, 101, 145–146, 149; commentaries of, 78, 162, 163, 165, 167, 178; as founding figure, 23
Liu Shipei, 53
"Liuzhuan zhang" (Fazang), 231n59
Li Yinchen, 61
Li Yuanjing, 83

Li Zikuan, 96, 113
Longquan, 111–112
Lotus Sutra, 43, 131–132, 163

Madhyamaka School, 134
Mahāyāna Buddhism, 41, 170, 182
Mañjuśrī, 27
Marxism, 202n6
mathematics, 96
meditation, 146; Amitābha Buddha meditation, 168; Chan meditation, 168–169, 177; in Chan School, 174; Chengguan on, 171; definitions of, 173, 175; at Dharmadhātu Institutes, 169; directive and nondirective forms, 174, 176; Gyōnen on, 172; Huayan curriculum and, 168–179; at Institute of the Xianshou School, 169; by Jiechen, 60; in monastic school curriculum, 176–178; at Qingliang Institute, 169; in Sinitic Buddhist tradition, 174; in Tiantai School, 172, 177; Xufa on, 172; of Yuexia, 52. *See also* Contemplation of the Dharmadhātu
Mei Guangxi, 45, 229n40
Mengcan, 107–108, 112; Huayan Sutra and, 120; imprisonment of, 119–120; as student, 90
mereology, 135
Method for Contemplation of the Dharmadhātu, 143, 164, 169–170, 175
Method for Contemplation of the Dharmadhātu Mysterious Teaching for Eliminating Delusions and Returning to the Origin (Fazang), 164–165, 171, 172, 235n32
Method of Contemplation on the Complete Interfusion of the Three

INDEX

Sages (Chengguan), 82, 149, 154, 172; study of, 164
Minnan Buddhist Institute, 45, 87, 88, 93, 158; curriculum at, 165
Modern Sangha, 93
monastic schools: Anhui Monastic School, 45, 69, 80, 85, 88, 158; closing of, 73; Jiangsu Monastic Normal School, 49, 54–55, 103; meditation in curriculum, 176–178; role in Chinese Buddhism, 1, 12, 48–50, 73, 157; Taixu at, 49; Yuexia at, 49–50; Zhiguang at, 49–50. *See also* Jetavana Hermitage; Qingliang Institute
moral restraint, 173
Muxi, 58, 61
Myōe, 146

Nāgārjuna, 22, 23
Nanjing Buddhist Pure Karma Society, 26
Nanjing Huayan Society, 83
Nanjō Bunyū, 149
Nanting, 23, 97–98, 229n40; at Huayan Lotus Society, Taiwan, 112–113; lectures of, 161; as student, 69, 80; as teacher, 80, 92–95
nature inclusion, 41
nature origination, 41, 171
Nirvana Sutra, 101
nondirective meditation, 174, 176
nonobstruction, 143, 170–171, 228n39
Northern Expedition (1926–1928), 63, 75–76, 101

Ocean Seal Samādhi, 139
Oda Tokunō, 23, 127, 147, 229n40
one and the many, 19, 228n39

One Hundred Entrances Into the Ocean of Meanings in the Huayan Sutra (Fazang), 149, 153, 154
One Mind, 171–172
One Vehicle, 40, 129–133; Perfect Teaching of the One Vehicle, 43, 131, 135, 171, 177
Origination of the Dharmadhātu, 135–136
Outline of Chinese Buddhism (Sakaino Kōyō), 133
Outline of the Four Teachings of Tiantai (Che'gwan), 127, 167
Outline of Xianshou's Five Teachings (Xufa), 13, 98, 115, 127, 133, 169; as required curriculum, 165–167
Ouyang Jingwu, 40–41, 50–51

Park, Jin Y., 142
patriarchs: Chengguan as, 9, 22, 134, 142; *Chronicle of the Buddhist Patriarchs*, 22–23, 36, 126–127, 146; Dushun as, 22–23; Fazang as, 21–23, 127, 132; Zhiyan as, 22, 136, 138; Zongmi as, 21–22, 132, 151
Peng Shaosheng, 153
People's Republic of China (PRC): Chinese Buddhism and, 104, 181; fear of, 109; founding of, 104; Huayan University network in early, 105–109
Perfect Teaching of the One Vehicle, 43, 131, 135, 171, 177
perspective, 138–139, 141. *See also* Ten Profound Gates
pervasion, 143, 171
phenomenon, 8, 19, 139, 229n39
philosophy, 51
pilgrimages, 27, 59, 77, 81
Pinjia Dazangjing, 214n24

[269]

INDEX

Practice of Chinese Buddhism, The (Welch), 160–161
Prajñāpāramitā Sutras, 130
PRC. *See* People's Republic of China
Primer on Buddhism, A (Yang Wenhui), 37, 39
principle and phenomena, 142–143
Profound Gates of the One Vehicle of the Huayan (Fazang), 138
psychology, 51
publications: *Buddha's Light*, 45, 100, 101, 177–178; *Buddhism Semi-monthly*, 207n36; Buddhist Books publishing house, 148, 207n36; *Buddhist Journal*, 55; *Great Cloud*, 153; Huayan Commentary and Subcommentary Publishing Committee, 82–83; of Huayan Sutra, 4–5, 9; Jinling Scriptural Press, 39, 50, 149–150, 152; *Modern Sangha*, 93; periodicals, 11; *Sound of the Sea Tide*, 28, 40, 85, 96, 103; of Taixu, 41–42; of Yang Wenhui, 5, 39, 149–150, 152; of Yingci, 44, 79, 81–83, 90, 107, 152, 161–162; Youzheng Press, 55, 151. *See also* specific publications
Puchang, 52, 212n12
Pure Land School, 20, 28, 37, 180, 182, 208n48

Qianlong Canon, 148–152
Qinghai (abbot), 78, 217n18
Qingliang Institute, 20, 78–80, 93–94, 158; Contemplation of the Dharmadhātu at, 176; Huayan curriculum in, 165; meditation at, 169; study in, 162, 163
Qingliang Temple, 217n18

Record of Investigation into the Profound (Zhiyan), 136, 138

Record of the Transmission of the Buddhadharma Through the Three Nations (Gyōnen), 36
Record of the Transmission of the Huayan Sutra (Fazang), 25, 150
Republican China: control of religion and, 76–77; establishment of, 74–75; Huayan Buddhism during, 3–7; Huayan sectarianism during, 38–46; recovered texts in, 147–154, 181
revelation, 140, 229n39
Roos, Liza. *See* Hardoon, Liza Roos

Sakaino Kōyō, 133, 203n18, 229n40
Śākyamuni Buddha, 128
Samādhi, 139, 153
śamatha, 174
"Sanbao zhang" (Fazang), 231n59
sangha, 49, 67, 73, *93*
Sanskrit, 51, 96
Schicketanz, Erik, 33
Scott, Gregory Adam, 148, 151
Second Sino-Japanese War (1937–1945), 76, 97, 105
sectarianism, 9. *See also* antisectarian trend; Huayan sectarianism
separateness, 137
Shanghai Lotus Society, 26
Shaodian, 28, 29–30
Sharf, Robert, 173
Sheng, Mrs., 79
Shi Dongchu, 6, 62, 95, 97, 157, 212n7
Shimaji Mokurai, 23, 127, 146, 229n40
Shiqing, 87
"Shishi zhang" (Fazang), 231n59
Shouye, 6, 29, 207n23
shū, 37–38
Sinitic Buddhist tradition, 17, 18, 27, 39, 126, 144; meditation in,

INDEX

174; as sect-centric, 145; texts of, 40, 90, 159, 164
Sino-Tibetan Teaching Institute, 153
Six Characteristics, 29, 99, 115; Fazang on, 137, 145; as key doctrine of Huayan, 99, 125, 136–137, 179, 182
Six Schools, 127, 168
Sound of the Sea Tide (HCY), 28, 40, 85, 96, 103
Sponberg, Alan, 175–176
student monks, 67–68
subject object pairs, 141, 239n39
Su Manshu, 53
Sun Liren, 112
Sun Yat-sen, 1, 55–56
Sun Yuyun, 53–54
superstition, 75–77
Śūraṅgama Buddhist Institute, 103, 176
Śūraṅgama Sutra, 44, 81, 83, 103, 158–159
sutras: Diamond Sutra, 44, 99, 120; Heart Sutra, 44, 84, 107; Laṅkāvatāra Sutra, 131; Lotus Sutra, 43, 131–132, 163; Nirvana Sutra, 101; Prajñāpāramitā Sutras, 130; Śūraṅgama Sutra, 44, 81, 83, 103, 158–159; Sutra of Bequeathed Teachings, 159; Sutra of Briefly Explained Admonishments, 233n6; Sutra of Perfect Enlightenment, 40, 44, 54, 135, 151, 159, 165; Vimalakīrti Sutra, 44, 54, 80, 131. *See also* Huayan Sutra
Su Zhouchen, 28

Taiping Rebellion (1850–1864), 59, 147
Taishō Canon, 231n59, 236n32
Taiwan, 104; Chinese Buddhism in, 109–112; Huayan Lotus Society in, 112–118; Zhenchan in, 121
Taixu, 39–40; *biguan* of, 27; criticism from, 10; initiatives of, 61; lectures of, 42–44, 153; on meditative practice, 146; at monastic school, 49; paradigm, 2; publications of, 41–42; at Wuchang Buddhist Institute, 51
Tang Dayuan, 45
Tang Junyi, 7
Tang Yongtong, 33
Tanyue, 66, 87, 88
Tathāgathagarbha theory, 129, 131, 180
Teaching of Humans and Gods, 132
temples: in Chinese Buddhism, 65–66; destruction of, 107. *See also specific temples*
Ten Meanings, 127, 168
Ten Profound Gates, 29, 115, 136, 177, 228n39; Chengguan on, 138; Fazang on, 138, 145; ideas in, 138–139; identity of reality in, 139–141; as key doctrine, 99, 125, 138–141, 165, 179, 182; perspective in, 141; Zhiyan and, 138
Ten Schools model, 133
Three Contemplations, 127, 168, 236n35
Three Natures paradigm, 145, 166
Three Times Study Association, 221n74
Three Vehicles, 129
Tianjin Buddhist Grove of Virtue, 154
Tiantai School, 20, 39–40, 43, 66–68, 101, 130, 236n35; meditation in, 172, 177; teaching of, 182; Tiantai lineage, 6, 9, 14; Xufa and, 167

INDEX

Tiantai Zhiyi, 20
Tiantong Monastery, 52, 81, 162
Tibet, 107
Tikong, 213n21, 215n53; as abbot, 64; as student, 58
Travagnin, Stefania, 2, 157
Treatise on the Five Teachings (Fazang), 13, 115, 129, 130, 135, 137, 150; access to doctrine in, 179; as required curriculum, 164–166; study of, 167; Three Natures in, 145
Treatise on the Golden Lion (Fazang), 130, 137, 178
Treatise on the Huayan Buddha Recollection Samādhi (Peng), 153
Tung Lin Kok Monastery, 108
Tzu Chi Foundation, 111

Ui Hakuju, 33
unity, 137, 180
universal inclusion, 177
Use Temple Property to Advance Education movement, 73

Vairocana Buddha, 18, 19, 28, 29, 114
Vasubandhu, 159
Verses on the Structure of the Eight Consciousnesses (Xuanzang), 159
Vimalakīrti Sutra, 44, 54, 80, 131
Vinaya, 44
vipaśyanā, 174
visualization, 174, 175
Voice of Buddhism, 113

Wang Guowei, 57
Wang Senfu, 61
Wang Song, 34
Weicheng, 69, 88–89
Weifang, 88, 220n74
Weinstein, Stanley, 31–32
Welch, Holmes, 5–6, 38, 106, 160–161, 168–169
Wenxi, 49
World Buddhist Federations, 61–62
World Buddhist Householder Grove, Shanghai, 100, 153
World War II, 105
Wuchang, Huayan University of (1928–1930), 63–64
Wuchang Buddhist Institute, 2, 51, 61–62, 64, 68, 75, 100; curricular influences on, 164–165
wuxiang, 134
Wu Zetian, 137

Xiandu, 66, 116
Xiangrui, 102–103, 154, 165, 169
Xianshou Dharma Collection, 149–150
Xianshou Fazang. *See* Fazang
Xianshou School, 20–22; Institute of the Xianshou School, 102–103
Xianyin, 100
Xianyue, 87, 97
Xiao Weisheng, 101
Xiding, 27
Xingfu Temple, 58–59, 66, 69; abbots of, 84–85, 87; lay assembly of, 86
Xingyun, 111
Xinyan, 79, 80
"Xuanyi zhang" (Fazang), 231n59
Xuanzang, 134, 159, 174–175
Xuefan, 95, 97; study of, 220n74
Xufa, 127–128, 133, 149, 165–166; commentaries, 10, 13, 39; on Contemplation of the Dharmadhātu, 179; creative thinking and, 202n5; Doctrinal Tiger of the Southeast, 167; on meditation, 172; schema of, 168; Tiantai School and, 167
Xu Weiru, 83, 153–154
Xuyun, 60, 90, 214n38

INDEX

Yang Wenhui, 20, 22, 50, 60, 147, 209n53; commentaries, 11; creative thinking and, 202n5; criticism by, 10; on Four Dharmadhātu, 229n40; Huayan curriculum and, 157–160, 162, 164–165; influence of, 36–37; on meditative practice, 146; publishing house of, 5, 39, 149–150, 152; students of, 54. *See also* Jetavana Hermitage

Yangzhou Huayan University, 98–102, 162, 165, 167, 168–169, 177

Yao Binbin, 6–7

Yekai (abbot), 52–53, 55, 66

Yincun, 94

Yingci, 9, 12, 72; *biguan* of, 27; curriculum and, 164; death of, 84; dharma transmission of, 66; lectures and publications of, 44, 79, 81–83, 90, 107, 152, 161–162, 217n18, 271n18; legacy of, 93, 104, 111; at Nanjing Huayan Society, 83; pilgrimages of, 81; programs of, 160; at Qingliang Institute, 78–80; second-in-command role of, 69; second university started by, 58; student and master in Huayan University network, 77–84; teaching by, 50, 105; vision of, 81–82; Yuexia and, 52–55

Yinguan, 28

Yogācāra, 40–41, 50, 130, 134, 145, 180; teaching of, 182. *See also* Consciousness-Only School

Youzheng Press, 55, 151

Yuan Shikai, 99

"Yuanyin zhang" (Fazang), 231n59

Yuexia, 3, 7, 23, 151; curriculum and, 164; death of, 58, 70; Huayan Sutra and, 70–71; lectures of, 44, 54, 55, 56, 70, 160; legacy of, 67–71, 93, 104, 111; meditation practice of, 52; at monastic school, 49–50; as primary teacher, 53; as religious authority, 183; revival of, 5; students of, 59; tutelage by, 70; university moved by, 57; Yingci and, 52–55; Yuzhu and, 54, 212n12

Yufo Temple, 107, 118–119

Yuzhu: impact on Yingci, 54; as student, 52; Yuexia and, 54, 212n12

Zen, 32, 33, 208n48

Zhang Qingyang, 112

Zhang Taiyan, 42, 45, 54, 57, 207n36

Zhanshan Temple Buddhist Institute, 91

Zhenchan, 83, 107–108; lectures of, 161; and revival of Huayan in mainland China, 118–119; as student of Yingci, 107, 161; in Taiwan, 121; in U.S., 119

Zhengdao, 88

Zhengyan, 111

Zhenhua, 69, 92; at Huayan Lotus Society, 115

zhiguan, 174

Zhiguang, 7, 68, 92, 95–96; dharma transmission of, 67; Huayan Lotus Society launched by, 112; at Jetavana Hermitage, 158; at monastic school, 49–50; as student, 58

Zhisheng, 35

Zhiyan, 129–130; Origination of the Dharmadhātu and, 136; as patriarch, 22; Ten Profound Gates and, 138

[273]

INDEX

Zhiyi, 43, 131, 172–175, 234n15
Zhou Guoren, 28, 29–30
Zhou Shujia, 229n40
Zhou Xuande, 110
Zhulin Buddhist Institute, 89, 91–95, 154, 158, 169, 232n1
zong, 12, 20, 37–38; model of Chinese Buddhism, 30–33, 35; multiple meanings for, 31–32
Zongliang, 29
Zongmi, 132, 151–153; classification scheme, 42; commentaries of, 171; as patriarch, 21–22, 132, 151
Zongyang, 55–56

THE SHENG YEN SERIES IN CHINESE BUDDHIST STUDIES
Edited by Daniel B. Stevenson and Jimmy Yu

Sacred Economies: Buddhist Business and Religiosity in Medieval China
Michael J. Walsh

Spells, Images, and Maṇḍalas: Tracing the Evolution of Esoteric Buddhist Rituals
Koichi Shinohara

Living Karma: The Religious Practices of Ouyi Zhixu (1599–1655)
Beverley Foulks McGuire

*The Body Incantatory: Spells and the Ritual Imagination
in Medieval Chinese Buddhism*
Paul Copp

Emperor Wu Zhao and Her Pantheon of Devis, Divinities, and Dynastic Mothers
N. Harry Rothschild

The Science of Chinese Buddhism: Early Twentieth-Century Engagements
Erik J. Hammerstrom

*Spreading Buddha's Word in East Asia:
The Formation and Transformation of the Chinese Buddhist Canon*
Jiang Wu and Lucille Chia, editors

Recovering Buddhism in Modern China
Jan Kiely and J. Brooks Jessup, editors

*Chinese Esoteric Buddhism: Amoghavajra, the Ruling Elite,
and the Emergence of a Tradition*
Geoffrey C. Goble

*Thriving in Crisis: Buddhism and Political Disruption
in China, 1522–1620*
Dewei Zhang